The Complete Guide to Portfolio Construction and Management

For other titles in the Wiley Finance series
please see www.wiley.com/finance

The Complete Guide to Portfolio Construction and Management

Lukasz Snopek

A John Wiley and Sons, Ltd, Publication

This edition first published 2012
© 2012 Lukasz Snopek

Translated by Jessica Edwards from the original French edition: *Guide Complet de Construction et de Gestion de Portefeuille* published in 2010 by Maxima Laurent du Mesnil Editeur, Paris.

Registered office
John Wiley & Sons Ltd, The Atrium, Southern Gate, Chichester, West Sussex, PO19 8SQ, United Kingdom

For details of our global editorial offices, for customer services and for information about how to apply for permission to reuse the copyright material in this book please see our website at www.wiley.com.

Wiley publishes in a variety of print and electronic formats and by print-on-demand. Some material included with standard print versions of this book may not be included in e-books or in print-on-demand. If this book refers to media such as a CD or DVD that is not included in the version you purchased, you may download this material at http://booksupport.wiley.com. For more information about Wiley products, visit www.wiley.com.

Designations used by companies to distinguish their products are often claimed as trademarks. All brand names and product names used in this book are trade names, service marks, trademarks or registered trademarks of their respective owners. The publisher is not associated with any product or vendor mentioned in this book. This publication is designed to provide accurate and authoritative information in regard to the subject matter covered. It is sold on the understanding that the publisher is not engaged in rendering professional services. If professional advice or other expert assistance is required, the services of a competent professional should be sought.

Library of Congress Cataloging-in-Publication Data

Snopek, Lukasz.
    The complete guide to portfolio construction and management / Lukasz Snopek.
        p. cm.
    Includes bibliographical references and index.
    ISBN 978-1-119-97688-2 (hardback)
 1.   Portfolio management.   I.   Title.
    HG4529.5.S63 2012
    332.6 – dc23

                                                                            2011039046

A catalogue record for this book is available from the British Library.

ISBN 978-1-119-97688-2 (hardback) ISBN 978-1-119-95304-3 (ebk)
ISBN 978-1-119-95305-0 (ebk)   ISBN 978-1-119-95306-7 (ebk)

Set in 10/12pt Times by Laserwords Private Limited, Chennai, India
Printed in Great Britain by CPI Group (UK) Ltd, Croydon, CR0 4YY

Contents

Foreword

Since the mid-1990s, the world of asset management has seen a large number of its main principles, both quantitative and qualitative, collapse one after the other, leaving investors and their portfolios at the mercy of market fluctuations. At the risk of sounding somewhat cynical, it can be said without regret that it was high time. Most of these grand principles had in fact been suggested in the mid-1950s in a very different financial world from the one we know today. The tools available were simpler and the markets more segmented. Volatility remained contained and crises – excepting the odd occasion in a few emerging countries – were rare. Good diversification in stocks combined with a few good choices of securities or markets, plus a few government bonds, were enough to avoid the main pitfalls. A few measures of risk taken from the Greek alphabet and some probabilities based on normal distribution were usually enough to convince any diehard sceptics.

Today, the financial universe is very different. Portfolio management has become global – as have its crises and its tools. The equity risk premium has been negative for the last 10 years and interest rates are at record lows. Volatility regularly experiences violent explosions sparked by investor sentiment and macroeconomic news. "Accidents" supposed to occur once in a thousand years in a normally distributed world can now be observed several times a decade. Correlations between assets are weak, except when they should be weak in order to limit the damage. Finally, the most exotic and undesirable risks are securitised, then carefully hidden in products that are sold on to the general public. As for the ability of the big States of yesteryear to honour their debt, this is – and will be – more and more often called into question, while emerging countries seem to be making a better go of it. But for how long?

Faced with such an environment, it has become crucial for investors to give thought to their true objectives and, especially, the best way of meeting them. One could reasonably suppose that most investors aim above all to preserve their capital and, if possible, to generate a certain amount of capital growth if investment opportunities present themselves. But opportunities and growth also mean taking risks and therefore risking losses. When establishing their portfolio, wise investors should be principally concerned with their exposure to the risk of losses. Unfortunately, there are a whole set of questions that most models ignore, or cover only partially. How do you adequately measure these risks, if we assume that volatility is only an approximation of risk, solely valid in a symmetrical and Gaussian world? Furthermore, a company's true risk profile should not be based on the volatility of its shares, but on whether or not the company is well run. How can we succeed in analysing the various asset classes in terms of the nature of the risks being run, instead of according to an arbitrarily imposed classification? How can we include hedge funds and private equity, which are not new asset classes but different ways of investing in traditional assets? Finally, how can we reconcile the old approaches to investment, which were based solely on the analysis of fundamentals – profits or the development of macroeconomic data – with new theories such as those issuing from behavioural finance and which admit the influence of irrational factors, such as excessive confidence, mimicry, misperceptions, and investors' other psychological biases, on the formation of stock prices?

Lukasz Snopek's book seeks to answer all these questions. Challenging the dogmas of yesterday is never easy, and he or she who tries runs the risk of destroying without trying to rebuild. Very fortunately, the author has carefully avoided this trap. Not only does he discuss and illustrate perfectly the limits of existing investment models, he suggests a new framework for portfolio construction based on strategic long-term allocation combined with "multi-force" tactical allocation. Thanks to this last aspect in particular, the whole range of macroeconomic, fundamental, technical and behavioural factors that can influence prices in a financial market can be included. Therefore, it offers an overall framework for reflection that is applicable to all types of investment and portfolio.

As Warren Buffett liked to say, "Over his lifetime, it is impossible for an investor to make hundreds of good decisions. One a year is enough." For many investors, reading this book will no doubt be it for 2012.

Francois-Serge Lhabitant
Chief Investment Officer, Kedge Capital
Professor of Finance, Edhec Business School

About the Author

Lukasz Snopek has been working for many years as a wealth manager and investment consultant in the private banking sector. His qualifications include a Master of Law and a Master's degree in Business Administration (HEC), the Swiss Federal Diploma for Experts in Finance and Investments and the International Wealth Manager Certificate (CIWM). Lukasz Snopek is also a corrector for the Swiss Financial Analysts Association and teaches portfolio construction and management at the Institut Supérieur de Formation Bancaire (ISFB) in Geneva.

Acknowledgements

I would like to thank the following people, without whom this book would not have existed:

- my wife Jennifer for her support throughout the writing process, and especially for her advice and attentive reading of the manuscript;
- my friend Antoine Courvoisier for our innumerable discussions, his advice and the time he was kind enough to devote to reading these many pages;
- my friend Marc Munz for reading and commenting on the manuscript;
- M. Thierry Lacraz for reading and commenting on the manuscript;
- Professor Thorsten Hens, and Martin Vlcek for his comments on the Behavioural Finance chapter;
- Professor Martin Hoesli for his comments on the Real Estate chapter;
- my friend Thomas Lufkin for his comments on the Macroeconomic section;
- Jessica Edwards for the translation of the manuscript into English;
- all the people at John Wiley & Sons who contributed to the English version;

and, of course, Professor François-Serge Lhabitant for his wonderful foreword.

Their pertinent and constructive remarks helped to improve both the content and the presentation of this book.

Introduction

In managing their assets, investors seek above all to preserve the capital invested by trying to generate a level of growth higher than or equal to average inflation. Various approaches exist in practice, but recent financial crises – with their often dramatic consequences for individuals and their wealth – argue for a more flexible process, no longer based on rigid asset allocation but, as we will see, on the attractiveness of asset classes.

The approach to portfolio construction and management suggested in this book favours risk-based management rather than a focus on expected returns, which are difficult to predict. To help investors fully optimise their returns and minimise risks, deep and intrepid reflection was called for.

It is not easy to question what we have been taught and have acted upon for many years. Can this be put down to conviction, habit, loyalty to a certain philosophy or just to facility? Or is it rather due to a lack of courage, curiosity or pragmatism?

Of course, the answer depends on each individual. But in a world that demands constant adaptation and review, it is necessary now more than ever to reconsider the way we invest, and to cast a critical eye over financial theories frequently based on fragile assumptions. Today, it seems increasingly clear that market movements cannot be satisfactorily explained by these theories and that new paths must be explored.

What if volatility were not an appropriate measure of risk? And what if Markowitz's modern portfolio theory and other financial models were outdated? What if fundamental analysis and technical analysis were complementary rather than opposing?

And, finally, what if it were impossible to predict market movements, making all models or attempts at modelling obsolete?

As the mathematician Mandelbrot observed, "we must understand, in a more realistic way, how different types of prices develop, how risk is measured and how money is made or lost. Without this knowledge, we are destined to undergo crashes again and again."[1] The time is ripe to give these issues serious consideration.

Part I defines the objectives sought by any investor and the risks to which they expose their capital, before examining the various risk measures used in finance. At the end of this analysis, a more appropriate measure of risk is suggested.

In Part II, we define the different asset classes and the various risks associated with each, culminating in a classification according to their degree of risk.

The notion of market efficiency is dealt with in Part III, as are fundamental and technical analysis. The valuation of each asset class previously defined is covered in Part IV.

Next, three practical approaches are presented in Part V, namely those of Warren Buffett, Benjamin Graham and Peter Lynch.

Part VI addresses behavioural finance, with an exploration of the different investor biases in terms of information selection and processing, as well as in the use of assets.

Part VII considers whether it is possible to anticipate market movements, by examining various approaches including the macroeconomic approach. We will then suggest in Part VIII an investment model that takes into account the conclusions reached throughout our analysis.

The second to last section presents a study of portfolio construction and management including, first of all, the different approaches used in finance, such as Markowitz's modern portfolio theory, the Capital Asset Pricing Model (CAPM) and Value-at-Risk (VaR). Finally, a new, simple and practical path is suggested based on the model developed beforehand.

The relative attractiveness of different asset classes for investors is examined in the tenth and last part. The objective here is to suggest a new framework for portfolio construction and management, thus helping investors to achieve their goal of preserving and growing their capital in the best possible conditions.

---

[1] Mandelbrot, Preface, V.

Part I
Investors and Risk

1
Basic Principles

1.1 INVESTORS

Before beginning our analysis, it is worthwhile noting that this book ultimately aims to help a particular type of individual: investors.

These individuals, who have **capital** to invest deriving from various sources (savings, inheritance, proceeds from the sale of real estate, etc.), are those most concerned by what follows.

They want to invest this sum of money so it yields a profit, thereby increasing their capital over time. So investors look first and foremost for a return, which may take the form of **regular income**, **capital gains**, or both at once.

At this stage, it should be noted that the **expected return** for the given time horizon must be **positive** in order to achieve the desired growth. It must also be **higher** than **average inflation** so that investors can **preserve** their **purchasing power** over time, and therefore their real wealth. Furthermore, net return – that is return after tax – should ideally be taken into account.

So, along with the **risk of capital loss**, **inflation** is one of the two greatest **risks** for investors, as it can seriously affect their capital over time. As such, it is worth defining more precisely.

1.2 INFLATION

Inflation can be defined as an **increase** in general price level, with the chief consequence of a decrease in consumer purchasing power. Conversely, **deflation** is defined as a **decrease** in general price level.

Salaries, retirement pensions and other social security benefits are generally indexed to inflation, thus enabling consumers to maintain their purchasing power over time. As Marc Faber suggests, "to explain inflation to your children, buy a $100 US bond and frame it, then watch its value diminish to almost nothing over the next 20 years".[1]

As shown by the graph below (Figure 1.1), inflation can indeed strongly affect the value of assets over time. Excluding any investment generating annual interest and considering an inflation rate of only 2%, the capital's value is halved in about 35 years. With an inflation

---

[1]Marc Faber. Interview with Tom Dannet. "Five Books: Marc Faber on Investment." 23.10.2009 (www.fivebooks. com/interviews/marc-faber-on-investment).

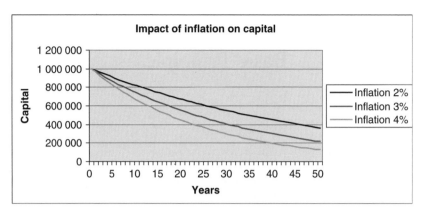

Figure 1.1 Impact of inflation over time with an interest rate of 2%, 3% and 4%.

rate of 3%, this period drops to 23 years and at a rate of 4%, "only" 17 years are necessary to halve the initial capital. The importance of investing money at a rate which covers at least that of inflation is obvious.

The **objective** generally fixed by **central banks** for inflation is around **2%**. However, in absolute terms, this figure should be revised upwards from an investor's point of view, considering the product categories most relevant to consumers in the price index. Indeed, when focusing on price increases for food, housing, energy or health-related spending, the average rate of inflation appears to be much higher.

In general, a market basket is used to calculate price changes. This basket includes a representative selection of goods and services consumed by private households. It is subdivided into various categories of expenditure, and each main category is weighted according to the share it represents in household expenditure. The following examples are of the consumer price index calculation for Switzerland[2] and England[3] (Table 1.1).

Table 1.1 Allocation of items to IPC and CPI divisions in 2010

Items	IPC weight	CPI weight
Food and non-alcoholic beverages	11.063%	10.8%
Alcohol and tobacco	1.784%	4.0%
Clothing and footwear	4.454%	5.6%
Housing and household services	25.753%	12.9%
Furniture and household goods	4.635%	6.4%
Health	13.862%	2.2%
Transport	11.011%	16.4%
Communication	2.785%	2.5%
Recreation and culture	10.356%	15%
Education	0.669%	1.9%
Restaurants and hotels	8.426%	12.6%
Miscellaneous goods and services	5.222%	9.7%

---

[2] Source: www.bfs.admin.ch.
[3] Source: www.statistics.gov.uk.

Ultimately, the impact of inflation depends on the category of the population being considered and its type of consumption. In light of this, an interesting tool has been made available in the UK. Individuals can make use of a personal inflation calculator[4] to calculate inflation specifically based on their own personal expenditure, which can then be compared to national inflation.

Generally speaking, an annual rate of 2% is the minimum conceivable threshold and a rate of 3% is more realistic.

By setting a target rate of return of 2%, investments may only just cover inflation, while a target of 3% will begin to generate a certain level of growth. It is interesting to note that Graham, in his work written in the 1950s, already believed "that it is reasonable for an investor [. . .] to base his thinking and decisions on a probable (far from certain) rate of future inflation rate of, say, 3% per annum".[5]

So investors must bear in mind that their final return, which we will call the real rate, should be calculated in the following way:

Real rate = nominal rate − inflation rate

Example:

Nominal interest rate of a savings account = 2.5%

Inflation = 2%

Final (real) rate = 2.5% − 2% = 0.5%

Our Advice

Given that periods of deflation also exist, we ultimately suggest allowing for an **average inflation rate** of **2%**. The important thing is to take this minimum threshold into account in the investment process.

1.3   CHOICES FOR INVESTORS IN TERMS OF INVESTMENTS

Investors may choose to invest in an asset with virtually no risk. This investment, commonly known as a **risk-free rate investment**, offers a very low return, usually only partially covering inflation, except of course during periods of deflation.

However, a feature of this type of investment is that it is always **positive**, generating capital **growth** which, though **modest**, is **stable** over time. Some investors settle for this type of low return investment, even though their purchasing power may be affected over time.

---

[4] www.statistics.gov.uk.
[5] Graham, p. 50.

For other investors, a risk-free rate investment is not enough. Investment in other asset classes must therefore be considered in order to improve returns and avoid capital being affected by inflation in the long term. As we will see further on, domestic stocks (national firms), for example, provide good protection against inflation.

Investors can turn to **risky assets** such as stocks, bonds or real estate. They certainly generate **higher returns** than risk-free rates, but they may be either **positive** or **negative**. Because of fluctuations in their price over time, the possibility of capital loss is the main risk for investors here.

It is now time to begin our analysis by examining how this risk is defined in finance, and determining how well this is adapted to reality.

2

Measures of Risk

2.1 VOLATILITY OR STANDARD DEVIATION

As we have just mentioned, the price of certain assets can fluctuate over time, either upwards or downwards. The amplitude of these variations around the mean was the first tool used to define risk, particularly by Markowitz in establishing the foundations of modern portfolio theory. According to this approach, the greater the variation around the mean, the riskier the asset.

In finance, the **standard deviation** is often used to measure the risk of a financial asset. This is an index of dispersion around the expected result (mean). The higher this variation from the mean, the riskier the financial asset is considered to be, given the variability of its outcome.

Based on historical data for the price of a financial asset, it is possible to determine the frequency of occurrence of a certain profitability, or of a return interval, and to obtain what is called a **probability distribution**.

These same data allow the **expected return** and the aforementioned standard deviation to be calculated. Given the shape of the distribution and for practical reasons, a particular distribution called **normal distribution** is used, which has the following characteristics:[1]

- it is completely characterised by its **mean** and **variance** (standard deviation squared);
- it is **symmetrical** around its mean.

Furthermore, according to this distribution, there is (see Figures 2.1–2.4):

- a 68% chance of falling within +/− 1 standard deviation of the mean;
- a 95% chance of falling within +/− 2 standard deviations of the mean;
- a 99% chance of falling within +/− 3 standard deviations of the mean.

However, not all distributions are symmetrical, and the probability of **rare events** (distribution tails) or **financial crises** occurring is **underestimated** by normal distribution.

Furthermore, positive deviations from the mean should be considered positive factors for investors, as they entail no capital loss. If we take the example of an asset that generates only positive, though highly variable, returns over a given period, the strict application of this concept would lead to the conclusion that this is a very risky asset in terms of its

---

[1]Statistical graphs taken from http://www.astro.ulg.ac.be/cours/magain/stat/stat51.html.

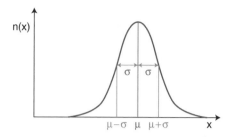

Figure 2.1   Illustration of the normal law.

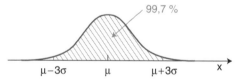

Figure 2.2   Illustration of the normal law.

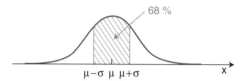

Figure 2.3   Illustration of the normal law.

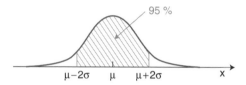

Figure 2.4   Illustration of the normal law.

standard deviation. This would be a rather surprising conclusion for an investor who had not made any capital loss.

Empirical studies also show that *ex post* returns differ from those calculated using models (*ex ante*). Moreover, the idea of time horizon or holding period is key here. The total return obtained by an investor specifically depends on the moment when the purchase or sale takes place.

For example, take two investors who entered the market at the same time with the same probability distribution, but who sold at different moments. The investor who sold earlier made a different return from the investor who held the position longer, although the expected return was initially identical. We could also consider two investors who entered the market at different moments with different probability distributions, and who then exited at two different moments, but who achieved the same performance. This shows that returns will essentially depend on investors' entry and exit decisions.

As we can see, normal distribution is not really suitable. Another distribution, called the **gamma distribution**, might be more appropriate. The gamma distribution takes into account not only the mean and variance, but also skewness and the thickness of tails (kurtosis), which are the third and fourth moments in statistics. However, it too is based on probabilities.

The problem with probabilities is that extreme events do occur. This probability is underestimated by normal distribution and better taken into account by the gamma distribution, which implies that the probability of a negative return is in fact greater than commonly thought.

In addition, studies related to behavioural finance indicate that **low probabilities** are often **overestimated** while **higher probabilities** are **underestimated**, showing a distortion of probabilities by investors.

As part of risk management analysis, four cases can be distinguished according to their degree of occurrence:

Risk management table

low probabilities with significant consequences on performance (2)	high probabilities with significant consequences on performance (4)
low probabilities with insignificant consequences on performance (1)	high probabilities with insignificant consequences on performance (3)

Generally, it is preferable to avoid situations no 2 and no 4 as they can have negative consequences if they do take place. However, as we saw earlier, low probabilities with significant consequences do exist, and can strongly influence investor decisions.

On the stock markets, events supposed to happen "occasionally" actually occur much more frequently than expected. From a statistical point of view, very strong corrections, such as that of 19 October 1987 when the Dow Jones index fell over 29%, or 29 September 2008, when Wall Street lost nearly 7% in one day, should never happen. However, these major losses did happen despite the infinitesimal chances of them occurring.

By considering the daily variation in the Dow Jones Industrial index, Mandelbrot[2] demonstrated these discrepancies in a very interesting way (see Table 2.1).

Table 2.1 Dow Jones Index variations according to the theory and in practice (period 1916–2003)

Variations	According to the "theory"	In practice
>3.4%	48 days	1001 days
>4.5%	6 days	366 days
>7%	Once every 300 000 years	48 days

---

[2]Taken from Mandelbrot, p. 31.

These theoretical probabilities of occurrence seem poorly adapted to market reality and the variations in stock prices do not, therefore, seem to follow normal distribution.

As Taleb summarises perfectly, "our world is dominated by the extreme, the unknown, and the very improbable (improbable according to our current knowledge) – and all the while we spend our time engaged in small talk, focusing on the known, and the repeated".[3]

We must not fail to mention the **luck factor**, which can play a significant role. If we were to examine the characteristics of successful entrepreneurs who have started their own business and become millionaires, we would find characteristics such as courage, risk-taking, optimism and a very strong will. Looking at entrepreneurs who have failed, it seems that they also possess these personality traits. Aside from a few differences in individual capabilities, "what truly separates the two is for the most part a single factor: luck. Plain luck."[4]

"Luck is far more egalitarian than even intelligence. If people were rewarded strictly according to their abilities, things would still be unfair – people don't choose their abilities. Randomness has the beneficial effect of reshuffling society's cards."[5] So, for a given period, a fund manager will do better than his or her peers, before being replaced by another fund manager who will do better than the first, and so on. However, while this luck factor exists, it is undeniably related to a person's individual and intellectual skills, but these aspects will be examined in the later sections of our analysis.

Using **standard deviation**, or volatility, as the **only measure** of **risk** is **insufficient**, and an approach based on probabilities seems difficult to implement in order to anticipate markets and model their movements. Indeed, for each new movement, no one can know in advance which scenario is going to play out even with the knowledge of the different probabilities associated to each scenario. Although the most probable scenario is likely to occur, another scenario with a lower probability may also occur due simply to the fact that it exists.

Finally, we can also note that for each new movement, new scenarios may emerge with their own related probabilities, or even unanticipated scenarios that exist without us realising it, making modelling based on probabilities even more complex. To make decisions about investment, it is therefore preferable to **focus** on **consequences**, which are easier to determine than an estimation of probabilities.

As Frank Knight summarises, "human knowledge is often largely insufficient to determine the probabilities of the various events possible".[6] Furthermore, it can sometimes be dangerous to draw conclusions about statistical relationships that are due only, or at least partially, to chance.

---

[3] Taleb, p. xxviii.
[4] Taleb, p. 106.
[5] Taleb, p. 222.
[6] Taken from N. Beiner.

Our Advice

For the reasons that have just been outlined, we recommend that **volatility not be considered** as the **only measure of risk** for portfolio construction. However, as we shall see later, it provides an **important indication** of the **level** of **activity** of a market or security.

According to a recent EDHEC study, "portfolio managers state that they lack sufficient knowledge to manage risk optimally [. . .] and do not fully take into account extreme risks when constructing portfolios. They also fail to employ techniques that avoid generating overly-concentrated portfolios because of poor input estimation."[7]

In the report published by Morningstar in the February/March 2009 edition of its journal *Morningstar Advisor* entitled "Getting a Read on Risk", it emerges "that there's much more risk than there appears to be and that the standard deviation doesn't capture all the risk".[8]

In conclusion, as shown by the mathematician Mandelbrot, markets are much wilder and more frightening than theory would have us believe. You might then wonder if investors are truly willing to invest in a market whose risk is much higher than they think.

2.2 BETA AS A MEASURE OF RISK

Another criterion was then developed, focusing this time on the degree of an asset's price variation in relation to the market, measuring in a sense its "reactivity" and therefore its degree of risk relative to market variations.

This is **beta**, which is a **measure** of **sensitivity** in relation to the **market**. It is generally used to measure what is called market risk.

The market's beta is set at 1. If the value of beta is higher than 1, the asset is said to overreact in relation to the market, and is therefore "riskier". When the value is lower than 1, it underreacts, and may be considered "less risky". Use of this criterion also implies defining the idea of the market, and as such we might wonder if, for example, the S&P 500 should really be regarded as the market.

A new **relationship** between **risk** and **return** was developed as part of the **Capital Asset Pricing Model** (CAPM) developed by William Sharpe.[9] To summarise, investors demand the payment of a premium for the risk taken. The greater the risk, the higher the premium should be and therefore the higher the return. Also note that only market risk should be taken into account, as specific risk can be eliminated through diversification.

---

[7]EDHEC Survey.
[8]*Morningstar Advisor*, pp. 8–13.
[9]See Sharpe and the CAPM in his article published in the *Journal of Finance* in 1964.

Specific risk is the intrinsic risk linked to an individual security, which depends only on factors specific to that security (management of the company, obsolescence of a range of products, etc.) and is therefore independent of factors that affect securities as a whole. When combined with market risk, this gives total risk.

So expected return can be defined as follows:

Expected rated of return =

Risk-free rate + Beta * (expected market return − risk-free rate)

Consequently, in order to raise the long-term rate of return, it is simply necessary to increase the beta, considered as a new measure of risk.

Besides the difficulty of measuring it with precision, the **beta changes constantly**, solely in relation to market fluctuations. Furthermore, use of beta assumes that the upside potential and downside risk are equal, although this is not necessarily the case in practice.

It was demonstrated in 1992 by Fama and French[10] that there is no relation between securities' return and their beta, which does not therefore seem to be a decisive factor. Ratios such as the Price to Earnings Ratio (P/E) or the Price to Book were much more effective in explaining differences in returns between securities.

These results were confirmed in a study by Malkiel a few years later.[11] Furthermore, "recurring anomalies between expected and actual returns, attributed to pockets of market inefficiency, are demonstrated by various empirical studies". Thus, he identified that with an equal beta, the shares of small capitalisation companies got an average return significantly higher than large-cap stocks. Similarly, "growth companies' stock (low book-to-market ratio), for the same beta, got a lower return than value companies' stock (high book-to-market ratio)".[12] Certain risk factors are therefore not completely taken into account by the beta.

It would seem that **beta** is **not** an **adequate measure** of **risk**, as other elements influence market risk; it depends on a large number of macroeconomic variables, such as interest rates, inflation, changes in GDP, etc. Other than the difficulty of selecting an index that can be regarded as representative of the market, the market rate of return is difficult to estimate and it is an *ex ante* return.

At this stage, is it also worth noting that the CAPM is often used to determine the cost of equity, one of the components of a company's cost of capital. This is the rate of return required by shareholders, but it is difficult to estimate in practice.

---

[10]Article nicknamed "The Beta is Dead" by financial economists. *Journal of Finance*, 1992.
[11]Malkiel, p. 207.
[12]Grandin, Hübner, Lambert, p. 11.

> **Our Advice**
>
> We believe that investors should **focus** on the **factors** that **influence** price fluctuations and try to **determine** the **forces** that **cause prices** to rise or fall.
>
> Therefore, the sole criterion of volatility or reactivity in relation to the market is too simplistic as a measure of risk.

2.3   VALUE-AT-RISK (VaR)

Using the criterion of volatility, the same weight is given to upside and downside deviations, although positive variations do not really constitute a risk of capital loss for the investor.

Consequently, a new approach was developed to better take into account and focus on downside fluctuations, which in the end are the only fluctuations responsible for capital loss. This is the concept of Value-at-Risk (VaR).

VaR makes it possible to determine, assuming normal markets, the **maximum level** of **loss** over a **given time period** to a **given level** of **confidence**, generally set at 95%.

For example, the VaR of a position at 5% probability is a threshold value that indicates that the portfolio has a 5% chance of losing more than this limit. A VaR (5%) of 10% means that the investor has a 5% probability of making a loss of over 10%, or over 95% probability of doing better than this threshold, i.e., a 95% chance of making less than a 10% loss.

However, VaR calculations are based on the strong assumption that the distribution of returns is normal or log-normal.[13] It follows that if the distribution is not normal, it is impossible to use VaR. As we have already seen, market and stock price movements do not really follow normal distribution and, as such, VaR should be rejected for that reason alone.

In addition, as Nicole Beiner[14] points out, the VaR tells us nothing about amounts that can be lost with a low probability, and a low probability does not mean never.

Conditional VaR, or CVaR, was developed in response to this criticism and can be applied whatever the type of distribution. The CVaR indicates the expected losses in the worst 5% of scenarios. In other words, the average of the 5% of worst outcomes is calculated to give an idea of the loss distribution in the critical zone considered. This measure is more stable and reliable than VaR.

However, different parameters such as expected return, volatility and correlations are estimated. Consequently, any error in these estimates will give a false VaR or CVaR.

Compared to volatility, this approach does have the **advantage** of **concentrating** on **potential losses**, also known as downside risk, but like all probabilities, the very existence of a probability is already a risk in itself.

---

[13] A random variable follows log-normal distribution if its logarithm follows a normal distribution.
[14] See Beiner, p. 65.

> **Our Advice**
>
> In our view, a **statistics-based approach** is **unsatisfactory** and the concept of VaR and CVaR as measures of risk should therefore be rejected.

2.4   INVESTOR BEHAVIOUR TOWARDS RISK

Statistical laws do not seem **well adapted** to **finance** and any statistical measure of risk or measure aimed at building a model should be rejected. So, is there a more appropriate measure of risk and how should investors apprehend it?

We have already established that a risky asset may produce a negative return, i.e., its value can decrease over time. Of course, the magnitude of this decrease can vary from one asset to another, but this **potential loss** of value is in our view the key characteristic of risky assets. Consequently, once investors decide to enter the world of risky assets, they accept the risk of losing all or part of their capital, but can in return expect higher returns.

By adopting a new definition of risk, and accepting that **markets are risky "in absolute terms"**, independently of their volatility or probability distribution, we stand to achieve much more profitable performances. Moreover, the criteria of volatility as the sole and uniform measure of risk for all investors does not allow for the variety of individual behaviours. Indeed, attitude in the face of risk depends on individuals, who do not always act in a rational or uniform manner.

According to a given degree of risk, **risk-taking** could be represented by the **decision to invest or not to invest** in the market or in a certain asset class at a given moment.

Investors who take the risk of investing in the market must accept the potential risk of losing money and obtaining a lower performance than the cash rate (risk-free rate).

If they do decide to invest, they wish to make a higher return than the risk-free rate with the greatest certainty in the market context at the moment they have to make their decision. In a case of major uncertainty, they may even prefer to avoid the market. Investors have **complete flexibility** as they can decide to enter or exit the market at any moment.

The term "conviction" is essential and must be distinguished from probability related to distributions and different scenarios. Conviction is more a subjective, human and behavioural sentiment that influences decision-making. This conviction is based on several factors that form a part of the analysis.

In a way, investors must ask themselves when they should invest or not invest in the market or in a particular asset class. The question of when to enter or exit is obviously crucial, and models exist to help investors with this decision.

> **Our Advice**
>
> We believe that the real **risk-taking** happens at the moment of **making** the **decision** to **buy** (to **keep**) or to **sell** a **risky asset** according to a defined degree of risk.
>
> So, while **risky assets** are **risky by definition**, there are **specific risks** related to each **type** of **investment**.

Before making a decision, investors must first understand the range of assets available, the different risks associated with them and finally their classification according to their degree of risk. These various aspects are the subject of the next section.

Before beginning this new section, it is worth mentioning here the three golden rules that a friend, former trader turned administrator of financial companies, outlined one day:

1. If you do not understand a business, do not invest (smart principle).
2. Do not put all your eggs in the same basket (diversification principle).
3. Analyse your worst-case scenario. If it is really bad, go away!

These three principles summarise the logical approach to follow as part of any investment process: **understand**, **diversify** and **manage risks** by avoiding the most significant.

Part II
Asset Classes and their Degree of Risk

3
Asset Classes and Associated Risks

At the start of our analysis, we indicated that investors seek to make a return in the form of income and/or capital gains.

To achieve this objective, they must be familiar with the **investment universe** available before making their investment choices.

We define an **asset class** as a set of goods or securities (equity, debt or contracts) which exhibit the same characteristics, behave in the same way on the market and are governed by the same rules. Furthermore, an asset must be able to be **traded** on an **organised market** and **generate** an **income and/or capital gains** in the future. The main **purpose** of **acquiring** an asset is **investment**, i.e., to seek a return.

This section begins with a review of the different asset classes and, more importantly, an analysis of the risks associated with each. Asset price fluctuations depend on whether or not different factors, or more precisely risks, materialise, and these risks are usually specific to each class. After identifying the risks, we will determine whether it is possible to hedge against them and, if so, how. The list of risks will be as comprehensive as possible.

At the end of this section, we will classify the asset classes according to their degree of risk using several criteria.

3.1 MONEY MARKET INVESTMENTS

3.1.1 Definition

Money market instruments include all **short-term instruments** with a **maximum maturity** of **12 months**.

These are highly liquid, high-quality debt investments that generate a **modest** yet **regular income**, such as government debt securities, certificates of deposit, commercial paper or fiduciary deposits.

For private management, in terms of the form of investment, fiduciary investments are usually distinguished from money market funds. Although bonds with a maturity of less than one year belong to the money market category, they will not be considered in detail here as they are covered in the next section.[1]

---

[1]See 3.2.

A **fiduciary deposit**[2] is an investment made **in the name** of a **bank**, in the form of a short-term deposit in another bank, but **on behalf** and at the **risk** of the **investor**, who therefore bears the risk of default or bankruptcy of the borrower. Counterparty risk may be mitigated by demanding a minimum rating (AA or AAA for example) or by counterparty diversification.

The interest rate earned is usually lower than the LIBOR (*London Inter Bank Offered Rate*) on the market for the given maturity. The LIBOR is the interest rate at which banks borrow on the interbank market, while investors who wish to lend money for a given period ask the bank to borrow from them and what interest rate they may obtain. As the loan is instigated by the lender, a lower interest rate is justified. This is a useful means of financing for banks, allowing them to borrow money at a better rate from their clients. The **interest** and **principal** are **paid** at **maturity**.

A **money market fund** invests in **short-term debt securities** of the highest quality. **Income** may be **distributed or capitalised**. Their main advantage over fiduciary investments, which often impose a fixed term, is their high liquidity. However, this type of investment can undergo price fluctuations over time because of the greater variety of investments.[3]

It is interesting to note that during the 2008 liquidity crisis, investors turned massively to money market funds or government debt securities to the detriment of fiduciary investments, seen as overly risky. Fiduciary rates suffered extremely high volatility during this period and sometimes banks even offered a rate higher that the LIBOR to attract investors.

Finally, the choice between these two types of investment rate will be influenced by the rate of income and capital gains tax in the investor's country of residence.

3.1.2   Risks associated with money market investments

Money market investments are not risk-free. The following risks may all be encountered:

a) Counterparty risk (default risk)

As mentioned above, the **quality** of the **borrower** is the essential risk involved in money market investments, as **bankruptcy** is the ultimate risk borne by investors (default risk).

Counterparty risk can be mitigated by careful **selection** and **diversification** of borrowers, and a high **credit rating** requirement. Because of its structure, an investment in a money market fund ensures greater diversification than a fiduciary deposit invested in a single bank.

b) Liquidity risk

This risk essentially concerns only fixed-term **fiduciary investments**, as money market funds are very liquid. A fiduciary investment subject to 48 hours' notice is obviously very liquid also.

---

[2]Fiduciary deposits are very common in private banking in Switzerland.
[3]Essentially short-term bonds whose prices vary over time.

Short maturity instruments **limit** this **risk** for investors.

c) Interest rate risk

Investors often think that quality money market instruments are risk-free, forgetting that they bear the **risk** of **interest rate fluctuation**, which can be significant. Every time a fiduciary deposit is renewed, there is a risk it will be reinvested at a different interest rate, which may be lower than the previous rate. We are referring here to short-term rates, i.e., under 12 months.

When **interest rates** are **rising**, short-term **fiduciary deposits** are preferable as they are quick to take advantage of any new rate rises, unlike money market funds that are slow to adjust to new rates.

Conversely, when rates are **falling** or expected to fall, it is best to make a longer-term **fiduciary deposit**, and then to **favour money market funds**. These are less sensitive to falling interest rates, integrating rate changes more slowly than fiduciary investments. Money market funds are invested in instruments with a longer maturity (though under 12 months), meaning they can benefit from rates that have been fixed for a longer period.

d) Inflation risk

As previously mentioned, returns offered by money market investments usually only **just cover inflation** in the **long term**. Inflation can therefore reduce the future value of the investment.

This risk can be reduced by investing in **other asset classes**, with a view to diversification. The proportion of money market investments will obviously depend on the investor's risk profile. It will be larger for conservative portfolios and very low for more dynamic profiles.

e) Currency risk

When denominated in **currencies other** than the **reference currency**, fiduciary deposits or money market funds represent an additional risk, as the currency risk borne by investors can be significant.

Investors often hope to take advantage of a higher interest rate in a foreign currency, but frequently forget that the conversion of these funds into the reference currency can ultimately lead to capital loss. Exchange rate movements can in fact be very violent, and affect investments. Therefore, large money market investments in a foreign currency should be avoided.

However, a need for liquidity in several currencies may justify money market investments in different currencies. In other cases, investors can either **limit** themselves to fiduciary investments in their **reference currency**, or **hedge** against the negative effects of exchange rate fluctuations by using forward currency contracts, for example. This will be looked at in more detail later on.

> **Our Advice**
>
> Regarding money market investments, we recommend:
>
> - focusing on borrower quality;
> - taking the direction of short-term interest rates into account;
> - favouring investments in the reference currency.

3.2   BONDS

3.2.1   Definition

A **bond** "represents a fraction of a **loan** made to a company or a public authority by a large number of investors. This type of security is issued in series, with the same issue price, interest rate, maturity and repayment conditions."[4]

These are **debt instruments** with maturities of over one year, as short-term bonds (maturity of under 12 months) are regarded as money market instruments.

In principle, investors who buy bonds get a **regular return**, paid out in the form of interest (**coupons**), and can also make a **capital gain** if the initial purchase price was lower than the resale price or redemption value. Bonds bought with the intention of being held until maturity (in which case we speak of yield to maturity) should be distinguished from bonds bought for a shorter period with speculative intent.

A bond's **total return** can be defined as follows:

$$\text{Bond return} = \text{fixed regular income} + \text{conditional capital gain}$$

a) Types of bond

Firstly, regular **fixed-rate bonds** are to be distinguished from **zero-coupon bonds** which, as their name implies, pay **no interest**, but make a capital gain when **redeemed** at maturity. These bonds are bought at a substantial discount to par value, i.e., below 100%, and are redeemed at par (100%).

Floating rate notes pay a **coupon** that **varies** over time. The coupon is equal to a **reference rate** like the LIBOR, plus a spread, i.e., a certain percentage (for example, LIBOR + 2%). In this case, investors are affected by interest rate fluctuations between two coupon dates.

Perpetual bonds have no **set maturity** and pay fixed coupons for life. Because of their "infinite" maturity, they are **very sensitive** to **interest rate fluctuations** and can experience

---

[4]Novello, p. 88.

major price fluctuations. Consequently, they should only be considered by investors seeking to earn a fixed income over time, who are unconcerned about the fluctuation of the bond's value.

Perpetual bonds are often "**callable**", giving the issuer the right to redeem the loan before maturity at a predetermined date and price. By exercising this option, the issuer can refinance at a lower rate if interest rates have dropped significantly since the initial date of issue. This type of clause reduces the bond's value for investors, as they run the risk of being redeemed before maturity and having to reinvest at a lower rate.

Some bonds are "**puttable**", meaning the holder is entitled to request early repayment at a predetermined price. However, they are rarer in practice and, because of this right to early redemption at the holder's request, more expensive.

Inflation-linked bonds provide protection against this threat and help preserve real value over time. Technically, every year, the nominal amount is adjusted to inflation based on the consumer price index. The coupon rate remains the same, but the nominal amount varies over time. However, this type of bond has low liquidity.

Finally **convertible bonds** allow the holder to convert the bonded debt to stocks (equity) according to defined conversion procedures, but they are not commonly encountered in practice.

b) Types of bond issuer

The first distinction in terms of issuer lies between **government**, **sovereign** or supranational bonds and **corporate bonds**.

As we mentioned earlier, government bonds with a maturity of less than 12 months, such as American Treasury bills (T-bills) or German "Bubills", are considered money market instruments because of their maturity, in the same way as commercial paper or certificates of deposit.

Government bonds from **developed countries** are **high-quality debt instruments**, but their creditworthiness depends on the country in question and the state of its finances. Greece is a recent example of a developed country with worrying financial health. Bonds from most **emerging countries** are of a **lower quality**, due to greater uncertainty about their ability to repay their debts.

By emerging countries, we mean all countries that are not considered advanced. According to the criteria defined by the International Monetary Fund (IMF), the 33 advanced (developed) countries are:[5]

---

[5]See list at www.imf.org (Data and Statistics).

• Australia	• Greece	• Norway
• Austria	• Hong Kong	• Portugal
• Belgium	• Iceland	• Singapore
• Canada	• Ireland	• Slovakia
• Cyprus	• Israel	• Slovenia
• Czech Republic	• Italy	• South Korea
• Denmark	• Japan	• Spain
• Finland	• Luxembourg	• Sweden
• France	• Malta	• Switzerland
• Germany	• Netherlands	• Taiwan
• Great Britain	• New Zealand	• United States

However, in the current economic environment, it is important to **examine** the **level** of **indebtedness** of the country in question carefully and to favour those with solid finances. It appears that several countries still do not respect the Maastricht criteria, which set the upper limits of indebtedness at 60% of GDP for public debt and 3% for budget deficit.

It can also be useful to study the distribution of the debt to find out who the other creditors are. This is particularly true of Europe, a club where everyone "knows everyone else".

Moving on to **corporate bonds**, it can be worthwhile to classify these according to company type and, more importantly, industry. In our view, an in-depth examination of the outlook of the industry in which the company operates, as well as the company's fundamentals, is key to determining the quality of the issuer.

The type of issue is also essential, as it determines the level of creditor protection in case of bankruptcy. **Subordinated bonds** pose an additional risk to creditors, as they are only entitled to have their debt repaid once the other (priority) creditors have been repaid. Bonds with an embedded call option also pose a risk to creditors.

Bonds issued by companies that benefit from a **State guarantee** or, because of their capital structure, benefit from an **implicit State guarantee**, also exist. They are generally of a quality equivalent to government bonds, but offer lower returns than ordinary corporate bonds of a similar quality.

c) Issuer quality, credit rating agencies and bond rating

Bondholders seek first and foremost a regular return in the form of coupons. However, interest is not paid if the issuer goes bankrupt or finds itself in **default**. Consequently, the choice of bonds should be based on the credit quality of the borrower.

Investors can refer to the **rating** assigned by **credit rating agencies** to determine the quality of an issue. Standard & Poor's, Moody's and Fitch are the main credit rating agencies. To rate the loan, they carry out a detailed analysis of the company's economic sector and financial state. The interest rate at which the company is able to finance itself on the market directly depends on the rating obtained, and therefore determines the cost of financing.

Loans rated **AAA** are the **most creditworthy**, and the lower limit for investment grade bonds is **BBB** (*Standard & Poor's*), at which **creditworthiness** remains **adequate**. Under this threshold, bonds do offer higher returns (they are called **high yield bonds**) but they carry a higher risk of default.

Sources

The main credit rating agencies are present on the internet:

www.standardandpoors.com

www.moodys.com

www.fitchratings.com

Bond issues with a BB to B rating are not very creditworthy. Bonds with a CCC to D rating are vulnerable to non-payment and are therefore highly speculative securities.

It is important to note that a **rating applies** to a **specific debt issue** and not to a company. Subordinated bonds issued by the same borrower will have a lower rating than regular bonds.

As such, it is useful for investors to study the rating of the bond issue before making an investment decision.

The following table[6] (Table 3.1) details the various ratings that can be given to bond issues.

Table 3.1   Description of ratings given by ratings agencies S&P and Moody's

S&P	Moody's	Description
AAA	Aaa	Prime, extremely strong capacity to pay interest and repay principal.
AA	Aa	High grade, slightly lesser financial strength.
A	A	Strong capacity to pay interest and repay principal. Changing circumstances and the economic environment can have a noticeable influence.
BBB	Baa	Medium grade, adequate capacity to pay interest and repay principal. Changing circumstances and the economic environment can have a significant adverse affect on the company.
BB	Ba	Currently meeting its financial commitments, however faces future uncertainties.
B	B	Less certainty that the company can continue to meet its financial commitments.
CCC	Caa	Speculative loan. The company is almost or already defaulting on interest payments and principal repayments.
CC	Ca	Extremely speculative loan. Great danger of default.
C	C	Very low probability that the debt will be serviced in full and on time.
D	–	In default.

---

[6]BankingToday.ch, June 2002.

Ratings agencies can sometimes be slow to change ratings, and the subprime crisis has caused doubt as to their precision and reliability. Moreover, besides the increasing complexity of products requiring analysis, the fact that these agencies are paid by issuers can lead to potential conflicts of interest.

These ratings are a good indication of creditworthiness, but cannot by themselves justify an investment decision. As we suggested earlier, an analysis of the industry and its prospects must also be carried out. In addition, we recommend examining trends in prices for **Credit Default Swaps** (CDS), which "provide precious information about the perception investors have of debtor risk".[7]

These instruments will be covered in more detail in the following subsection on risks.

d) Forms of bond investment

Investors can decide to invest directly in individual bonds or in bond funds, but management fees and expenditure involved in these funds often affect their performance. Another option is a bond index tracker, i.e., a fund that replicates the performance of such indexes. Passive (or index) management is often favoured where bonds are concerned.

e) Taxation of bonds

Coupons paid are regarded as income and are taxed at various rates depending on the country. Capital gains, however, are treated differently in different countries. For example, capital gains are taxed in France, while in Switzerland there is no capital gains tax on private property.

3.2.2   Risks associated with bonds

a) Default risk associated with bonds

This risk relates to the quality of the borrower and its ability to meet its financial commitments, i.e., to pay coupons and/or repay the borrowed amount. Bankruptcy of the borrower results in the loss of all or part of the capital invested. However, the position of creditors is preferable to that of shareholders. Regular bond debt is paid first, followed by "subordinated" debt, and only if there is anything left over will shareholders receive a liquidation dividend.

This risk can be **mitigated** by investing in **high-quality debt**, such as government bonds, favouring countries with solid finances.

It is also possible to hedge against such a risk by buying **CDSs (Credit Default Swaps)**. For the payment of a premium, this derivative protects the holder against issuer default, such as bankruptcy or moratorium. The event giving rise to payment must be clearly specified in the contract between the buyer and seller. The amount of the premium depends on the

---

[7]*Swiss Derivative Guide 2010*, p. 73.

issuer's credit quality and its future development. In this case, the default risk is transferred from the buyer to the seller of the CDS.

"Trends in CDS prices are a suitable instrument for measuring the perception of risk on financial markets."[8]

b) Risk associated with the type of issue and risk of early termination

The type of debt being issued also represents a risk for investors. Senior debt offers better protection than subordinated (junior) debt that may be assimilated to capital.[9]

In case of bankruptcy, creditors of unsubordinated debt have **priority** over holders of a subordinated bond, who are only entitled to repayment of the debt once the other (priority) creditors have been repaid. Stockholders only have a claim on the company's residual equity.

Subordinated bonds, being callable, also carry the risk of early termination. As we have seen, an embedded call option is a reinvestment risk for investors, who could be forced to reinvest at a lower rate. For this reason, the price of these bonds is lower than that of regular bonds.

It is difficult to hedge against these risks, apart from avoiding a certain type of issue and only considering regular, unsubordinated bonds.

c) Liquidity risk associated with bonds

Depending on the **size** of the loan and the levels of **supply** and **demand**, the price of an issue can be particularly sensitive to a lack of liquidity on the secondary market. Therefore, investors may risk not being able to sell their bonds quickly or at a good price if demand is weak or if the spread (gap between the purchase price and the sale price) is significant.

Once again, it is difficult for investors to hedge against this risk, but an examination of the size of the issue and of prior market liquidity conditions for the type of bonds in question helps limit this risk.

In practice, an issue of over 500 million euros is generally considered to be adequately liquid. The spread also provides a good indication of liquidity.

d) Ratings risk associated with bonds

A ratings drop will negatively influence the price of bonds, because of the lower debt quality implied by the new rating.

---

[8] *Swiss Derivative Guide 2010*, p. 73.
[9] Tier 2 Capital for example. According to capital standards set by the Basel II agreement, Tier 2 capital includes undisclosed reserves, revaluation reserves, general provisions, hybrid instruments and subordinated term debt. See www.bis.org/bcbs/index.htm.

Investors can hedge against this risk through careful **monitoring** of a bond issue's **rating**. For example, comments made by ratings agencies, such as "negative credit watch", must be taken into account.

Furthermore, it is worth noting that there are often constraints in management contracts that prohibit investments below BBB (investment grade level). Consequently, a credit rating downgrade – from BBB to BB for example – can trigger a rush to sell on the market, further precipitating the downward price movement.

e) Interest rate risk (price risk and reinvestment risk)

Interest rate variations influence both fixed-rate bond prices and the **reinvestment rate** of coupons, but with opposite effect. When rates drop, coupons are reinvested at a lower rate, whereas the price of the bond itself rises. Conversely, when rates rise, coupons are reinvested at a higher rate, but the price of the bond falls.

Before buying a bond, investors need to find out its yield to maturity, which is a good estimation of the bond's annual return assuming that it is held to maturity and rates do not change. If investors want to sell before maturity, they run the risk of having to sell at a loss if interest rates rise in the future. If they keep it, they have to accept price fluctuations. Therefore, the shorter the maturity, the lower the risk.

However, exposure to **price risk** can be limited in several ways.

i) Approach according to context

We can distinguish two main situations and determine the appropriate approach for each, taking into account the term structure of interest rates.

"Exact" positioning in terms of maturity will depend on the expected evolution of the yield curve (flat, normal or inverted yield curve).

Environment of rising interest rates:

As stated earlier, when interest rates rise, bond prices fall. So, if this scenario is anticipated, it is better to buy **short-term bonds** which are less sensitive to interest rate variations due to their low duration.[10] This will attenuate the drop in bond prices.

As soon as the rise is over and rates have stabilised, investors should switch to long-term bonds to lock in the higher returns and protect themselves against any future fall in interest rates.

Indeed, if rates subsequently drop, the price of these bonds will rise due to the greater appreciation of long-term bonds, which have a higher duration. However, coupons will be reinvested at a lower rate.

---

[10]For more detail on the idea of duration and modified duration, see below.

Environment of falling interest rates:

We have seen that when interest rates fall, bond prices rise. **Long-term bonds** are preferable when such a scenario is expected, as their higher duration means they are more sensitive to interest rate variations. This will improve the bond's price appreciation.

As soon as the fall is over and rates have stabilised, investors should switch to short-term bonds so as not to be locked in for too long a period in case of a future rates rise.

Moreover, a subsequent rise in interest rates will result in a fall in bond prices, but short-term bonds will suffer less from this depreciation due to their lower duration.

ii) Approach according to the hedge ratio

Exposure to price risk can be further limited by using what is called a **hedge ratio**. Using the duration of a hedging instrument for long-term interest rates, it is possible to calculate the amount of the instrument needed to hedge a bond portfolio. A bond futures contract or an interest rate swap can then be used.

The **duration** of a bond is a weighted average of successive interim maturities and final redemption. In other words, it represents the time it will take investors to recover their initial investment, considering the bond's purchase price, the coupon, its maturity and, finally, interest rates.

A higher time to maturity, a lower coupon rate and a lower yield to maturity all mean a higher duration.

Modified duration gives the sensitivity of the bond's price to interest rate movements.

The aim of this hedging strategy is to bring the portfolio's overall modified duration to zero, thereby protecting it against the influence of interest rate changes on prices.

For a given bond position with a precise modified duration, it is simply necessary to calculate the number of futures contracts to be sold[11] to bring this modified duration to zero. Therefore, if rates were to rise, the overall value of the portfolio would change very little if at all, as the decline in the bond's price would be compensated by the gain made on the sale of the futures contracts.[12]

This strategy is valid in the short term, but in the long term the hedge must be adjusted according to interest rate movements or the change in modified duration, not to mention the cost of the hedge.

---

[11] Number of contracts $= \dfrac{\text{Bond price} * \text{Bond's modified duration}}{\text{Price of the hedging instrument} * \text{Instrument's modified duration}}$.

[12] As their price is set by subtracting the interest rate from 100*, a higher rate decreases their price.

iii) Use of options as a hedging strategy

A strategy adapted to the context of interest rate trends reduces this risk substantially. Investors can also make use of "caps" or "floors", which allow them to hedge against rates increases or decreases respectively.

When interest rates are expected to rise, investors can buy a "**cap**" (interest rate call option) to hedge against rates rising above a certain level (strike price). If this threshold is passed, the buyer receives an amount corresponding to the difference between the observed rate and the strike price. This protection is often offered in conjunction with floating mortgage rates, where the borrower benefits from falls in interest rates but risks having to suffer higher interest rates in the future.

Where a decline in interest rates is expected, a "**floor**" (interest rate put option) may be used, giving protection when interest rates fall below a certain level. The holder of floating-rate debt securities who uses a "floor" will be paid an amount corresponding to the difference between the strike price (precisely defined level) and the observed rate at the moment of coupon payment.

iv) Immunisation strategy

In order to **hedge** against both **price risk** and **reinvestment risk** – "immunising" against these two opposite effects – a so-called immunisation strategy can be adopted to compensate for each.

While a hedging strategy aims to eliminate price sensitivity by selling a certain number of derivatives to bring the duration to zero, immunisation aims to **immunise** the **expected return** for a given period against interest rate fluctuations.

Of course, there is an investment that guarantees a predetermined expected return for a given period: the zero-coupon bond. Most bonds do pay coupons however, meaning that they are exposed to reinvestment risk.

To set up this strategy, a bond should be chosen whose **duration** corresponds to the **investor's time horizon**, in order to protect the underlying bond against any fluctuation until the next coupon date. Consequently, the portfolio must be reconfigured just after the coupon date, so that the portfolio duration is kept in line with the residual time horizon. Depending on the case, one effect may outweigh the other slightly.

It is important to note that immunisation is based on duration, and relies on the (strong) assumption of the parallel shift in the term structure of interest rates. In other words, this means that short- and long-term rates should develop in parallel, but this is not always the case in practice. It is therefore more effective on long-term strategies, as short-term rates are more volatile.

The complex implementation of this strategy is reserved for professionals and, like all hedging strategies, it generates an additional cost for investors.

f) Inflation risk

This risk is obviously linked to the risk of interest rate fluctuation that we have just discussed, as an interest rate rise to contain inflation has a negative impact on bond prices.

It is possible to hedge against this risk using **inflation-indexed bonds**. However, investors must be conscious of the reduced liquidity of this type of bond on the market.

Furthermore, as with money market investments, returns from debt investments may sometimes only just cover inflation in the long term. This risk can be reduced by considering other asset classes.

g) Currency risk associated with bonds

In the case of investments in a foreign currency, i.e., a currency other than the reference currency, **exchange rate fluctuations** can have a significant impact on the final return.

For a foreign currency investment without foreign exchange risk hedging, the return will be divided into two parts: the gain or loss on the investment itself, and the gain or loss on the exchange rate between the reference currency and the investment currency.

When the currency risk is eliminated, returns will be made up solely of the gain or loss on the investment, minus the **cost** of the hedge. During some periods, a portfolio hedged against currency risk can outperform one that lets foreign currency fluctuate, but in other periods, the opposite may be true.

As such, is it worth hedging against currency risk, or should exchange rate fluctuations simply be endured?

In general, the answer to this question depends firstly on the **weight** that the **foreign currency** position represents in the portfolio. If it is very low (a few percent), it may be justified not to hedge, as the impact on the overall portfolio is negligible. However, if the position is significant (20% or 30%), the question is worth asking.

h) Risks specific to emerging markets

It is difficult for investors to hedge against the various risks involved with emerging markets. Nonetheless, they must be conscious of these risks, and the specific context of a company established there and of the developing country in question must be analysed in advance.

- Political risk

  A government's lack of political experience, or the instability of the political system, leads to an increased risk of rapid and intense political and economic upheaval. This risk is obviously greater in emerging countries.
- Economic risk

  The economy of an emerging market is more reactive to fluctuations in interest rates and inflation than that of a developed country – it is also more exposed to them. A given event can therefore have much stronger repercussions. Furthermore, emerging markets often have a weaker financial base. Finally, their financial markets do not have an adequate structure and monitoring systems. As the assessments are different and ratings non-existent, it is much more difficult to assess credit risks.

- Credit risk

  Investments in government or corporate debt in emerging markets tend to involve higher risks than in developed countries, because of lesser creditworthiness, high public debt, debt conversions, a lack of market transparency or a lack of information.

- Currency risk

  The currencies of emerging markets undergo stronger and more unpredictable fluctuations than the currencies of developed countries. Some countries have introduced foreign exchange controls, others are likely to do so at any time, or may abandon their indexation to a reference currency.

  For example, many export-focused Asian countries use the US dollar for their transactions. These countries have indexed their currencies on the USD to avoid excess exposure to exchange rate movements. However, countries have an increasing tendency to dismantle this system.

- Inflation risk

  Due to strong price fluctuations and an underdeveloped financial market, the central banks of emerging countries can have difficulty meeting their inflation targets. Inflation may therefore fluctuate more than in developed countries.

- Market risk

  In emerging countries, monitoring of financial markets is faltering if not inexistent, and so regulation, market transparency, liquidity and efficiency are all lacking. In addition, these markets often display major volatility and significant price differences. Weak regulation accentuates the risk of price manipulation and insider trading.

- Liquidity risk

  An asset's liquidity depends on supply and demand. However, the social, economic and political developments, as well as the natural disasters that emerging countries experience, can influence the supply and demand mechanism more quickly and enduringly.

- Legal risk

  The absence or lack of monitoring of financial markets can result in investors being unable to have their legal rights respected, or only with difficulty. An inexperienced justice system can lead to major legal insecurity.

  Furthermore, requirements aimed at protecting the rights of shareholders or creditors (disclosure requirements, insider trading prohibition, management obligations, protection of minority interests, etc.) are often insufficient, if they exist at all.

- Execution risk

  Clearing and settlement systems often vary from one market to another. Often obsolete, they are a source of processing errors, as well as of considerable delays in delivery and execution. Not to mention that some emerging markets do not have these systems.

Our Advice

In regard to bonds, we recommend:

- favouring bonds issued by governments with strong finances;
- favouring corporate bonds issued by companies with low debt levels and/or solid fundamentals (industry);

- ideally choosing unsuborddinated loans;
- favouring issues that provide adequate liquidity;
- considering the direction of interest rates;
- hedging large foreign currency positions according to the degree of conviction.

3.3   STOCKS

3.3.1   Definition

A stock is an equity security that makes its holder one of the **owners** of the company that issued it. "Shareholders therefore benefit from **social rights** (right to vote at shareholders meetings, right to elect and be elected to the Board of Directors) and **economic rights** (right to dividends, right to receive a share of the proceeds of liquidation if the company goes bankrupt and a preferential right to buy new shares in case of capital increase)."[13]

Investors who buy stocks have the right, if the company is doing well, to a **share** in the **profits** generated, paid in the form of **dividends**, which are the returns generated by the investment. In addition, if the value of the company increases, which is reflected in a rise in its share price, investors can also make a capital gain on their initial investment.

Total return of a stock = conditional income + conditional capital gain

a) Types of stock

So-called **common stocks** are those which give their holder all the rights mentioned above. **Dividend-right certificates**, however, only confer the economic rights. This type of stock is limited in practice and the most common example is the dividend-right certificates of the pharmaceutical company Roche.

Firstly, we can distinguish **value stocks** or **income stocks**, which pay regular, high dividends. Investors looking for regular returns will try to identify stock that is considered good value for their level of earnings and dividends.

Growth stocks are generally characterised by a very high market value in relation to current profits, but offer the prospect of future earnings growth. They do not usually pay high dividends as they reinvest practically all their profits to ensure their growth. Price fluctuations are more significant and they are considered more risky than value stocks.

Secondly, we can distinguish **small** and **large capitalisations**, but the size and definitions vary from country to country.

Stocks are also differentiated[14] according to their reaction to the economic climate. Companies sensitive to economic cycles, such as airlines or auto manufacturers, are called **cyclical**

---

[13] Novello, p. 46.
[14] See Novello, p. 49.

stocks. Conversely, companies less sensitive to cyclical fluctuations, such as those in the healthcare or food industries, are called **defensive stocks**.

Finally, **preferred stocks** are **hybrid securities** between stocks and bonds. They give preferential rights to dividends; preferred stockholders are paid before any dividend payout to common stockholders. A fixed preferential rate is promised, provided that the company can distribute dividends. If not, dividends may accumulate to the following year. These are known as cumulative preferred stocks. In case of bankruptcy, holders of these securities are below bondholders in the order of reimbursement but above common stockholders.

b) Developed and emerging countries

Stocks can be classified in two main categories depending on the country: those of developed countries and those of emerging markets. By emerging countries, we mean all countries that are not considered advanced according to the criteria defined by the International Monetary Fund (IMF). This list is the same as the one mentioned above.[15]

c) Industry

Other than the cyclical and defensive sectors defined above, it can also be useful to distinguish between different industries in order ultimately to select individual securities (stock picking). We can define the sectors and industries[16] as shown in Table 3.2.

d) Forms of investment

Investment in this asset class can consist of buying **individual stocks** directly, **equity funds**, market or sector **index funds** (tracker funds), or **futures contracts**.

An **equity fund** offers the advantage of investment **diversification** with low capital, and management by specialists who can react quickly to market information.

However, most equity funds practice so-called "**relative management**", that is in relation to a benchmark or reference index. They measure their performance in reference to the benchmark. In practice, 80% of funds underperform their benchmark and a fund that outperforms its benchmark never stays at the top of the rankings for 10 consecutive years. Moreover, equity funds suffer from mild illiquidity as investors cannot exit the market immediately, unlike with selling stocks or index funds. They must await the NAV (Net Asset Value), calculated daily at best, to find out their exit price.

Finally, equity funds generally involve a significant fee structure. We recommend instead investing directly in the benchmark, by simply buying a market or sector index fund, or using futures.

An **index fund** (or tracker fund) offers more flexibility by making it possible to set purchase or sale limits, or even stop losses[17] (which is not possible with equity funds), costs investors

---

[15]See 3.2 b).

[16]Taken from Credit Suisse, "Research Monthly" (Swiss edition), 18 May 2009.

[17]See also point 3.3.2 c).

Table 3.2   Suggestion for segmentation by sector and industry

Sector	Industry
Energy	Energy
Materials	Chemicals
	Construction Equipment
	Metals and Minerals
	Pulp and Paper
Industry	Capital Goods
	Business Services
	Transport and Logistics
Consumer	Automobiles and Automobile Components
Discretionary	Consumer Durables, Apparel, Textile and Luxury Goods
	Hotels, Restaurants and Leisure
	Media
	Distribution
Consumer Staples	Food and Staples Retailing
	Beverages
	Food Products
	Tobacco
	Household Products and Personal Care
Health	Health Equipment and Services
	Biotechnology
	Pharmaceuticals
Finance	Banks
	Diversified Financial Services
	Insurance
	Real Estate
Information Technology	Software and Services
	Technology Hardware and Equipment
	Semi-Conductors and Equipment for their Manufacture
Telecommunications	Diversified Services
	Mobile Communications
Utilities	Utilities

less and provides attractive diversification in terms of exposure to a market or a particular sector. Counterparty risk must however be taken into account for this type of investment. Indeed, it is important to be familiar with the product structure and how the positions are held (directly or by borrowing).

Nonetheless, index funds can be criticised on several points. Firstly, equity funds specifically allow gambles to be taken in relation to an index with the aim of outperforming it, while an index fund will at best achieve the same performance as the index.

Furthermore, because of their construction based on the market capitalisation of companies, securities included in some indexes may represent a huge proportion, thereby biasing the homogeneity of the index. In some cases, a few securities may represent over half the index, as with the SMI[18] (*Swiss Market Index*). An equally weighted index can be an attractive

---

[18]Nestlé, Roche, Novartis and UBS alone account for nearly 60% of the SMI.

answer to the problem of market capitalisation weighting, but investors have to accept a performance gap compared with the initial index.

Performance may also sometimes be inferior to that of equity funds for a given observation period. Moreover, when the cost of rebalancing is considered, tracker funds' performance can sometimes be lower than that of the index. Finally, some empirical studies have shown that securities included in an index perform less well than those excluded.[19]

The choice of either a broad market index fund or a sector index fund is very important, as it will define the desired market exposure. A sector index fund may be more suitable as it is more selective than the market as a whole, or even a tracker certificate on a basket of securities, which ultimately amounts to stock picking.

It is also possible to use index **futures contracts**. These are standardised contracts between investors and a clearinghouse, with the advantage of being publicly traded and therefore highly liquid. Costs, moreover, are very low, with much lower minimum investment amounts than those for buying stocks or index funds directly.

In fact, only an **initial margin** need be deposited in a **margin account**, the size of which will depend on the volatility of the underlying security (generally between 5% and 15%). Profits and losses are calculated on a daily basis, using the "marking to market" process. At the end of each trading day, according to the future's price movement, the margin account is readjusted to reflect the gain or loss of the open position. If the balance of the margin account falls below the **maintenance margin requirement**, the investor receives a **margin call** and must pay into the account to return it to the initial margin, or the broker will close the position.

As we will see later, the use of options is another form of investment, as is integrating structured products linked to equities into a portfolio.

Our Advice

In view of the above, we suggest **combining the use of broad market or sector index funds or futures with a selection of individual securities**, which amounts to adopting a so-called classic or improved "core-satellite" approach. This will be covered in the following sections.[20]

3.3.2   Risks associated with stocks

In view of the various risks listed below, it is difficult to maintain that volatility alone constitutes an appropriate measure of risk. In our view, stocks are risky assets by definition.

a) Total risk

Generally speaking, **total risk** comprises the **specific risk** associated with shares in a particular company and **market risk**, which depends on macroeconomic conditions and fluctuations in the stock market in general.

---

[19]Observations made by Schroders on the Swiss market.
[20]See point 8.2, part IX.

It is possible to reduce exposure to specific risk through **diversification**, leaving only market risk. Inadequate diversification can lead to **concentration risk**: for example, one stock representing 25% of a portfolio.

Moreover, it is essential to have an intelligent diversification strategy that helps minimise exposure to the same risks. This implies being fully aware of the portfolio's different positions. For example, judging by the number of securities, a portfolio made up of 25 financial stocks appears at first glance to be diversified, but in fact remains strongly exposed to a particular sector.

However, too great a diversification may lead to overdiversification, which is expensive and may potentially reduce returns. Investors must find a good balance and, to do so, we suggest considering the following principles:

- do **not invest** in **a single** asset **class**;
- **avoid very small positions** in a portfolio that have a negligible impact on overall performance. Invest a minimum of 1%–2% in a position;
- maintain **sufficient diversification** between **industries** and **regions**. Do not accept too much exposure to a single industry or particular region;
- **avoid large concentrations** in a portfolio. In general, an individual position should not account for more than 10%. However, much depends on the type of product.

b) Risk associated with speculation

At this stage of our analysis, it is worthwhile for investors to consider what they are really buying when they acquire a stock.

Besides the equity instrument giving them economic and social rights, and the potential income and capital gains, investors also acquire a certain number of risks that we will list below, including the risk associated with speculation.

Speculators, whose primary goal is **short-term profit**, constitute a specific category of investors. With improved access to information and the globalisation of trade and financial markets, their number has increased considerably over the last few years. They aim to get rich quickly and easily by taking advantage of various opportunities that present themselves on the market.

Chartists – followers of technical analysis – often belong to this category. They try to predict market entry and exit points in the short term by analysing graphs and their forms. We will examine technical analysis in more detail in the next chapter.

Investors, on the other hand, usually adopt investment strategies with longer time horizons, and take into account various factors to determine the attractiveness of an asset class and its prospects for future development. For them, graphical analysis is an additional decision-making tool.

When investing in stocks, investors must accept exposure to price fluctuations which, due in large part to speculators who enter and exit the market quickly, may prove to be considerable in the short term. They must therefore be capable of holding a position for the time horizon they have set themselves.

In this analysis, we consider that **market risk encompasses** the risk associated with **speculation**. Any investor who buys a stock is, at the same time, buying a share in speculation over which they have very little influence. However, investors can attempt to profit from this, as we will see later. As Graham pointed out early on, "everyone knows that speculative stock movements are carried too far in both directions, frequently in the general market and at all times in at least some of the individual issues".[21]

If we take this analysis to the extreme by assuming that the share of speculation is very large, the market becomes a veritable casino manipulated by speculators, and the only factor that can generate returns is luck. In some markets, speculation is so strong that investors would be forgiven for wondering what exactly it is that they are buying. The satisfaction that comes from stock betting would thereby replace satisfaction from returns, turning stock markets into giant lotteries or racecourses where the horses are stocks to gamble on. Some may believe that there is nothing random about this type of race, and that only the best may win, but here we will let the investor or the gambler make up their own mind.

The profitability of casinos and gambling is generally very high, just like exploitation of the stock market. One may sometimes wonder whether it is worth risking one's money by investing in the stock market, as the likelihood of significant losses is often greater than commonly believed.

Investors must be conscious of this. They must understand and analyse market mechanisms and the various stakeholders involved, all of which will have an influence on the price of their securities. Using the tools described below will help to limit the risk of losses.

c) Risk of falling stock prices

When the stock market and stock prices fall, investors suffer a **loss** of value of the **capital invested** that can be significant depending on the size of the downturn. In the event that a decline is anticipated, it is possible to hedge against this risk in several ways.

i) Placing a stop loss order

Investors may decide to set a price **limit** at which a **sale order** will be triggered. In the event of a sudden downturn, the final execution price may be lower than the stop loss level, as the order is executed at the first available exit price. Investors should note that depending on the type of instrument and the market under consideration, it is not always possible to place stop loss orders.

Stop losses are **free** to place and **easy** to **renew**. However, once executed, they leave investors with cash although the drop may only be temporary. As we will see below, a put

---

[21]Graham, p. 31.

option on the other hand allows investors to profit if the price of their security recovers before the option expires.

ii) Buying a put option (right to sell)

This insurance has the advantage of eliminating risk asymmetrically, i.e., it **protects** investors against **downside risk** while allowing them to **participate** in **rising markets**.

Unlike stop losses, this insurance has a **cost**, which may be high depending on the option's strike price, time to expiration and volatility. The higher the coverage sought, the more expensive the put. Furthermore, as with all strategies using options, **timing** is an important aspect and future development is uncertain. It is possible to be right, but too early (the put expires too quickly) or too pessimistic (a correction does occur but the strike price is set too low).

Moreover, often only **American options**[22] are available, which means having to pay more for the possibility of exercising the option at any time. Differences between the bid (sale price) and the ask (purchase price) are sometimes large and it is often difficult to master the costs of such a strategy.

iii) Sale of futures contracts

The sale of futures contracts lets investors reduce their exposure to stocks and thereby limit the loss of value of their investments in case of market downturns. In this case, they eliminate market risk symmetrically, that is, they **hedge** against any market **downturn** but do **not participate** in market **upswings** (in the case of complete hedging).

When a downturn is expected, they can sell a certain number of futures corresponding to the amount to be hedged. If the downturn does occur, the profit generated by the sale of contracts (closure of the position by buying back the same number of contracts) therefore compensates for the loss in value of the stock.

However, this strategy requires setting aside an initial margin and daily calculation of variation margins. Open futures contracts are **marked to market** daily, i.e., the process of evaluating gains or losses is carried out every day, and this can lead to margin calls. Consequently, investors must have enough cash to meet potential margin calls if the maintenance margin requirement is no longer met.

This strategy is certainly **simple** to set up, but investors must monitor the **movement** of futures prices **carefully**, and consider placing **stop loss orders** to limit losses on the futures contracts if the market were to move in the opposite direction.

Finally, this hedging strategy is often imperfect; the number of contracts is often rounded off, variations in stock prices do not necessarily correspond to the variation in the futures

---

[22]The holder of an American option has the right to exercise it at any time until the expiration date, unlike a European option that can only be exercised at expiration.

contracts and the expiry of the contract used does not always correlate to the time horizon of the hedge (basis risk). Therefore, the hedge is often partial and the futures contract used does not perfectly represent the positions held in the portfolio (correlation risk).

iv) Sale of stock

If a **strong decline** is **expected**, it is better to sell the stock directly so as not to suffer the loss of value.

Obviously, for investors who are unwilling to accept potential capital losses, and for whom preserving capital without risk of fluctuation is essential, this asset class should not be considered.

d) Liquidity/solvency risk associated with stocks

Liquidity risk is the risk that a company will no longer be able to meet their short-term financial **commitments**, such as interest payments, principal repayments, payment of suppliers, etc.

It is difficult for investors to hedge against this type of risk, but before investing, examining the ratios used to measure short-term liquidity may prove useful. The most commonly used in practice are the **current ratio**,[23] which generally should be higher than 2, or the **quick ratio**,[24] which should at least be equal to 1 to be sure that the company has enough cash and liquid assets to cover their short-term debts. It is important to be able to monitor the movement of these ratios over a three to five-year period, and to know their average value for the industry the company operates in so that comparisons can be made.

A short **cash cycle** will not pose any **cash flow** problems, while a longer cycle may, clients paying their invoices too slowly in relation to the payment of supplier invoices by the company. Cash is therefore essential for its survival, as even if it is making a profit, a company can go bankrupt if it lacks cash.

Long-term **solvency risk** is the risk that a company will not be able to meet its financial **obligations** in the **long term**, which can ultimately lead to the company going bankrupt.

Once again, it is difficult for investors to hedge against this type of risk, but examining the ratios used to measure long-term solvency may prove useful before investing. The **debt ratio**[25] and the **interest coverage ratio**[26] are the most commonly used in practice. Here again, it is important to be able to monitor their movement over a three to five-year period, and to know their average value for the industry the company operates in, so that comparisons can be made. For example, looking at changes in the debt ratio of the former airline Swissair between 1997 and 2000, we can see that it went from 3.76 to 13.95, a progression that should immediately have discouraged any potential investor.

---

[23]Current ratio = Current assets/Current liabilities.
[24]Quick ratio = Cash + Marketable securities + Accounts receivable/Current liabilities.
[25]Debt ratio = Total liability/Total assets.
[26]Interest coverage ratio = EBIT/Interest expense.

e) Bankruptcy risk associated with stocks

This is the **ultimate risk** associated with the company's future survival. In the event of bankruptcy, stockholders can only hope to recover a share in the proceeds of liquidation.

It is difficult to hedge against this type of risk, apart from avoiding investment in stocks altogether. Examining the various ratios indicated above and a more comprehensive analysis of the company's operations both help limit exposure to this risk. Nonetheless, it is associated with any stock investment.

f) Operational risk of the company

Human error, **fraud**, **corruption**, **exceptional expenditure** and the **loss** or **unavailability** of **employees** or **managers** are operational risks that can prove to be significant, or even catastrophic for a company.

Everyone remembers the operational loss of several billion euros caused by Jérôme Kerviel at the Société Générale, or the loss of 2.3 billion dollars by a trader at UBS, the Enron scandal, or the bombing of a Pan Am flight that led to the airline's bankruptcy.

Investors holding shares in a company are obviously powerless to control these risks, making it practically impossible to hedge against such consequences. There are hazards and, unfortunately, black sheep in every profession, but exposure to this risk can be limited by swift reactions to news and rumours circulating about companies held.

g) Reputation risk associated with stocks

This risk relates to events that affect the **company's image** (defective products, court cases, reputation in the industry, with clients or suppliers, etc.).

It is difficult for investors to hedge against this type of risk, but this factor must also be considered as part of the investment process. Following news related to the company again helps limit this risk.

h) Risk related to the economic environment/industry risk

Macroeconomic conditions, the **economic climate** and the various **seasonal** or economic cycles obviously have an influence on companies. Interest rate movements, changes in growth and unemployment rates or commodity price movements affect various industries and therefore companies directly. The degree to which companies are affected and react will vary from one industry to another.

It is difficult for investors to protect themselves against this type of risk, but a detailed analysis of macroeconomic conditions, the relevant industry and future prospects help to limit it and to find an appropriate position within this asset class.

i) Political risk associated with stocks

A **lack** of **political stability** in a country can affect assets held within it and have an impact on the companies operating on that soil. This risk is more manifest in emerging countries.

Economic conditions can also incite governments to make decisions that affect particular industries and their long-term profitability.

It is difficult for investors to hedge against such a risk, apart from avoiding investing in stocks in emerging countries. Taking this factor into consideration can help select stocks with a low political risk by turning to the developed markets.

j) Legal/regulatory risk associated with stocks

The legal and regulatory framework defines the **limits** of a **company's operations** and any modification can have significant consequences. Changes in Swiss bank secrecy and their consequences for banks are a prime example.

Once again, apart from belonging directly to a major lobby, it is difficult for investors to protect themselves against this risk, but taking these factors into account during the process of investment in an asset class, a sector or a particular security helps limit exposure to it.

k) Risk associated with emerging countries

Besides political and liquidity risk, it is often **difficult** for investors to **obtain information** about a company operating in an emerging country. In addition, there are often **restrictions** on foreign investment and stakes in these companies. Finally, transaction **costs** are often very high and can sometimes be ten times higher than those paid on the American or English markets.

On this type of risk, please refer to indications given above for bonds.[27]

l) Monetary risk associated with stocks

Some countries may pursue **monetary** and **fiscal policies** leading to higher inflation, interest rates, borrowing costs and, ultimately, a recession. This can also have an impact on domestic currency.

A **weak currency** favours exports, but penalises imports, while a **strong currency** penalises exports and favours imports. Therefore, the impact will vary according to the company's business activities and whether it is import or export focused.

Investors have difficulty hedging against this type of risk, but their decision to focus on export or import companies should depend on their expectations for currency movements.

m) Currency risk associated with stocks

In the case of investments in a foreign currency, i.e., other than the reference currency, exchange rate fluctuations can have a significant impact on the final return.

---

[27]See 3.2.2 h).

Hedging currency risk

Exchange rate movements are **virtually unpredictable**; the best forecast for tomorrow's rate (and the following days') is today's exchange rate. In the short term, partly because of the considerable number of speculators and stakeholders, it is very difficult to forecast exchange rate movements. An established trend may continue until a turnaround, but further than that, any forecasting is very problematic.

However, many experts recognise that currencies tend to follow a "mean reverting process". In other words, even if the price deviates over short periods from the long-term mean (which may itself change), in the end, the net result should be neutral. Over short periods, however, the impact can be significant.

A recent study by Frank Russell Canada Ltd has shown that over a 23-year period from 1981 to 2003, the annual return of a "hedged portfolio" was practically identical to that of an "unhedged portfolio".[28]

The time horizon and the asset's holding period may provide some clues as to whether it is worth hedging or not.

If investors intend to hold the asset for a short period, they should consider hedging against short-term exchange rate fluctuations, which can impact significantly on returns. On the other hand, if investors intend to keep certain investments for a very long period, hedging against currency risk may not be necessary. In the long term, although it undergoes fluctuations, the average performance of the exchange rate can approach zero and only the performance of the asset will have been decisive. However, even in the case of long-term asset holding, it may be feasible to hedge at certain times against currency risk and not at others, wagering on both the asset rise and appreciation of the foreign currency. The following example on Apple stock (Table 3.3) illustrates this.

First of all, it is interesting to note that the performance over five years of a European investor's portfolio (the reference currency being the euro) made up only of Apple stock

Table 3.3   Impact of exchange rate EUR/USD on Apple stock (period 2004–2009)

Title	Stock price on 31.12.2004	Stock price on 31.12.2005	Stock price on 31.12.2006	Stock price on 31.12.2007	Stock price on 31.12.2007	Stock price on 31.12.2009
Apple (USD)	32.2	71.89	84.84	198.08	85.35	210.86
Annual return		123.26%	18.01%	133.47%	−56.91%	147.05%
Return over 5 years				554.84%		
Exchange rate EUR/USD	1.356	1.184	1.3196	1.459	1.398	1.4316
Apple (EUR)	23.75	60.72	64.29	135.76	61.05	147.29
Annual return	155.69%		5.89%	111.17%	−55.03%	141.25%
Return over 5 years				520.26%		

[28]Taken from BWMG Team, October 2004.

in USD is higher in the case where currency hedging was carried out, and that only the security's return was decisive. The investor makes a return of +554%, compared to +520% if he is exposed to EUR/USD exchange fluctuations over this period – a 34% difference.

The cost of hedging does, however, have to be taken into account, and will essentially depend on the differential in short-term interest rates. A large differential can have an impact of a few percentage points on performance. In an environment of low short rates in most countries, as has been the case since 2009, there is practically no differential and the cost of hedging has become insignificant. Having said that, this factor should be considered.

Looking at the yearly return, however, we can see that in 2005 it would actually have been better not to have hedged against currency risk, and to have let the US dollar appreciate. The 2005 performance was +123% in USD, but +155% in EUR. Taking the above example, if the position had only been hedged from 2006 onwards, performance over five years would have been +650%! So, it would have been preferable not to hedge against currency risk in 2005, but to have opted for hedging the following years.

Time horizon and holding period do not appear to be decisive criteria. Analysing the **forecast** for the investment currency is essential, but in our view it is the investors' **degree of conviction** and their **capacity** to accept **exposure** to **risk** which will mainly determine the decision to hedge against currency risk or not.

In practice, if investors have no particular conviction about a currency, they will remain neutral. If they are comfortable taking the risk of foreign currency fluctuation, they will not hedge. On the other hand, if they do not want to be exposed to this risk, they will ensure the position is hedged appropriately, in order to focus solely on the asset's return. In case of a strong conviction, they will hedge if they expect the investment currency to weaken.

The question of what **proportion** to hedge (100%, 50% … of the position?) will again depend on the degree of conviction and the risks investors are willing to take. The **volatility** of the **asset class** should also be considered. Certainly, for bonds, seeking an additional 1%–2% return while risking a currency loss of 3%–4% seems unjustified. It may be useful to compare the volatility of the currency with the volatility of the asset class. The use of limits or stop losses helps limit the risk of losses.

The use of **forward exchange contracts** as a hedging instrument provides protection against the currency risk associated with positions in foreign currency, and investments in the investor's reference currency avoid this risk entirely.

Finally, some consider currency as an asset class in itself or as a form of diversification that must be managed accordingly. We will leave this question open but, in our view, investors must first decide what to invest in and then contemplate whether the investment currency is worth hedging.

Investors can also limit their exposure to this risk by investing in their reference currency.

Our Advice

For investing in stocks, we recommend:

- combining individual stocks with index funds or futures;
- diversifying intelligently;
- using effective hedging instruments wherever possible (stop losses, puts, futures);
- examining liquidity and solvency ratios;
- carrying out a strategic analysis of the company and its industry;
- taking into account the political and regulatory framework;
- hedging large foreign currency positions according to the degree of conviction.

3.4 REAL ESTATE

3.4.1 Definition[29]

It is possible to invest directly in real estate by buying a property in one's own name or, in some countries, by holding it through a non-trading real estate investment company,[30] which has the advantage of facilitating the transfer of assets to heirs.

Direct purchase requires a **large amount of capital**, a **long investment horizon**, and a **comprehensive knowledge** of the sector and the location of the property. It implies a certain amount of work on the part of the investor, as housing stock must be managed in a professional manner. Investors unwilling to get personally involved must pay a property management company at an often considerable cost.

It is also possible to invest in this asset class **indirectly**, by investing in listed or unlisted **real estate funds**, or shares in property investment companies or real estate investment trusts (REITs) that provide access to a real estate portfolio.

Indirect purchase requires **less capital**. In addition, real estate funds and real estate investment companies can reduce risks if they are diversified geographically and by real estate category. Real estate funds are often focused on residential property, and are generally more diversified than real estate investment companies, which own mainly commercial offices and warehouses. Consequently, real estate investment companies are more heavily indebted, more sensitive to the economic climate and, most importantly, more closely tied to market trends.

Real estate funds and investment companies are rarely traded at their **net asset value** and prices include a **premium** or a **discount** in relation to this value. For example, in Switzerland, on 31 December, 2009, the average premium of listed funds was 21.9%.[31]

---

[29]See also Hoesli, *Real Estate Investment.*

[30]For example, in France the société civile immobilière or SCI is the most common form of holding property.

[31]Credit Suisse, Datastream, annual and interim fund reports.

Interest rate movements play an important role here – an interest rate rise will push the premium down, while a fall in interest rates will push it up, in this case constituting a premium to pay for access. Investor demand for this type of investment, as well as tax benefits, also maintains the premium at a high level.

Many studies have demonstrated the **weak correlation** between **direct real estate** and **stocks/bonds**. Consequently, including direct property in a portfolio helps to reduce overall risk and plays a valuable role in diversification strategies. The **optimum share** is between **15** and **20%** of the investor's total wealth.

On the other hand, **indirect** property is **closely correlated** to **stocks** and **bonds**, and so is less attractive in terms of diversification. It is generally recommended to allocate **about 5%** to this asset class, while also taking into account the degree of correlation between the relevant real estate market and the type of assets in the investor's portfolio.

For this analysis, we will only consider the merits of indirect property in a portfolio.

Finally, property investments are often seen as good **protection against inflation**. When inflation is rising, the value of a mortgage used to finance property declines over time. In other words, the value of the debt will be lower tomorrow than it is today because of inflation, which has a positive effect for borrowers.

3.4.2   Risks associated with real estate[32]

a) Risk associated with the physical nature of the asset

Land and buildings are physical assets – a fact which makes them unique – for which there is **no regulated trading**. They are not traded on a centralised stock market. **Transaction costs** are **high**, as are **maintenance costs**.

Investing in real estate funds helps reduce this risk significantly, and delegates the management of real estate.

b) Liquidity risk

Direct property is far less liquid than the stock market. Selling a property can take several months or even years. Direct investment requires significant capital outlays and generates a liquidity risk, as investors are slow to receive proceeds from the sale of their property.

Indirect investment in real estate funds or investment companies helps reduce this risk considerably, as most of these funds offer better liquidity.

c) Risk associated with the structure of the real estate market

Real estate markets are often opaque, and require detailed knowledge of the local context. It is essential to refer to **local experts**, which limits access to the market. In addition,

---

[32]See also *Specific Risks in Securities Trading*.

information is often **asymmetrical** and difficult to come by. In other words, this means that some of those active on the market have more information than others.

Consulting experts, carrying out comprehensive analyses of the property market or purchasing real estate funds specialised in this area all help deflect this risk, and funds let investors delegate the management of real estate to professionals.

d) Risk associated with supply and demand

The value of real estate fluctuates according to supply and demand and the economic climate. Tax incentives or attractive credit terms can also stimulate the property market and tend to boost prices.

Only a thorough analysis of the macroeconomic variables and of the relevant property market will reduce this risk. Investors must therefore determine the attractiveness of this asset class and the future prospects of the market in question (country, residential or commercial property, etc.) in order to make a decision.

e) Interest rate risk

Real estate is affected by interest rate movements. When interest rates are low, mortgages are cheap and it is easy to make higher than average returns. Conversely, high interest rates mean dwindling returns.

As such, it is interesting to note that when rates are low and inflation is expected to rise, the value of debt will be lower in the future, thereby favouring borrowers.

It is possible to use **OTC (over the counter)** interest rate products to hedge against the risk of fluctuation. When a decline in interest rates is expected, a **"floor"** (interest rate put option) may be used, giving protection when interest rates fall below a certain level. The holder of a "floor" will be paid an amount corresponding to the difference between the strike rate and the observed rate at a set maturity date.

Conversely, when interest rates are expected to rise, investors can buy a **"cap"** (interest rate call option) to hedge against rates rising above a certain level (strike rate). This protection is often offered as part of floating mortgage rates, where the borrower benefits from rates falls but risks having to suffer higher interest rates in the future.

Finally, a **"collar"**, which is a combination of a floor and a cap, makes it possible to set a minimum and maximum level of interest rate fluctuation. As with all insurance, this type of protection comes at a cost that must be evaluated in relation to the expected risk of interest rate movement and its consequences for the investment.

f) Currency risk

When investing in a foreign currency, investors are also exposed to foreign exchange risk in relation to their reference currency. As previously discussed, it is possible to hedge against this risk.[33]

---

[33] See 3.3.2 m).

Our Advice

For (indirect) real estate investment, we recommend:

- favouring listed and very liquid funds;
- consulting experts and carrying out detailed analyses before selecting specialised real estate funds;
- deciding on the geographic exposure and the type of property preferred (residential and/or commercial);
- taking into account the level of interest rates and their expected movement;
- hedging large foreign currency positions according to the degree of conviction.

3.5   COMMODITIES AND METALS

3.5.1   Definition

By commodities, we mean physical goods produced by agriculture or the mining industry, for example, and standardised in order to be used as underlying assets in a trade.

Commodities (energy, precious and other metals, agricultural products) are usually traded on **futures markets**. Under contractual agreements, investors can buy or sell futures contracts related to the price movement of a given commodity.

The price of these different commodities fluctuates according to supply and demand on each of these markets, but this asset class provides attractive future prospects. **High demand** due to **world population growth**, **finite reserves**, the development of **renewable energy**, and the appearance of a **middle class** in some **emerging countries** are all increasing the attractiveness of commodities.

It is worth noting that meat consumption is related to GDP growth, and that several kilos of grain and hundreds of litres of water are required to produce a kilo of meat.

From a **social** and **ethical** perspective however, it is debatable whether investors "should" invest, or speculate, on price rises for basic foodstuffs. In our view, this speculation, which can contribute to world hunger, should be excluded from any investment decision, and only the energy and precious or industrial metals sectors should be considered.

At this stage, it is also important to mention the development of socially responsible, ethical and environmentally respectful investments with various themes and involving various industries. For example, **"responsible" investors** who share this approach to investment can favour clean energy or alternative energy equity funds, which invest in the development of renewable energy or alternatives to highly-polluting traditional energy sources.

Commodities are organised into three broad categories: energy, agricultural products and precious and industrial metals.

a) Energy

Prices in the energy sector essentially depend on **supply** and **demand** in the market, influenced in particular by **geopolitical factors**, which also cause a risk premium to be included in pricing. Natural gas is perhaps destined eventually to replace or supplement the oil supply. There is also significant growth in demand for electricity, requiring modifications in terms of supply and capacity.

As for **oil**, price increases for black gold seem inevitable in the long term. Demand, linked to the economic climate, as well as the level of US oil stocks, are essential factors in price setting.

However, oil resources are not infinite and will eventually be exhausted. This rarity helps sustain price rises. Moreover, demand from rapidly developing countries such as China and India is constantly increasing. The risk of dollar depreciation, future inflation and risks related to equity and property markets have also prompted investors to buy oil as a safe investment in the same way as gold.

In addition, oil extraction, which takes place in increasingly difficult conditions and at greater and greater depths, is increasingly expensive for companies.

Finally, **speculation** on the oil futures market helps sustain high prices. In a recent study, the International Monetary Fund (IMF) even admitted that soaring prices in 2007–2008 could largely be explained by speculation. In general, renewable energy only becomes profitable once the price of oil rises above 60 dollars per barrel.

b) Agricultural products

Agricultural products are reputed to be **volatile**, **difficult** to **access** and depend above all on the **structural conditions** governing the market in question (assessment of the planting or operational area relative to demand). For example, producers earn two times less by planting cotton than soya beans. A smaller production surface and the appeal of natural products can therefore help sustain cotton prices. As for timber, prices have fallen sharply due to problems triggered by the real estate crisis. The recession in the construction industry has pushed prices down, offering new investment opportunities.

It would be overambitious to review each of these markets here. We will simply note that overall, **economic** and **climate conditions** influence levels of supply and demand and therefore, ultimately, prices. Furthermore, speculators often abound on these markets. For these reasons, a detailed analysis is essential before making any investment.

c) Precious metals[34]

For centuries, **gold** has been coveted for its rarity, beauty and near inalterability. **Central banks** hold **gold stockpiles** as reserves of wealth. Gold is mainly used for jewellery,

---

[34]Taken from "Metals" Bulletin.

electronics, coins, dentistry and decoration (art). India is the biggest consumer of gold, followed by China and the United States.

Malkiel[35] considers that gold plays a limited role in a portfolio, in that it does not generate income and can undergo severe fluctuations. Nonetheless, gold is a highly appreciated investment and is usually present in portfolios, especially those of conservative clients. The financial crisis and fears of banks going bankrupt have boosted demand for physical gold, which has seen its price rise above 1000 dollars – recently up to almost 2000 dollars – an ounce. It is truly considered to be a **safe investment** by investors and probably seen as an alternative to weak currencies such as US dollar.

Silver is the best conductor of heat and electricity. It is used for antibacterial purposes, electricity, jewellery, silverware and photography. Unlike gold, silver is not really regarded as a safe investment, and its price fluctuates in a more cyclical manner due to its **industrial use**.

Palladium is used mainly for catalytic converters, electronics, jewellery, dentistry and chemistry. Finally, **platinum** is used for catalytic converters, jewellery, chemicals, electronics, glass and oil.

d) Industrial metals[36]

The **prices** of industrial metals change in a more **cyclical** manner due to their link with industry and the economic climate.

Aluminium and its alloys are included in the composition of many industrial and commercial products for uses ranging from soft drink cans to aeroplanes, aluminium foil, and power lines.

Copper has many household, industrial and technological applications. It is both ductile and resistant to corrosion, and is a good conductor of heat and electricity. Its main uses are electricity, coins, water pipes, microprocessors and construction.

About 70% of **nickel** is used to produce austenitic stainless steel, 10% for superalloys (aerospace) and 20% for alloy steels, rechargeable batteries, catalysts, chemicals and coins.

Zinc is mainly used as corrosion protection for iron and steel. It is also an essential micro-nutrient for human, animal and plant health. It is mainly used for galvanisation, pharmaceuticals, casting, construction and brass.

Tin is mainly used as a protective layer or alloyed with other metals. It is found in containers, receptacles, electronics and transport.

Lead is a dense, malleable, corrosion resistant metal used in construction, electrical systems, batteries and radiation-proof screens.

---

[35]Malkiel, p. 306.
[36]Taken from "Metals" Bulletin.

3.5.2   Risks associated with commodities and metals

Commodities and metals are exposed to the following risks.[37]

a) Risk of price fluctuation related to supply and demand

As we have already noted, the price of commodities depends on fluctuations in supply and demand over time, which vary according to the **economic climate** and **economic cycles**. The presence of **speculators** also puts pressure on prices.

In our opinion, demand generally has a greater stimulating effect on prices than supply, as to a certain extent supply has to adapt itself to demand.

The price of oil, for instance, is influenced more strongly by demand than supply; however, it is also worth following OPEC (Organisation of the Petroleum Exporting Countries) meetings, which set production quotas – and therefore supply – specifically according to demand. Member countries may decide, as was the case at their meeting on 10 March 2010, to maintain quotas when supply is sufficient to satisfy demand.

In terms of precious metals and gold in particular, the influence of central banks must be reiterated, as they buy and sell gold according to their desired level of reserves.

It is difficult for investors to hedge against this risk, but it can be limited by undertaking a comprehensive analysis of the market being considered in order only to invest at opportune (favourable) moments and avoid investing when conditions are difficult.

b) Climate risk and natural disasters

The climate and natural disasters also have an influence on prices. However, weather conditions mainly affect supply. A good (abundant) harvest has the effect of lowering prices, whereas a bad harvest pushes prices up to compensate for the small quantities produced. This risk is less significant for precious metals.

Producers usually protect themselves against this type of event by using insurance or futures contracts. It is difficult for investors to hedge against this risk, but it can be mitigated by a comprehensive analysis of the relevant market, which takes into account prevailing weather conditions that will affect the market.

c) Risk associated with government intervention, embargoes and trade barriers

When conditions of supply or demand become exaggerated, governments reserve the right to intervene in these markets in order to rebalance them by setting **quotas** or **restrictions**. The objective is to maintain or return to a fair equilibrium price. This risk exists mainly for commodities.

---

[37]Taken from *Specific Risks in Securities Trading*.

Recall, for example, the intervention of the Cambodian, Pakistani and Indian governments, which temporarily prohibited rice exports during the period of excessive demand in 2008. This was to curb rising prices, favour the domestic market and avoid local uprisings caused by famine. More recently (May 2010), India decided to ban cotton exports to force producers to favour the domestic textile market. This measure penalised neighbouring countries that import cotton, such as Pakistan, Bangladesh and China.

Once again, it is difficult for investors to hedge against this type of risk, which should really be considered as characteristic of the commodities market (essentially for agricultural products) and constantly borne in mind.

d) Risk associated with fluctuations in interest rates and other variables

The price of commodity futures[38] changes mainly according to **interest rate** movements, but it also depends on variations in **storage costs** and in the **convenience yield**, which is linked to stock levels and their seasonal fluctuations. Depending on the case, holding the commodities themselves (i.e., immediate availability) does confer advantages that holders of futures contracts do not have.

For example, in the case of heating oil in winter, the spot holder (who buys today for immediate delivery) has an immediate advantage over futures holders, implying in this case a high convenience yield that creates a situation of backwardation (see below – point f). This convenience yield is lower in summer.

e) Risk associated with exchange rate fluctuations

As with any investment in a currency other than the reference currency, investors are exposed to currency risk.

Commodities are **often listed** in **dollars**, the movement of which can have various different consequences.

"A rising U.S. dollar normally has a depressing effect on most commodity prices. In other words, a rising dollar is normally considered to be noninflationary. One of the commodities most affected by the dollar is the gold market [. . .], the prices of gold and the U.S. dollar usually trend in opposite directions."[39] Nonetheless, there are observable instances of gold and the dollar both rising in tandem, perhaps indicating that this relation is waning.

"Commodity prices are considered to be leading indicators of inflationary trends. As a result, commodity prices usually trend in the opposite direction of bond prices."[40]

---

[38]Future price = spot price * (1 + risk-free rate) + storage costs – convenience yield.
[39]Murphy, p. 419.
[40]Murphy, p. 418.

So the dollar influences commodities, which in turn influence bonds, which finally influence stocks.

f) Risk associated with futures market cycles

In a situation of **normal backwardation**, futures prices are lower than the spot price (cash price), and they decrease over time. In this case, the market demands a premium, so to speak, for short-term availability.

Conversely, in a so-called **contango** situation, futures prices are higher than the spot price, and they are therefore rising over time. In 2009, the structure of the oil futures price curve clearly showed a contango situation (upward sloping).

As we said to begin with, futures contracts are the main instrument for investing in this asset class. Depending on the economic situation and on supply and demand levels, one or other of these two situations may present itself and it is very important for investors to position themselves correctly. Poor positioning is an investment risk. During backwardation, it is better to buy futures contracts, while during contango, buying at spot is preferable to buying futures. But this is not always possible in practice, especially for consumable commodities where the use of futures contracts is necessary.

Therefore, with futures contracts, "rollover gains are made when a forward curve is in backwardation, as the expired contract can be replaced by a more advantageous contract. On the other hand, when a commodity market is in contango, rollover losses are inevitable."[41] Indeed, in the first case, a gain is made because a new, cheaper contract can be bought, whereas in the second case, a new contract must be bought at a higher price than the futures contract that has just been sold, thus generating a loss (see Figure 3.1).

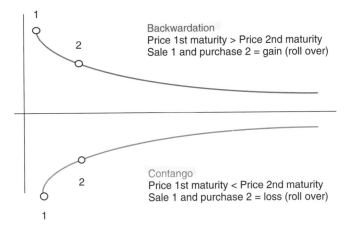

Figure 3.1   Forward curve – *Backwardation* and *Contango*.

---

[41] *Swiss Derivative Guide 2010*, p. 81.

> **Our Advice**
>
> When investing in energy and precious or industrial metals, we recommend:
>
> - studying supply and demand levels according to the economic climate and cycle;
> - taking weather conditions and natural disasters into account;
> - keeping a close eye on state intervention;
> - taking into account interest rate levels and, more importantly, the situation of *backwardation* or *contango*;
> - monitoring the US dollar;
> - hedging large foreign currency positions according to the degree of conviction.

3.6   PRIVATE EQUITY

3.6.1   Definition[42]

Private equity is a **form** of **venture capital financing** for companies that are not publicly traded on a stock exchange or, exceptionally, who wish to delist. These investments usually occur at the early stages of a company's development, when future prospects are uncertain and risks are higher.

Private equity investments made in young companies or start-ups with high growth potential are often referred to as venture capital. But private equity can also take the form of capital made available to a young company just before its initial public offering, or IPO, for example (mezzanine financing).

Generally, this form of financing is structured so that the proceeds from the IPO are sufficient to repay the company's shareholders all or part of their participation. When used to finance a change of owner, in the case of a delisting for example, this is more often called a buyout.

This type of investment may be made **directly**, or **indirectly** through a **private equity fund**. However, in this case, there is no guarantee that the fund manager will be able to acquire the shares and make the capital gains expected of this type of investment. The manager's skills are decisive for the success of an indirect investment.

3.6.2   Risks associated with private equity

a) Liquidity risk

A private equity investment usually has **very low liquidity** due mainly to the existence of lock-up periods, which prevent investors from exiting before a certain date.

This risk cannot be avoided. In fact, lack of liquidity is more a characteristic of this type of investment than a risk.

---

[42]Taken from *Specific Risks in Securities Trading*.

b) Risk associated with unlisted investments

As private equity is **not publicly traded**, valuation of the investment over time is difficult.

Investment in listed private equity funds helps limit exposure to this risk, but as in practice there are very few of these, we tend to consider this risk as one of the characteristics of this investment.

c) Risk associated with limited regulation and a lack of transparency

The absence of an organised, regulated market specifically allows this type of investment to be conducted within a **less regulated framework**, which is also **less** stringent in terms of **transparency**.

Investors can reduce this risk by requiring that the manager invest where there are stronger regulations, which depend on the country, and that they provide greater transparency about their investments.

d) Major insolvency and bankruptcy risk

When investing in venture capital, future prospects are uncertain and the ultimate risk of bankruptcy is obviously more pronounced. Investors can lose practically everything.

It is difficult for investors to hedge against this type of risk, even when using financial instruments such as puts or futures. In our view, the best possible hedge for investors who can't manage this risk is simply to avoid this type of investment altogether.

e) Risk associated with the lack of diversification

Private equity typically implies a **large concentration** of investments in order to allocate considerable initial resources to projects in the development stage, when financing needs are high. Although it is a characteristic of this type of investment, this approach does therefore suffer from a lack of diversification.

Diversification into other asset classes, and investing in private equity to a limited extent (a small exposure in the portfolio), will help limit this risk.

f) Leverage risk

The use of debt is one of the characteristics of private equity and exposes investors to **additional financial risk** due to leverage, i.e., using debt to increase the investment's profitability. The borrowed capital must therefore generate an additional profit relative to the risk taken. If the risk pays off, gains will be multiplied but, conversely, the same goes for losses.

In our view, it is difficult for investors to hedge against this risk.

g) Currency risk

As with any investment in a currency other than the reference currency, investors are exposed to currency risk. Please refer to the previous discussion on this point.[43]

h) Risk associated with the human factor

Finally, in young companies where the personalities of executives in key positions play an essential role, any change in the team can have extremely negative repercussions on private equity investments.

Private equity is therefore a highly speculative investment, and should be considered the **riskiest asset class**. It may only be suggested to a limited number of investors.

In conclusion, although private equity can be considered an asset class, the activity of venture capital is highly specific and should only be included in a portfolio with the utmost caution. The frequent lack of listing, the high degree of risk, and the lack of transparency are all issues which must be of paramount concern to investors.

Our Advice

If investors wish to include private equity in their assets, we recommend deciding on the amount to invest, then delegating management to professionals.

Such an investment is somewhat similar to the activity of a business angel or venture capitalist keen to invest actively, i.e., with significant participation in both capital and decision-making. Indirect investment is an alternative, but the choice of fund and manager is paramount.

3.7   OTHER ASSET CLASSES

Aside from currencies, which are often regarded as an asset class, we might consider including other assets such as **aircraft** or **boats**, as income is generated by their rental or commercial exploitation.

However, given the depreciation over time of these assets, maintenance and exploitation costs, and the limited number of individuals who own private jets or boats intended for hire, they should instead be regarded as the "non-investment, for personal use" part of an individual's fortune.

The same reasoning applies to cars, with the exception of **vintage cars** whose value can grow significantly over time. This type of investment can therefore prove very profitable.

The same is true of all **collectors' items** or **artworks** whose value can appreciate with time to be sold for more than their purchase price. Finally, we might consider **wine** and bottles of future "grands crus" that are also likely to grow in value over time.

---

[43] See 3.3.2 m).

In our view however, all the goods we have just listed depend on one essential factor: **passion**. Individuals have personal interests and particular pastimes and hobbies they are willing to spend money on. So although these assets do become part of an individual's fortune, they are acquired not as an investment but rather as the realisation of a dream or pursuit of a passion. These decisions are based on deep personal motivation and less on the profit motive.

A sailing or car enthusiast will buy a yacht or a vintage car. A modern art lover will buy a work by his or her favourite artist for the pleasure of owning it and being able to contemplate it at home. In the event that the work should be sold, this art enthusiast would probably use the proceeds of the sale to buy another one. As for wine, a "grand cru" is intended above all to be enjoyed on a grand occasion or at a special event, and the pleasure it gives to the palate is the main objective sought by wine lovers.

Obviously, some of these goods may be bought with a view to speculation, i.e., quick resale in order to make a gain on the capital invested. However, the market for this type of goods is often illiquid and valuation includes a significant level of subjectivity. Furthermore, the value is often related to the uniqueness of the item and its history. Finally, the term speculation often refers to short-term objectives, while the holding period of this type of asset is usually long and is not a factor that is appreciated objectively by an enthusiast.

For all these reasons, we do not consider these goods as "normal" investment assets as far as this analysis is concerned, although we recognise that they can be regarded as such, marginally, for some investors.

4

Particular Forms of Investment
within Asset Classes

4.1 HEDGE FUNDS

4.1.1 Definition

By definition,[1] hedge funds have an **absolute return objective**, allowing managers to take long and short positions on the market, rewarding them with **performance-related commissions** and allowing them a great deal of **flexibility** in terms of investment style and approach. Managers adopt a more active management style and seek to profit from the market's various inefficiencies.

"A hedge fund is a private investment association that uses a large range of financial instruments such as short selling of stocks, derivatives, leverage or arbitrage, all in different markets. Usually, the managers of these funds invest part of their own resources and are paid according to their performance. Hedge funds often require high minimum investments and access to them is limited. They are intended mainly for wealthy clients, whether private or institutional."[2]

Therefore, hedge funds should not be regarded as an asset class, but rather a **particular investment strategy**. Furthermore, because of the diversity of strategies used and the fact that returns are derived from the return made on other traditional asset classes, it cannot be maintained that hedge funds have the specific characteristics necessary to be regarded as a separate asset class.

In Switzerland, FINMA recognises[3] that "hedge funds are a special form of collective capital investment [. . .] subject to more lenient legal requirements than other forms of investment and therefore have greater freedom of investment".

It is possible to invest directly in individual hedge funds, or indirectly in **funds of hedge funds**, which provide diversified exposure to several different funds and management strategies. Selecting the best fund of hedge funds, adapted to market cycles, represents the added value essential in the management of this type of product.

Although hedge funds will not be studied comprehensively as part of our analysis, we will address the importance of the **strategy used** by the fund manager. It is particularly worth

---

[1]Capocci, p. 19.
[2]Capocci, p. 19.
[3]Former Swiss Federal Banking Commission (SFBC), considering no 1. Note that the SFBC has become FINMA.

mentioning the following strategies,[4] which clearly argue in favour of inefficient markets and are useful in demonstrating a flexible approach to investment.

- Equity Long-Short

  Funds using this strategy identify, on the one hand, undervalued stocks (long or buy positions) and, on the other hand, overvalued stocks (short or sell positions) in certain regions or market segments. They bet on the fact that sooner or later the liquidation of these positions will generate capital gains. In the Equity Long-Short strategy, there is no ongoing search for beta neutrality in terms of market risk. However, for so-called Equity Market Neutral strategies, managers seek a beta neutral position (long side beta = short side beta), i.e., the sums of the betas for the long and short positions are equal.

- Arbitrage

  Arbitrage strategies aim to exploit price differences in markets for identical or similar investments. These strategies include fixed income arbitrage, convertible bond arbitrage or mortgage-backed securities arbitrage.

- Event-driven

  Managers who apply these strategies aim to exploit certain events, such as coming changes in companies (mergers, acquisitions, restructurings, remediation, etc.). Merger arbitrage, distressed securities and special situations strategies also belong to this category.

- Global macro

  Hedge funds that pursue these strategies attempt to identify macroeconomic developments early (changes in interest rates and exchange rates in particular), and profit from them. Growth funds and emerging market funds are both part of this category.

- Managed futures

  In this category of hedge fund, futures contracts are traded on financial instruments, currencies and commodities.

As we mentioned previously, **flexibility** is an essential factor and it will form the basis of the approach to portfolio construction suggested later. If hedge funds manage to generate attractive returns with less historical volatility, this is due in part to the flexibility of their investment policy. Furthermore, relatively illiquid markets offer bigger investment opportunities, specifically because they are less efficient. As Swensen points out, "The most lucrative investments tend to be located in shady areas, rather than under [. . .] Wall Street's spotlight."[5]

Before briefly presenting the risks associated with this type of investment, it is interesting to note[6] that some studies (see in particular Brown, Goetzmann and Ibbotson, 1999) indicate that hedge fund returns cannot be adequately approximated by commonly used statistical distributions such as normal distribution. This is consistent with our earlier conclusion about risky assets.

4.1.2   Risks associated with hedge funds

This type of strategy does include a set of market-related risks, particularly **liquidity risk** and **leverage risk**.

---

[4]Taken from "Specific Risks in Securities Trading".
[5]Swensen, p. 116.
[6]Taken from Boris Arabadjiev, p. 2.

In fact, **quarterly or semi-annual liquidity periods** strongly affect entry and exit points for this type of investment, unlike stock or bond investments that offer virtually immediate liquidity.

In times of crisis, liquidity is particularly sought after and there is no doubt that many hedge funds were unable to fully meet exit requests following the massive demand for redemptions at the end of 2008. They found themselves having to stagger redemptions,[7] or sometimes even separate their illiquid investments from their more liquid assets into distinct classes (creating "side pockets").

Recently, some funds have modified their structure or created a new, more liquid investment class so that they can offer investors better liquidity, usually **weekly**, and sometimes even **daily**. Article 34 of the EU Directive[8] on the Undertakings for Collective Investment in Transferable Securities (UCITS) imposes a minimum of fortnightly or monthly liquidity periods, which has the advantage for investors of reducing the terms of redemption. This structure is particularly suitable for "long-short" strategies, which invest in more liquid assets than other types of strategy. It is still too early to get an adequate performance history for these new, more liquid classes, but the performance targets announced by managers are clearly set lower than those of traditional, less liquid classes. There is a price to pay for reasonable liquidity with this type of investment.

Leverage certainly helps multiply gains by borrowing from banks several times the amounts managed, but it can also multiply losses. The existence of this leverage, however, confers considerable power to lenders, who can request redemption of all or part of the funds according to market conditions and the value of assets used as collateral for loans. In the event of margin calls or demands for redemption, some hedge funds may be forced to sell assets or even to close the fund, as was unfortunately the case in 2008 with the Carlyle Capital and Peloton ABS funds, among others.

Using **derivatives** can also lead to a risk of significant losses on the fund's investments.

The **lack of transparency** linked with hedge funds can also represent a risk for investors, who are not always correctly informed about the strategies being used. This is often an opaque environment, and as Bing Liang of the University of Massachusetts showed in her study, "unfortunately, 35% of hedge funds produce misleading and unaudited data. [...] If these small deviations from reality were taken into account, the average annual performance of hedge funds would no longer be 10.7% for the last few years (before 2004), but 6.4%. A figure which pales in comparison to a performance of 6.9% for the stock market and 7.5% for bonds."[9] Moreover, dead hedge funds and those which choose not to reveal their performance are not included in hedge fund indexes, which are therefore biased.

In terms of **performance**, some studies show that compared to other financial assets (stocks, bonds and real estate), this type of strategy may be less profitable over a longer period. For example, "from August 2003 to late 2008, the SPI index of Swiss stocks rose by 26.16%,

---

[7]Legal procedure using the clauses contained in their prospectuses.
[8]Council Directive 85/611/EEC. See also UCITS III.
[9]Weinberg and Condon.

or 4.38% per year. For this period, the *CS Tremont Investissable* index shows a negative performance of −14.74%, or −2.90% per year for hedge funds."[10] Nonetheless, this type of strategy resisted far better to the 2008 bear market, an exceptional year in every respect, where the magnitude of the correction that occurred in the markets was simply unforeseeable.

It is useful to note that hedge funds target positive performance above all, independently of any benchmark. This **absolute return objective** is certainly an **interesting alternative** to the traditional relative return approach. Furthermore, it would obviously be a mistake to put all hedge funds in the same basket. There are excellent fund managers who are professional and competent, and who deliver satisfying performances independently of market movements.

Sources

Hedge Fund Research, Inc. is regarded as the leader in terms of indexes and the hundreds of indexes it produces are a reference for comparing the performance of these strategies with their benchmark.

   www.hedgefundresearch.com

Indexes provided by *Credit Suisse Tremont* are also used in practice, but are less recent and sometimes less diversified than some *HFR* indexes.

   www.hedgeindex.com

We will leave it to each investor's discretion to decide whether or not they want to include hedge funds in their portfolio. However, it is essential to understand what we are investing in, **how performance** is **delivered** and the risks associated with the strategy concerned. Unfortunately, the Madoff affair illustrated the lack of due diligence on behalf of certain banks and investment companies worldwide, who did not adequately question the way such a performance had been achieved over such a long period.

There are **inherent risks** in each **particular strategy** for hedge fund management, but these aspects do not fall within the scope of our analysis and we invite the reader to refer to specialised works in this area.

Malkiel[11] recommends avoiding hedge funds, as in his view they were responsible for promoting the Internet bubble from 1998 to 2000 and for having played a destabilising role in the oil market in 2005 and 2006. He believes that the doubling in price cannot be explained simply by changes in supply and demand and it would seem that speculative activities, driven mainly by hedge funds, contributed to this rise.

In our opinion, it is more appropriate to consider this type of strategy as **complementary** to a particular **asset class**, while bearing in mind their illiquidity. For example, a long/short hedge fund should be considered in a portfolio's equity exposure because the fund's underlying

---

[10]Taken from Thétaz, "Three Reasons to Avoid Hedge Funds".
[11]Malkiel, p. 235.

assets are really just stocks. A hedge fund using futures contracts on commodities should supplement exposure to commodities as they have the same underlying; only the type of strategy is different. The percentage invested depends on the investor and the share of funds that can be less liquid.

Our Advice

If investors decide to include hedge funds in their portfolio as an alternative strategy to a particular asset class, we recommend:

- favouring liquid funds, and accepting to pay the price for this liquidity;
- favouring funds that do not use much leverage;
- making sure they fully understand how the performance is achieved;
- selecting the strategies best adapted to the market context.

4.2 STRUCTURED PRODUCTS

4.2.1 Definition

By **structured product**, we mean "the **combination of derivatives** and **traditional assets**, such as stocks or bonds. The combination of these components results in a financial instrument in the form of a security."[12] Structured products are usually divided into **three categories**:[13]

1. **Participation products**, such as certificates, which accurately reflect the movement of the underlying asset.
2. **Yield enhancement products**, such as maximum-return products, that allow investors to forego the potential upside exposure to an underlying asset above a given threshold in exchange for compensation, in the form of either a discount or, as with a "reverse convertible", an enhanced coupon. These combine a bond with a short put option and at maturity either pay a high coupon, or the holder receives the securities according to the movement in the underlying.
3. **Capital guaranteed products**, which limit the risk of losses in the event of falling prices, while making it possible to participate in a rise in the underlying.

Structured products can behave both like stocks and like interest-generating investments. Furthermore, the nature of the product can change dynamically over its entire lifetime.

Thus, investors keen to gain exposure to a specific market can do so in different ways. They can buy a few individual securities of companies listed on this market, buy an index fund for the market in question or buy into an investment fund. Finally, they can buy a structured product linked to the price movement of this underlying, depending on their views and price or return objectives.

Consequently, structured products are not really an asset class, but rather a particular form of investment in one of the asset classes according to the relevant underlying asset, investment

---

[12]Tolle, Hutter, Rüthemann, Wohlwend, pp. 89–90.
[13]Taken from Tolle, Hutter, Rüthemann, Wohlwend, pp. 90–91.

theme or industry. Their inclusion must depend on the terms of issue of these products at the time they are being examined, and therefore on their attractiveness for investors.

Nonetheless, it is important to be conscious of the risks associated with investing in this type of product.

4.2.2   Risks associated with structured products

The main risk associated with the issue of structured products is **counterparty risk**, which depends specifically on the creditworthiness of the issuer.

The other risks are related to the **components** of the **structured product** and to the **movement** of the **underlying assets**.

The bank Wegelin & Cie offers an interesting approach: to decompose the structured product, by separating "the complicated financial instruments and reducing them to a few basic components".[14] This approach also has the advantage of separating the so-called "nominal" part from the real part, which constitutes the real exposure to the underlying asset.

For example, by decomposing a capital guaranteed product, we arrive at two components: the bond part (zero-coupon) that provides a capital guarantee at maturity, and the option part that makes it possible to profit from a rising market.

Besides counterparty risk, investors are exposed to the risks associated with investing in a zero-coupon bond (essentially default risk) and the risks associated with the movement of the underlying asset, with losses being limited at maturity however, thanks to the particular construction of this product. Even so, as part of this capital guaranteed product, if the underlying undergoes a strong decline compared to the initial strike price, the option is likely to become almost worthless, and its delta[15] will fall. In the event of a market recovery, the extent of the rise will not match the market rebound due to the option's low delta. Moreover, the method used to calculate returns (quarterly, over the last six months, etc.) may also affect the product's final performance.

So using options has its own particularities. The exercise price, the interest rate level and the volatility of the underlying will all affect the price movement of the option and, consequently, that of the product.

The reader should refer to the *Swiss Derivative Guide 2010*,[16] which covers structured products and the use of options in great detail.

---

[14] Taken from Tolle, Hutter, Rüthemann, Wohlwend, p. 194.

[15] The delta represents the sensitivity of the option's price compared to the movement of the underlying.

[16] It can be ordered for 28 EUR from Handelszeitung und Finanzrundschau AG, Axel Springer Schweiz, or through the Wegelin & Cie website (www.wegelinstp.ch/ueberuns/publikationen.asp). ISBN 978-3-9523456-6-5.

> **Our Advice**
>
> For structured products, some of which can be very attractive, we particularly recommend:
>
> - favouring quality issuers in order to minimise counterparty risk;
> - closely examining the product's terms of issue (protection, participation, method of calculating returns, etc.). They must be attractive enough to justify allocating capital;
> - favouring short-term products.

At this stage, it will be useful to spend a moment looking at how options work.

4.3   OPTIONS

4.3.1   Definition

Options are **derivatives** whose value is derived from the value of an underlying asset, which may be the price of a stock, an interest rate or the price of a commodity.

Consequently, they should not be regarded as an asset class, but rather as a particular form of investment, or more precisely as hedging or speculation instruments.

Holding a **call option** gives the right (not the obligation) to purchase the underlying at a predetermined price (strike price) at a set expiration date or up until a certain expiration date. This option makes it possible to hedge against higher prices if a price increase is expected. It can also be used to speculate on price rises.

Conversely, holding a **put option** gives the right (not the obligation) to sell the underlying at a predetermined price (strike price) at a set expiration date or until a certain expiration date. It allows its holder to hedge against an expected decrease in prices. It can also be used to speculate on price decreases, or even to purchase the underlying at a desired price.

It should also be clear that holding an option (long call or long put) only confers a right, whereas the sale of options (short call or short put) implies the obligation to deliver the underlying or to pay for it if the option is exercised by its holder.

A **"European" option** may only be exercised at the expiration date, whereas an **"American" option** may be exercised at any moment up until the expiration date.

Options are usually **evaluated** using the **Black-Scholes formula**. However, as we shall see in the following sections, it is not really suitable as it makes very strong and quite unrealistic basic assumptions, like for example the assumption of constant volatility over time.

The option's price will change over time depending on the development of certain factors such as price variations in the underlying (sensitivity measured by the option's **delta**), the passage of time (sensitivity measured by **theta**), variations in volatility (sensitivity measured by **kappa**), variations in the interest rate (sensitivity measured by **rho**) and even the variation of the option's delta compared to the movement of the underlying asset's price (sensitivity measured by **gamma**).

This price, called the "premium", comprises the **intrinsic value** and the **time value**. It fluctuates until the expiration date according to the variables cited above, reaching a time value of zero at expiration.

So investors are buying time, and the more time they buy, the more they have to pay. Their option, as with any insurance, has a far from negligible price if they hope to hedge the entire position invested in stocks.

Some investors, such as Peter Lynch or Warren Buffett, avoid options entirely, the latter even considering that *"derivatives are financial weapons of mass destruction"*. Nonetheless, they are a part of the financial landscape and without wanting to go into detail, buying and selling options poses many risks that will now be presented briefly with associated Figures 4.1 to 4.6.

4.3.2 Risks associated with options

a) Long call option (buying a call)

With a long call option position, where a price rise is expected, **losses** are **limited** to the premium paid to acquire the option. In this case, the potential **gain** is theoretically **unlimited** and depends on a price rise in the underlying asset.

Take, for example, a call worth 1 EUR on a stock trading today at 20 EUR with a strike price set at 22 EUR; the buyer here is anticipating a price increase in the security. He or she will start making money once the price rises above 23 EUR, as first he or she must absorb the premium (22 EUR + 1 EUR). Any loss is limited to the 1 EUR spent and the

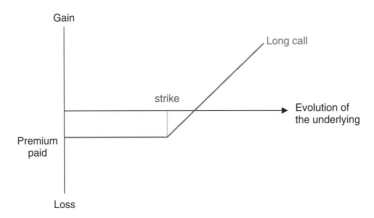

Figure 4.1   Payoff of a long call.

gain will be equal to the difference between the stock price at expiration and the strike plus the premium. So, if the expectation was correct, and the stock is worth 40 EUR, the call buyer will have made the sum of 17 EUR per option $(40 - (22 + 1))$.

b) Short call option (selling a call)

In a short call option strategy, the investor expects prices to remain stable or to decrease slightly, and wants to make a premium. The **gain** is therefore **limited** to the premium earned.

However, the risk of **loss** is theoretically **unlimited**, as if the buyer exercises the option, the seller will have to deliver the underlying security. If he or she does not own it, he or she will first have to buy it on the market at a price that may be far higher than the strike. Many banks limit this risk by only authorising short "covered" calls, where the investor already owns the underlying security in his or her portfolio.

It should be noted that selling covered calls is only appropriate if investors have a neutral or slightly bearish/bullish view of prices. In the event of a sharp decline, the premium received will not cover the loss in value of the position, and it is better to sell the stock if a major correction is anticipated.

Conversely, to take the example of a call sold for 1 EUR on stock currently trading at 20 EUR with a strike also set at 20 EUR, here the seller is anticipating a slight decline in the security. The premium earned represents the gain on the position. If the expectation was correct and the price drops slightly to 18 EUR, the call holder will not exercise the option as he or she can buy the security more cheaply on the market (18 EUR instead of 20 EUR, not counting the premium of 1 EUR). The seller of the call therefore wins in this scenario. However, if the security rises to 25 EUR, the option will be exercised and the seller will have to deliver the security in exchange for 20 EUR, which represents a loss of 4 EUR $((20 + 1) - 25)$.

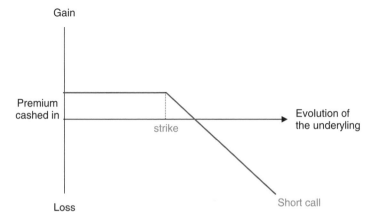

Figure 4.2   Payoff of a short call.

c) Long put option (buying a put)

In a long put position, a downward price movement is expected and **losses** are **limited** to the premium paid to acquire the option. In this case, the potential **gain** is also **limited**.

For example, by buying a put at 1 EUR on a stock worth 20 EUR with a strike price of 20 EUR, the buyer is seeking to hedge against an expected decline in prices. The loss is limited to the premium, and he or she will start making money when the price drops below the threshold of 19 EUR (20 − 1). The gain will be equal to the difference between 19 EUR and the price at expiration. If the expectation was correct and the security goes down to 10 EUR, the put holder will have made 9 EUR ((20 − 1) − 10).

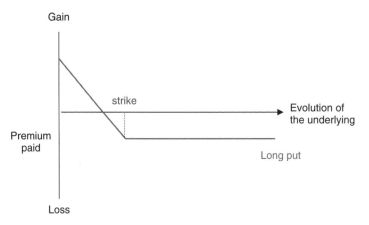

Figure 4.3   Payoff of a long put.

d) Short put option (selling a put)

In a short put position, prices are expected to remain stable or to rise slightly. Selling the option earns a premium. It also makes it possible to acquire an underlying security at a certain price (strike).

However, unlike selling a call, here the risk of **loss** is **limited**, except in the event that the company goes bankrupt where the risk of loss becomes unlimited, as if the option is exercised, the put seller has to buy the security at the strike price. So he or she must pay, but receives the underlying in exchange, which may still be of some value. Blocking certain positions or liquidities can mitigate this risk for banks.

Conversely, to take the example of a put sold for 1 EUR on stock currently trading at 20 EUR with a strike set at 21 EUR, the seller is anticipating here a slight increase in the security. The premium earned represents the gain on the operation.

If the expectation was correct and the price rises slightly to 22 EUR, the put holder will not exercise the option as he or she can sell the security for more on the market (22 EUR

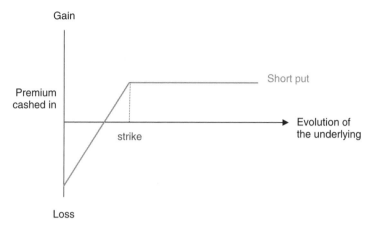

Figure 4.4 Payoff of a short put.

instead of 21 EUR, not counting the premium of 1 EUR). The seller of the put therefore wins in this scenario. However, if the security falls to 18 EUR, the option will be exercised and the put seller will have to buy the security at 21 EUR although it is only worth 18, representing a loss of 2 EUR $((18 + 1) - 21)$.

e) "Straddle"

Buying a call and a put at the same strike price and the same expiration date simultaneously is called a **"long straddle"**. A gain is made if the underlying security moves outside the interval [strike – premium paid; strike + premium paid].

Conversely, selling a call and a put at the same strike price and the same expiration date simultaneously is called a **"short straddle"**. A gain is made if the underlying security stays inside the interval [strike – premium received; strike + premium received].

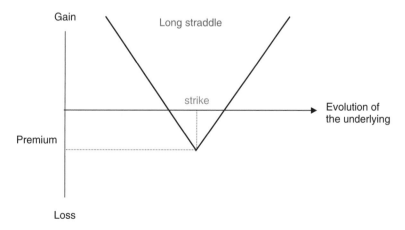

Figure 4.5 Payoff of a long straddle.

In the case of a long straddle with a strike price of 20 EUR on a security, the loss is limited to the premiums paid for the call and the put, or 1 EUR each (2 EUR in total). A gain starts being made when the price goes above 21 EUR (20 + 1) or drops below 19 EUR (20 − 1). Here, an increase or decrease greater than these two limits is expected.

f) Strangle

Simultaneously buying a call and a put with different strike prices is called a "**long strangle**". A gain is made if the underlying security moves outside the interval [strike of the put − premium paid; strike of the call + premium paid].

Conversely, simultaneously selling a call and a put with different strike prices is called a "**short strangle**". A gain is made if the underlying security stays inside the interval [strike of the put − premium received; strike of the call + premium received].

In the case of a long strangle with a put strike price of 15 EUR on the security and a call strike price of 18 EUR, the loss is again limited to the premiums paid for the call and the put, or 1 EUR each (2 EUR in total). However, a gain starts being made either when the price goes above 19 EUR (18 + 1) or drops below 14 EUR (15 − 1). Here, an increase or decrease greater than these two broader limits is expected.

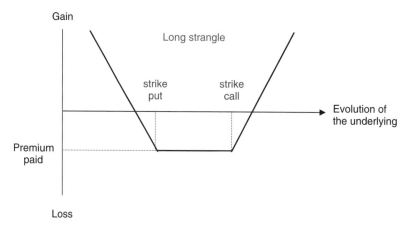

Figure 4.6   Payoff of a long strangle.

Our Advice

We believe that options should essentially be regarded as **hedging instruments** or **components** of a **structured product**, with, nonetheless, a considerable **speculative aspect**.

Furthermore, setting the strike price and choosing the expiration date are far from easy in practice, and it is common for investors to be right, but too early, or to hedge too late.

5
Classification of Asset Classes According to their Degree of Risk

It is now time to classify these different asset classes according to their degree of risk. We need to consider money market investments, bonds, stocks, commodities, real estate and private equity, with sub-sections within some asset classes. In our opinion, private equity is at this stage the most risky asset class (absence of a listed market, lack of liquidity, very high bankruptcy or default risk). So here are the assets to be classified:

- fiduciary deposits;
- money market funds;
- government bonds;
- corporate bonds;
- high yield bonds;
- stocks from developed countries;
- stocks from emerging countries;
- commodities;
- precious and industrial metals;
- real estate (indirect);
- private equity.

5.1 SELECTED CRITERIA FOR CLASSIFICATION OF ASSET CLASSES

It has already been stated that volatility (or standard deviation), beta and VaR are not appropriate measures of risk. So, one or more common criteria must be found, other than price variation, which allow a hierarchy of these asset classes to be established according to the risks associated with each.

As we mentioned to begin with, investors are seeking a return that can take the form of regular income, capital gains or a combination of both. A **regular income** is preferable in that it is determined in advance and therefore more certain for investors than a **potential income**.

According to this first criterion, fiduciary and money market investments, as well as bonds, are regarded as the least risky asset, because they generate fixed, regular income. Obviously, it is possible to make gains on bonds, but this would be a conditional capital gain, essentially depending on rate movements. As for real estate, in our view it comes between bonds and stocks as it combines an income and a capital gains component.

It is also interesting to consider the most pessimistic scenario possible, and to determine the investors' position in case of bankruptcy of the company issuing the security or of the counterparty. The **legal nature** of the **relationship** between the **creditor** and **borrower** is therefore worth taking into account.

In the event that the issuer goes bankrupt, money market investments and bonds fall into the bankruptcy estate. However, depending on the priority of their debt, creditors will be repaid first, unlike stockholders who are only entitled to a liquidation dividend if there are still assets to share. Holders of indirect (securitised) property are treated like stockholders. This criterion is inapplicable to commodities and precious metals.

Liquidity could be a selection criterion, but the existence of listed markets, which are generally liquid, does not really allow a more detailed classification. Certainly, emerging markets present a lower level of liquidity than developed countries, but it seems more appropriate to consider all the risks associated with emerging markets as additional risks.

As such, the **number of risks identified** can also constitute an important clue in helping to determine the degree of risk of an asset class. We will not consider currency risk, as it depends on the investment currency rather than the choice of asset class.

Finally, it is useful to examine, for a period of, say, 10 years, the **worst-case performance** for each asset class, as well as the **average loss** for this period. This will give an indication of the degree of losses, even if only historical, that investors have suffered and that may potentially occur again. In the table on the next page, we have indicated the annual perfor-mances of each of the proposed asset classes for a 10-year period for the US market, using different indices. We have given more weight to recent data over this timeframe, which we find very interesting.

The year 2008 is obviously rich in data, as it alone contains the worst-case performances for the given period.

It also shows an impressive correlation between all the asset classes, demonstrating that the financial crisis struck at every level and strongly attenuated the principle of diversification.

In our view, the average loss is useful because although it does not ignore the occurrence of any extreme results, which are important to consider, these are put into perspective by the other losses observed over the period. The performance of real estate in 2008 should therefore be compared to the other bad years for this asset class, in order to arrive at more reasonable conclusions.

Finally, these data are an additional evaluation criterion that will help us to arrive at a classification according to the degree of risk (Table 5.1).

So, using the various criteria that have been developed, we can construct Table 5.2.

Table 5.1 Asset class performances (2000–2009)

Asset class	2000	2001	2002	2003	2004	2005	2006	2007	2008	2009	Averave loss	Average return
Cash Index US COTR03 US T-Bills 3 months	2.36%	4.06%	1.71%	1.07%	1.25%	3.00%	4.81%	4.78%	1.75%	0.14%	n/a	2.49%
Gov. Bonds US GATR Index >1 year	13.38%	6.70%	12.11%	2.93%	3.47%	2.70%	3.12%	9.09%	14.21%	−3.81%	−3.81%	6.39%
Corp. Bonds Index US IBOXIG Investment grade	9.62%	11.30%	7.03%	7.28%	5.75%	0.84%	3.98%	4.01%	0.96%	12.79%	n/a	6.36%
Real estate Index RUGL EPRA/NAREIT	13.84%	−3.81%	2.82%	40.69%	37.96%	15.35%	42.35%	−6.96%	−47.72%	38.26%	−19.50%	13.28%
Equities (dev. countries) Index S&P 500	−10.14%	−13.04%	−23.37%	26.38%	8.99%	3.00%	13.62%	3.53%	−38.49%	23.45%	−21.26%	−0.61%
Commodities Index CRY	11.06%	−16.34%	23.04%	8.86%	11.21%	16.88%	−7.40%	16.74%	−36.01%	23.46%	−19.92%	5.15%
"High Yield" bonds Index IBOXHY High Yield	4.95%	0.17%	−8.84%	19.58%	10.14%	2.05%	9.66%	0.72%	−23.88%	44.46%	−16.36%	5.90%
Equities (emerging) Index MXEF	−31.80%	−4.91%	−7.97%	51.59%	22.45%	30.31%	29.18%	36.48%	−54.48%	74.50%	−24.79%	14.54%
Private Equity Index MSCI World	−14.05%	−17.83%	−21.06%	30.81%	12.84%	7.56%	17.95%	7.09%	−42.08%	26.98%	−23.76%	0.82%

Source: Bloomberg.

Table 5.2 Criteria used to classify different asset classes

Assets	Regular/conditional income	Possible capital gains	Position in case of bankruptcy	Number of risks identified	Worst-case performance (average)
Fiduciary Deposits	Regular	No	Priority Creditor	Low	Low
Money Market Funds	Regular	No	Priority Creditor	Low	Low
Government Bonds	Regular	Yes	Priority Creditor	Moderate	Low
Investment Grade Corporate Bonds	Regular	Yes	Priority Creditor	Moderate	Low
High Yield Bonds (including emerging countries)	Regular	Yes	Priority Creditor	Very High	Medium
Stocks from developed countries	Conditional	Yes	Residual Claim	High	Strong
Stocks from emerging countries	Conditional	Yes	Residual Claim	Very High	Strong
Real Estate (Indirect)	Regular/Conditional	Yes	Residual Claim	Moderate	Medium
Commodities	No Income	Only	n/a	Moderate	Medium to Strong
Precious and Industrial Metals	No Income	Only	n/a	Low	Medium to Strong
Private Equity	Usually No Income	Yes	Residual Claim	High	Strong

5.2   CLASSIFICATION OF THE DIFFERENT ASSET CLASSES

Based on the table above, we can now establish a classification of the various different financial assets studied. We have also organised them into different categories according to the level of risk (Table 5.3).

Table 5.3   Final classification of different asset classes

Money Market Funds Fiduciary Deposits Government Bonds	Categories with the **least risk**
Real Estate (Direct) Investment Grade Corporate Bonds	Categories with a **low to moderate risk**
High Yield Bonds Real Estate (Indirect)	Categories with a **moderate to high risk**
Metals and Commodities Stocks from developed countries Stocks from emerging countries Private Equity	Categories with a **high risk**

Part III
The Market

Once familiar with the investment universe and the various risks associated with each asset class as defined above, investors will need to study the market, which sets the price of these different assets.

However, they would be forgiven for wondering whether this price fully reflects all available information, and if it can indeed be regarded as "fair". This takes us to the famous notion of market efficiency.

6
Market Efficiency

According to the efficient market hypothesis, the price given by the market is always the **fair price** and **fully reflects all available information**.

"A market in which all available information is immediately reflected in the price of securities offers no opportunity for arbitrage. It is therefore difficult to beat the market with any consistency, making passive management the best choice."[1] Because the price is given efficiently by the market, any opportunity to generate excess returns will immediately be eliminated by the large number of market participants. Therefore, it is impossible for any investor to outperform the market in the long term.

"Conversely, if information is not always correctly nor immediately reflected in prices, this means there are pockets of inefficiency that may be exploited as part of an active portfolio management strategy."[2]

There are **three forms** of market **efficiency** originally defined by Eugene Fama in 1970.

6.1   WEAK FORM MARKET EFFICIENCY

"A market is weak form efficient if prices incorporate all **past information**."[3] All past information is reflected in the current price, making it impossible to predict future price movements based on past prices.

Many studies conducted using technical analysis methods (filters, moving averages) have reached the conclusion that after factoring in transaction costs, it is not possible to beat the market with any consistency.

Weak form efficiency also implies that the returns on securities are independent from one period to another, as information is immediately included in the price. However, many tests invalidate the hypothesis of serially independent returns.

Empirical studies, in particular by Bondt and Thaler (1985), have demonstrated that investors "overreact", tending to favour securities that are the subject of good news to the detriment of securities associated with bad news.

Evidently, weak form efficiency does not enjoy unanimous support.

---

[1]Grandin, Hübner, Lambert, p. 31.
[2]Grandin, Hübner, Lambert, p. 31.
[3]Grandin, Hübner, Lambert, p. 34.

6.2   SEMI-STRONG FORM MARKET EFFICIENCY

"A market is semi-strong form efficient if prices incorporate all **past and public information**. According to this definition, it is impossible to make any excess gains by trading on earnings, dividend or stock split announcements, etc., as this information can be used by anyone once it is made public."[4]

Event studies can be used to determine different price reactions following the release of information.

Prices may adjust immediately, thus implying that the market is efficient. However, when the price takes some time (several days or even months) to incorporate the information, this is referred to as under- or overreaction that can be exploited by investors.

Most studies show that investors react quickly, and that it is illusory to hope to make excess returns by trading on information such as dividend announcements, bonus share issues, stock repurchases, acquisitions, mergers, changes in accounting policies, etc. Nonetheless, some recent results show slow adjustment to events such as earnings announcements.[5]

We will examine investors' under- and overreaction to information in more detail at a later stage. At this point, we can assume that all publicly available information is **not immediately reflected** in prices, implying a certain level of market inefficiency.

6.3   STRONG FORM MARKET EFFICIENCY

"Finally, a market is strong form efficient if prices incorporate all **past, public and private information**. In this case, it is impossible to earn returns in excess of the market using insider information."[6]

However, in practice, the existence of **insider trading** invalidates this form; "abnormal" profits can be generated although this constitutes an illegal practice. Independently of any possibility of insider news, so-called **pockets of inefficiency** may exist. These take time to be corrected and to return to a situation of market equilibrium and efficiency.

Furthermore, "information is **not** a **free resource**; it entails **acquisition costs** that may be high. This is the case for many tools and services used by portfolio managers and traders. So this cost must be included in the definition of efficiency, particularly for testing the strong form. It was Grossman and Stiglitz (1980) who showed that prices should not perfectly reflect information."[7] Thus, "an investment fund, which requires constant information processing, must make a return in excess of the average market return to compensate for the cost of this information. If the fund's return exceeds market return and management costs, the market

---

[4]Grandin, Hübner, Lambert, p. 34.
[5]Grandin, Hübner, Lambert, p. 42.
[6]Grandin, Hübner, Lambert, p. 34.
[7]Grandin, Hübner, Lambert, p. 35.

may then be considered inefficient."[8] Of course, there are fund managers who succeed in beating the market after deduction of transaction costs, but they are unable to do so repeatedly, year after year. While the important **role** played by **luck** must not be forgotten, exploitation of these pockets of inefficiency should be considered.

6.4   CONCLUSION ON MARKET EFFICIENCY

According to this very strong assumption, variations in yesterday's prices do not influence today's prices, nor do they influence tomorrow's, so that each variation is independent from the last.

According to studies by Mandelbrot, in particular, it seems that prices have a sort of "memory" and that sometimes the market needs time to assimilate information and reflect it in prices.

Warren Buffett liked to joke that he would willingly subsidise university chairs on efficient-market hypothesis, so that professors could educate increasing numbers of misguided financiers whom he could then fleece.[9]

As Mandelbrot summarises, "efficient market hypothesis is nothing more than that, a hypothesis".[10] Graham already believed in his time that "when the price of a stock can be influenced by a 'herd' on Wall Street with prices set at the margin by the most emotional person, or the greediest person, or the most depressed person, it is hard to argue that the market always prices rationally. In fact, market prices are frequently non-sensical."[11]

Our Advice

In our opinion, independently of the form chosen, the **market should not** be regarded as **perfectly efficient**.

The degree of efficiency depends above all on the quantity, quality and reliability of information available on a market. Within the framework of future discounted cash flows, the certainty (reliability) of earning those flows will be decisive.

We believe that the **degree of efficiency** mainly depends of the **degree** of **certainty** regarding **future cash flows**.

In the case of government or other high quality bonds, the future cash flow is known (all the coupons have to be paid); therefore, this market seems efficient. Moreover, it allows very little room for active management.

On the other hand, if we look at stocks, where cash flows are conditional, or commodities, where cash flows may even be non-existent, these markets are far less efficient and allow more room for active management.

So asset classes have differing degrees of efficiency, with differences within each class.

---

[8]Ibid.
[9]Taken from Mandelbrot, p. 33.
[10]Mandelbrot, p. 216.
[11]Graham, p. 546.

However, is it possible to exploit these inefficiencies by trying to forecast and anticipate prices? Is the modelling of market movements feasible? We will attempt to answer these questions firstly by focusing on fundamental analysis, which seeks to determine the true value of an asset in order to compare it with the market price. We will then look at technical analysis, which concentrates solely on the market price and its movements, and aims to take advantage of past information.

Both these approaches aim to exploit pockets of market inefficiency so that investors can determine an asset's **"real" price** compared to that established by the market, which is not really the "fair" price. On the basis of these analyses, they can increase their chances of achieving their objective – capital preservation and growth – while reducing the risk of losses.

7

Fundamental Analysis

Fundamental analysis is based solely on market data and companies' financial results. It studies the various events within a company, its sector and the economic environment that are likely to cause its share price to rise or fall.

It principally examines the **balance sheet** to find out assets and liabilities, the **income statement** to assess revenues, expenses, and hence profits, and finally the **cash flow statement**. This important document reflects the company's ability to generate cash, an essential factor sought by any investor. Furthermore, unlike other documents, cash flows are difficult for accountants to manipulate. Obviously, it is better to have **financial statements audited** by recognised firms.

In any case, it is useful to stress the importance of **footnotes** in corporate financial reports, which often provide a wealth of information to anyone patient enough to read them.

As indicated above, we can first determine the company's **intrinsic value**, which will then be compared to its **market value** in order to decide whether to make the investment. However, the company can also be assessed using relative measures or, more precisely, certain ratios that we will describe below. Here we will focus on stocks.

Sources

Financial databases provide this type of information about companies. Access to the Bloomberg and Reuters financial information services for professionals must be paid for, but a great deal of information can be obtained at www.reuters.com (under *Financials* for the chosen company).

The following websites are also good sources of information:

www.bloomberg.com

www.boursorama.com

7.1 DISCOUNTED CASH FLOW

One method of stock picking involves determining the value of a stock by discounting its future cash flows.

Indeed, "a stock's value depends on the issuing company's ability to make profits in the future. The art of the financial analyst is therefore to try and predict this profit outlook and compare it to the price at which the stock is traded. This analysis helps determine if the stock is too expensive compared to its profit potential or, on the contrary, too cheap."[1]

---

[1] Novello, p. 60.

If this estimated value is higher than the market price, it is worth considering buying the stock. Conversely, if this value is lower than the market price, a short position or simply the decision not to buy the security may be envisaged.

The **dividend discount model** suggested by J.B. Williams or Gordon-Shapiro can be used to calculate this intrinsic value. However, it is based on the assumption that cash flows generated by a stock are the dividends paid out and that these grow over time either at a constant or a variable rate. Discounted free cash flows are used in practice to evaluate a company that pays no dividends and is not publicly traded, but we will not go into further detail on this point.

Gordon-Shapiro's formula is often used to determine this value by introducing the following parameters:

$$P0 = EPS1 * \text{Payout ratio}$$

$$\text{Cost of capital} - (1 - \text{Payout ratio}) * ROE$$

where
P0 = the price sought at time 0
EPS1 = estimated earnings per share in year 1
Payout ratio = amount of earnings paid out in dividends to shareholders
Cost of capital expressed as a rate
ROE = return on equity

However, the result obtained is very sensitive to the choice of parameters and of forecasts made about the expected growth rate of dividends. Companies often try to pay a steady dividend over time, which may imply accounting manipulations. It is also difficult to estimate the cost of capital.

Furthermore, unlike bonds, income generated by stocks is not fixed and can fluctuate over time. Finally, the time horizon considered to evaluate stocks using this formula is infinite, while the evaluation period is fixed for bonds (except for perpetuals).

Consequently, it is difficult to get a precise, reliable result using estimations and such a long time horizon.

In our opinion, this formula presents a number of disadvantages and should be rejected, at least from this analysis. We might consider that investors should pay no more than the intrinsic value calculated, or buy companies whose expected growth rates are above average over the next five years.[2]

Independently of whether or not to use this formula, the idea of intrinsic value has been decisive for one of the greatest and richest investors of our time: Warren Buffett. He is very

---

[2]Malkiel, p. 122.

much a follower of **value investing**, but this approach is rarely included in the programme of major business schools.

7.2 RELATIVE MEASURES

It is also interesting to examine the following ratios.

7.2.1 Price to Earnings Ratio (P/E)

The Price to Earnings Ratio represents the stock price divided by the earnings per share:

$$P/E = \frac{\text{Stock Price}}{\text{Earnings Per Share}}$$

In other words, it indicates to investors **how much** they have to **pay per unit** of **earnings** when buying this stock. So the higher the P/E, the more they have to pay. However, it is important to **compare** this ratio to the P/E of the **industry** the company operates in.

While it is very easy to use, the P/E ratio changes over time and can fall quickly when earnings or stock prices decline; it depends on corporate profits that fluctuate with economic conditions. So a low P/E is not necessarily attractive if the industry is in a downturn. Moreover, growth can differ from one company to another within the same industry, and this ratio ignores any such differentials.

It is also **sensitive** to the **financial structure** of the company and **depends** on **accounting data** that can be manipulated.

> **Our Advice**
>
> We advise **caution** in using the P/E ratio. It should not be used as the sole criteria for making an investment choice.

7.2.2 Price to Book

This ratio is a more useful indicator for determining the value of a company and its future growth.

$$P/B = \frac{\text{Market Value of Equity}}{\text{Book Value of Equity}}$$

In other words, it indicates **how many times** investors must **pay** the **value** of **equity** on the market. It should be **compared** to the P/B of the **sector** or industry. Too high a figure may suggest the risk of a bubble and, therefore, of correction. Generally, between 1 and 2 is regarded as a reasonable level.

Although easy to calculate, the P/B also depends on accounting data and can pose problems when evaluating companies with a large number of intangible assets. For that type of company, it is better to use the **Price to Cash Flow ratio**, which has the advantage of being **independent** of **accounting methods**.

On the matter of accounting, this anecdote from a company director who wanted to hire a new accountant is revealing. The first candidate enters and the company director asks him what he knows. The candidate replies that he knows all the rules of accounting extremely well, especially the American rules used by large multinationals. Unconvinced by this reply, our company director asks the second candidate the same thing. He gets the same type of reply, so he asks the third candidate to enter. This time, the candidate retorts: "Allow me to answer with a question of my own: what would you like to appear in your balance sheet?", to which the company director replies: "You're hired."

Our Advice

We also recommend that investors do **not** use the Price to Book ratio as the **sole criterion** when making an investment decision, and to favour securities with a P/B of **between 1 and 2**.

7.3   STRATEGIC ANALYSIS[3]

A more in-depth analysis of the company and its environment must be carried out, in line with the value investing approach advocated by Buffett and Lynch that we will cover in detail later. Firstly, it is necessary to understand the company's business model (how does it make money?) and its competitive advantages.

7.3.1   The business model

The aim here is to find out **how** the **company makes money** in practice. "The business model is the approach that the company has chosen to generate its income. In other words, it is the mechanism that will enable the company to make money."[4]

Generally, the final product or service is made up of many stages or, more precisely, many intermediary products or services. A company can either focus on the whole range of activities that make up the final **service** or **product**, or choose to concentrate on some in particular. It may concentrate only on **design**, **production** or **distribution**, or on a **combination** of two or even three activities. From an economic point of view, it will have to determine whether the income generated by the chosen strategy is higher than the expenses this choice entails.

A company's value is usually made up of **intangible assets**, otherwise known as intellectual property. These intangible assets can be used in various ways. "They can be sold, licensed,

---

[3]Taken from Snopek-Tripiana, p. 35ff.
[4]R. Cohen, *PME Magazine*, March 2001.

used as collateral or to guarantee a loan, as security to borrow money from friends, family, private investors and even banks."[5]

As part of the strategic analysis, assuming that knowledge is protected by intellectual property rights (patents, brands, etc.), the company must also decide how to exploit it commercially.

Thanks to this legal protection, a company's competitors will not be able to commercially exploit its own intangible assets, which therefore constitute its competitive advantage. However, this **protection** is of **limited duration**, and beyond a defined period competitors will in turn be able to exploit these intangible assets commercially. A company cannot hold a **monopoly** over an indefinite period. Furthermore, the protection only applies in the country in which the patent is used and registered. International procedures have to be undertaken, either in the countries concerned or via a system of international patents, in order to extend legal protection to other countries.

However, instead of exploiting its invention itself and "going to war" with its competitors, the company may decide to sell the **exploitation rights** and become, in some respects, the supplier of its competitors. Indeed, "when the product requires an overly large distribution network or logistics [...], assigning a licence to a strategic partner rather than owning production may be the best strategic option".[6]

A company may also "consider receiving royalties by licensing [the] patented inventions to other companies that are able to market them".[7] "Dolby" is a perfect example. Ray Dolby, after having designed and protected his system to improve sound recording, preferred to sell the exploitation rights for his invention to other companies, thus becoming a respected supplier rather than a hated competitor.

The reasoning is identical for the protection provided by a brand. Protection excludes the possibility of other companies using the brand, but once again for a limited period of time. It is important to distinguish the name of a company, which enjoys exclusive and unlimited protection, from the brand, which is always linked to the products or services of the company, and is protected for a limited period of time.

However, the sale of rights to use a brand – franchising for example – is rarely possible in the early stages of a company, as it must first acquire experience, a reputation and, above all, brand awareness for the products or services offered. Furthermore, the sale of rights to use a brand usually contributes to the company's activities by playing an advertising role and increasing brand awareness and, therefore, the company's profile.

Here we can give the example of "Caterpillar", which granted rights to use its brand to clothing manufacturer companies, in particular the famous Caterpillar shoes. These in fact are only manufactured under licence. Instead of producing shoes itself, the company preferred

---

[5] M. Piaget, p. 40.
[6] R. Cohen, *PME Magazine*, May 2001.
[7] M. Piaget, p. 40.

to sell exploitation rights to other companies with better knowledge of the manufacture of such items. Similarly, the "Délifrance" bakeries usually only hold the rights to use the brand.

Determining how the company makes money in practice is essential, but it is almost equally important to assess the **quality of the management**. This is a difficult factor to estimate for a private investor, but for a fund manager who wants to invest several millions, meetings can be arranged with the company's management. Therefore, investors can delegate this assessment to a fund manager and decide to invest some of their money. They leave it to the manager to conduct the stock analysis and selection.

At this stage, we might wonder if it is really possible to exert any influence whatsoever by investing in a company. Indeed, investors put their trust in the management, whose interests are often at odds with those of shareholders. Managers are often there for a short time only and have objectives of maximising short-term profit, while investors have a long-term approach and objectives. It can be taken as a very **positive** factor if **managers** are also **shareholders** in the company, ideally in the majority group. The ideal situation is when the founder is still in charge of managing the company.

However, we do suggest that investors undertake this analysis so they can at least be familiar with what they are buying, and how their stock will be able to grow over time.

The next step is to undertake a more **thorough strategic analysis**,[8] like the one developed by Snopek and Tripiana to be used in the start-up process and that we would like to outline below.

7.3.2   External analysis

Companies offering similar products or services can generate different turnovers and, more especially, profits. A company's **profitability** will mainly depend on its **chosen strategy**, but also on **market imperfections**.

Firstly, what is called an external analysis should be undertaken, examining the structure of the relevant market segments, such as the existence of barriers to entry or exit, the intensity of competitive forces and the potential market and its growth. Critical success factors must also be considered.

a) Barriers to entry

As we mentioned above, profitability will essentially depend on the barriers to entry to the correspondent sub-industry.

By barrier to entry, we mean **any factor that makes the expected profitability of a new entrant to a market lower than that of already established companies**. Expected profitability is therefore directly related to barriers to entry; the business will only be profitable

---

[8]Snopek-Tripiana, p. 28ff.

if it is difficult for new competitors to enter the sector, as each new entrant threatens to cause a drop in prices and, consequently, margins.

We will now present the main barriers to entry, whether induced by **differences in costs** or by **differentiation**.

First to be considered are **economies of scale**, which can be defined as lower costs per unit achieved once a certain volume of production is reached. However, beyond a certain volume, the unit cost per product stops decreasing, a phenomenon referred to as diseconomies of scale. Large purchases are entitled to certain discounts, which can also be described as economies of scale. These are essentially related to the technology used to manufacture the product and to experience, but depend heavily on the industry. So in some cases, it is unnecessary to be too large and size may even be a disadvantage.

Market size is another barrier to entry, in that it determines the possible number of competitors within a market. If the development of a new product is very expensive and the market is small, few products will be able to be sold and it will be hard to make a return on investment. Such is the case, for example, for the market for very large aircraft; the development of a Boeing 747 is very expensive (about $10 billion) and the market is very small with a very limited number of units sold. Consequently, the number of competitors in this market is very small.

As such, the **maximum number of competitors** can be easily calculated by dividing the total market size by the minimum size for efficiency. Total market size corresponds to the total number of units sold per year, while the minimum size for efficiency refers to the minimum size a company must be to benefit from economies of scale. For example, considering that about 12 million vehicles are sold on the European automotive market and that the minimum size for efficiency of a manufacturer is 3 million cars, this market can support a maximum of only four competitors. Above this point, the market becomes saturated and concentration will be necessary, as was the case in the audit industry with the "Big Five" becoming the "Big Four". Furthermore, if the market is saturated, a new arrival will have to force out a competitor, who will not necessarily give in easily.

Privileged access to raw materials and a consequent reduction in transport costs is another type of barrier.

Special production processes, such as the existence of patents protecting product manufacturing methods, also help protect the industry. Furthermore, certain company-specific particularities or ways of working are "private" processes that can be difficult to copy, and as such constitute another type of barrier.

Costs are also barriers to entry, especially when the prices charged by the market leader correspond to the costs of potential competitors, as the prices set are such that business is unattractive for the latter companies (this is called the "Entry Deterring Price"). The possibility of sharing costs between different products (cost sharing) also belongs to this category.

The **money** required to be able to enter a market and operate a business is not, in principle, a barrier to entry, as if the project is interesting, feasible and promising, investors can be found relatively easily. However, in some cases, financial resources can be difficult to muster, especially if the level of investment necessary is very high.

The product provides certain values sought by clients, who accept to pay a given margin for the value and quality that it brings them. Thus, the **branding, quality** and **reputation of the product** or company are other types of barrier to entry. As we indicated earlier, consumers or buyers are willing to pay a certain margin for a quality product. As such, the market leader can set a price which, without this margin, corresponds to the costs of potential competitors, thereby discouraging them from entering the market.

Similarly, the company's **prestige, reputation, know-how** or **experience** are all barriers to entry, which can prove very strong in some industries.

Finally, **government interventions** aiming to create monopolies can also be barriers, as they limit the entry of other competitors. **Subsidies** granted to certain companies, **agreements** with the government, or specific **legislation** can also be protection factors in a particular industry.

To conclude, it is important to understand that the higher the barriers to entry, the better the industry is protected, and therefore the greater expected profitability.

b) Barriers to exit

By barrier to exit, we mean anything that stops companies from exiting the market easily when business is bad.

The main obstacles are **sunk costs** (large investments that are hard to recover), the difficulty of **converting factories**, or a **lack of flexibility** due to contracts.

Furthermore, **switching costs**, i.e., the costs of switching suppliers, may also be a barrier to exit, but are considered here instead as **barriers to mobility** (preventing the free "movement" of the company).

It should be noted that if these barriers are strong, it may create unhealthy competition, as the "bad" companies cannot exit, spoil the market and prevent others from developing properly. Occasionally, some believe that a sector is "strategic", to the point that they are willing to lose money just so they can be present.

To conclude, it is worth bearing in mind that the greater the barriers to exit, the harder it will be to exit the industry if business is going badly.

c) Competitive forces

Barriers to entry are certainly necessary to guarantee good profitability, but they are not enough on their own. There are other factors in play, particularly competition within an industry. So profitability will also depend on the degree of rivalry between competitors.

There are **five competitive forces**[9] that influence both the profitability of a particular industry and the business strategy to follow.

i) Competitive rivalry within an industry

The term "competition" is difficult to define, as too broad a definition leads to too high a number of competitors, some of which are not worth "attacking". Yet if the definition is too narrow, it reduces the company's "battle field" excessively.

We can use the notion of need to help define competition. Two companies are competitors, in our view, if they meet the **same demand**, i.e., the same specific need. For example, on the Paris-Geneva line, the TGV is in competition with Air France-KLM, which itself is in competition with other airlines.

Consequently, competition "includes anything – person, organisation or group – that is likely to take money from your clientele. Thus, cinemas are now in competition with DVD hire and cable television companies [. . .]. Today, competition must be seen as all the different ways the customer has of getting what he wants, not as a precise list of companies working in your industrial field who try to beat you by lowering their prices or improving their performances."[10]

Rivalry between current competitors depends first of all on the **number of competitors**. If there are few competitors, rivalry will be weak, while a large number of competitors means strong rivalry.

Product differentiation also plays a role in terms of rivalry, as highly differentiated products entail the creation of small monopolies with little rivalry, where competition is only involved for the first customer.

Switching costs, i.e., the costs for the customer of switching suppliers, and therefore companies, can make the customer resist trying the competition. Again, if these costs are very high, we may see the creation of monopolies, where competition is only apparent for the first customer. Here we can give the example of Johnson & Johnson, which managed to increase switching costs by using a different terminology and different diameters from its competitors, making it more difficult to change suppliers.

In addition, **fixed costs** can also influence competition within an industry, as if costs are essentially fixed and demand fluctuates, a price war will occur. Conversely, if costs are predominantly variable, prices will usually be fixed.

Industry growth also influences rivalry. When growth is strong, there is little competition between companies as ultimately they all make money. If growth is weak on the other hand, competition will be fierce, everyone having to fight for their "bread".

Finally, in industries where the additional capacity offered is far higher than demand, the **size of increases in companies' supply** can also be a competitive factor. For example, the

---

[9]Porter's 5 forces.
[10]M. Robert, M. Devaux, pp. 26–27.

construction of a factory may provide an enormous production capacity compared to the increase in demand, making the factories too large for the market. Similarly, the creation of a new connecting flight significantly increases the supply of seats that then have to be filled, and this does not always correspond to the increase in demand.

As we mentioned earlier, barriers to exit can also influence competition within an industry.

ii) Potential competitors

Still, it pays to be wary of potential competitors who may come looking for their slice of the cake and constitute a threat for the companies already present.

The existence of strong barriers to entry or of low growth provides effective protection.

iii) The threat of substitute products

By substitute products, we mean all kinds of products and services "similar" to those of the company. These must also be taken into consideration. They enter into direct competition with your products because they meet the same need. Sugar and artificial sweeteners are a perfect example. Accordingly, products that can serve the **same purpose** for the customer with an advantageous cost–benefit ratio must be closely monitored. We advise paying particular attention to the characteristics of these products, their price, and especially their development, in order to avoid seeing your customers move towards the competition.

iv) The bargaining power of customers

It is also important to be aware that, in some cases, customers have strong bargaining power, which may influence the profitability of a given industry.

If customers are concentrated, if their purchases represent a large amount of the company's sales, if their supply options are many, if their switching costs are low and, especially, if the product is standard or undifferentiated (customers are only sensitive to price), then customers have strong bargaining power.

v) The bargaining power of suppliers

As with customers, suppliers may also have bargaining power.

When there is a limited number of suppliers, few substitutes for the product or service, when the cost of switching supplier is high and, especially, the product is unique or differentiated, suppliers have strong bargaining power.

Ultimately, it must not be forgotten that anyone can have a good idea, and that therefore competitors will always exist and, more importantly, act.

d) The potential market and its growth

The **current** and **potential** market size is relatively difficult to estimate, in that it is based primarily on quantitative data, such as sales or market shares.

However, it is possible to find information related to the **growth** of a given **industry** in newspapers, specialised journals and especially on the Internet, which is a considerable source of information. By using search engines and surfing company websites, the websites of marketing firms or any sites dedicated to a particular subject or field, a great deal of information about the potential or current market can be found.

It will be important to find out whether the market is growing, shrinking, or even stagnant. Industry growth provides an invaluable indication, but also useful is the idea of a **product life cycle**, which usually includes **four stages**.

In the **introduction** stage, the product starts to be distributed on the market, which is usually characterised by slow growth. Earnings are often negative during this period, in large part because of high development costs.

In the **growth** stage, sales volume increases swiftly, demand grows and profits are generated.

In the **maturity** stage, demand for the product begins to stagnate and the market stops growing. Profits reach their maximum level, and begin to drop slightly due to the expense of marketing to maintain demand.

In the **decline** stage, sales fall sharply, as do profits, and the market begins to shrink or decline. Innovation resulting in a new product is essential at this stage so that a transition may occur.

Bear in mind that the **duration** of each of these stages depends on the product. Some products have very short life cycles and others very long ones. For example, fashion items and IT products have very short life cycles.

Determining which stage the market is in is essential. Some companies wait until the product leaves the introduction stage, to avoid losses due to product development and launch and enter directly into a period where it is possible to make a profit. It doesn't necessarily pay to be a pioneer.

Finally, particular attention must be paid here to the size of supply increases or, more precisely, to the risk of providing additional capacity higher than demand, especially during the decline stage.

e) The political/economic/legal/social/technological environment

It is also important to analyse the general environment, political stability and the social or legal context.

The influence of **political forces** or **labour unions** on an industry and, therefore, on a company must be taken into consideration, as must the legal framework within which the company will operate.

Legal standards define many duties and obligations, both for individuals and for companies, and these standards change over time. The company must be aware of any new regulations, constraints, and even opportunities that may appear.

The **economic context** is obviously to be considered, without forgetting that economic health varies from one industry to another, making generalisations about the overall economy unrealistic.

The **social context** or, more precisely, **public opinion** must also be taken into account, as it is important that customers see the company's activities as "socially" and "ethically" acceptable according to current moral and social values.

Finally, the **technological environment** is extremely important for two reasons. Firstly, it tells the company which technologies it can or will be able to use as part of its business activities. In addition, the company should also look at "general" technological developments that are not necessarily directly related to their products or services, but which may however influence their very existence.

f) Critical success factors

Critical success factors are the **elements necessary for a company's success** in a given industry for a certain period.

At this stage it is worth emphasising that these critical success factors not only vary according to sub-industry, but also **change over time**. So, it is necessary to identify the "rules of the game" that will ensure success, according to the demands of customers and the business in question. It should be noted that it is entirely possible to modify the rules of the game, if the current success factors are unsuitable and a change will obviously be required at some stage in the future. Consequently, a company may well decide to alter the competitive playing field, based on the development of its distinctive skills.

As critical success factors depend on each sector, it is practically impossible to compile an exhaustive list. Nonetheless, a few examples will help provide a clearer idea of the concept.

In the agri-food industry, brand marketing, reputation, diversity of supply, and the distribution network are all critical success factors. The efficiency of industrial facilities and an efficient distribution network are two of the critical success factors for automotive manufacturing. In retail distribution, it is important to have sufficient purchase volume to ensure bargaining power vis-à-vis suppliers. For other sectors, price, product quality, reputation and customer loyalty may constitute other critical success factors.

It is therefore important to ascertain which resources and skills are required to run the business and, more importantly, to examine whether the company has skills which make it stand out from its competitors. This is precisely the purpose of internal analysis.

7.3.3   Internal analysis

After the external analysis, it is necessary to reflect on what, on an internal level – i.e., given their different resources and skills – could give a long-term competitive advantage to a company aiming to succeed better than others and to be as profitable as possible.

a) Resources

Resources are generally separated into **five categories**, and to run the business in question the value and adequacy of each of these must be appreciated.

Physical resources include all the tangible elements available, such as premises or equipment.

Financial resources are made up of equity or debt as well as borrowing capacity and cash flow.

By **human resources** we mean the "individuals available", including their education and training, their skills, experience and especially their motivation.

Intangible resources are essentially the technologies mastered and patented by the company, as well as their supply and distribution networks.

Finally, in terms of **organisational resources**, particular attention must be paid to the company's structure and the style of leadership and human resource management.

It will be essential to determine the **strengths** and **weaknesses** for each of these resource categories, so that the necessary measures can be taken if certain resources have to be sought externally.

Thus, by combining these resources, the company will be able to develop specific capabilities. Over time and through a process of improvement and development, these will become core competencies that distinguish the company from its competitors.

b) Core competencies

Core competencies are the **competencies** specific to a company that it sees as having a **strategic value**.

These competencies generate **value** for the **customer**, as they contribute strongly to creating the benefit the customer seeks in the product. Moreover, these core competencies must be **rare**; current or potential competitors must not have them. They also have to be **difficult** and **costly** to **imitate** for other companies. Finally, there must be no strategic equivalents for these competencies, i.e., it must be impossible to substitute them with other competencies.

In light of these distinctive capabilities, the company may determine which competitive advantage to focus on, in line with the critical success factors of the industry.

c) Competitive advantage

We will see that ultimately, profitability depends on uniqueness, to the extent that a company with a strong competitive advantage, and a unique product or service that is difficult to copy, will clearly have a profitable business.

Competitive advantage can be defined as a **characteristic of a company that differentiates it from other companies and can give it an advantage in both the medium and the long term**.

A company can develop a competitive advantage through the differentiation of its products or by exploiting cost differences with its competitors.

For example, strong branding, an excellent reputation, low production costs or the use of cutting edge technology are various characteristics that distinguish one company from the rest.

A company can gain a competitive advantage either by exploiting market imperfections, or by improving the operations of its value chain, its efficiency (low production costs with perfect quality), its flexibility (extremely short cycles), research and development (continuous innovation) or through cooperative arrangements or strategic networks.

However, in some industries, differentiation no longer depends on the products or the technology used, as they can ultimately be used by competitors, but on the quality of customer relations. Indeed, it is essential for a company to understand thoroughly the characteristics and requirements of demand, in order to be able to satisfy it in the best and fastest possible way. So for a company, competitive advantage means being as closely aligned as possible to the market on which it has decided to position itself. As stated by Arie de Geus of Royal Dutch Shell, "the ability to learn faster than your competitors may be the only sustainable competitive advantage".

d) Industry profitability

Here we will turn to an essential factor for strategic analysis: profitability ratios. These make it possible to ascertain the profitability of a given industry.

Return on investment (ROI) measures the amount of capital that must be invested to make a profit. It is divided into two parts: the **net profit margin** (NPM), which represents the amount earned on each dollar value of revenue, and the **total asset turnover** (TAT), which is an indicator of the volume of business done by the company for one year. It therefore reflects the level of capital intensity.

$$ROI = NPM * TAT$$

The NPM is calculated by dividing the company's net profit (revenue minus total costs) by its revenue. Meanwhile, the TAT is calculated by dividing total revenue by the company's assets, including needs for working capital.

$$ROI = Net\ Profit * Revenue$$

$$Revenue\ Assets$$

In a growth environment, the **net margin** on products will increase, as your revenue, and therefore net profit, will increase (assuming that charges are identical). However, in a period of recession, the challenge is to achieve the same revenue with fewer available resources and especially with fewer sales. Therefore, particular attention should be paid to this ratio.

It is also important to examine the second ratio, the TAT, as it gives an indication of the speed at which assets are circulated (see below).

Thus, the examination of an industry consists primarily in determining its profitability using the two ratios we have just presented. The rates of these ratios will provide a diagnosis of the sector in question, but it should be noted here that these two ratios are always opposed.

Sector	ROI	NPM	TAT
Industrial sector	8–12%	>6–10%	0.5–1.1
Distribution sector	8–12%	<6%	>1.1
Services sector	High	Fairly high	Moderate

By examining the financial statements of other companies operating in the chosen industry, it is possible to get an idea of the value of the rates of these two ratios. However, these are specific to a particular company and cannot be extended over an entire sector.

If the **NPM** is **high** and the **TAT** is **low**, this means that (attractive) margins on products or services can be achieved, and that these are specialised or differentiated markets. Competitive pressure is normally quite low. However, fixed assets are significant and the movement of assets within the company is not very fast. In this sector, a **differentiation** and positioning strategy is entirely suitable.

On the other hand, if the **NPM** is **low** and the **TAT** is **high**, this means that margins are fairly low and the environment is very competitive. Furthermore, this also implies that assets, particularly cash, must circulate quickly within the company. In this sector, such as supermarket retailing for example, a **cost leadership** strategy is ideal.

7.3.4   The SWOT table (Strengths, Weaknesses, Opportunities and Threats)

The results obtained should be summarised on a **SWOT table** (Strengths – Weaknesses – Opportunities – Threats).

Relevant aspects that emerged from the external analysis must be entered either in the "**Threats**" column, if they indeed pose a threat or risk to the company, or in the "**Opportunities**" column if the company can take advantage of certain possibilities or a favourable context for doing business.

Then, in the light of factors gleaned from the internal analysis, the company's advantages and strengths should be placed in the "**Strengths**" column and any negative aspects, shortcomings and weaknesses in the "**Weaknesses**" column. The table is presented like this:

THREATS	OPPORTUNITIES
STRENGTHS	WEAKNESSES

This simple table helps the company steer its business over the long term as, using the table, it can determine whether it should engage in a given activity or abandon it. Another advantage is that it presents the positive and, more importantly, negative points of the company; it indicates which aspects leave room for improvement and which competencies should be sought externally.

Above all, the table will help investors decide whether or not they should invest money in the company.

7.4   CRITICISM OF FUNDAMENTAL ANALYSIS

"In the **real world**, causes are usually obscure. **Key information** is very often **unknown** or **unattainable**, as with the 1998 Russian financial crisis. It can be **hidden** or **misrepresented**, as with the bursting of the dotcom bubble or the Enron and Parmalat group scandals. It can also be misinterpreted: the precise mechanism that links news to prices, or cause to effect, is mysterious and apparently incoherent. For example, for the same piece of news, two opposite effects might occur. Threat of war: the dollar falls. Threat of war: the dollar rises. Which of these will actually happen? In hindsight, it seems obvious; in retrospect, fundamental analysis can be reconstructed, and always appears brilliant."[11]

Moreover, **conflict of interest** can be a real concern, pushing analysts employed by a bank to issue recommendations on securities simply to generate commissions for their employer or to "favour" important clients.

---

[11] Mandelbrot, p. 27.

The possibility of **forecasting** expected price movements is also subject to debate and criticism. "In a study comparing them with weather forecasters, Tadeusz Tyszka and Piotr Zielonka document that the analysts are worse at predicting, while having a greater faith in their own skills."[12]

Warren Buffett recommends that investors ignore analysts, brokers and experts, and instead make their own investment decisions based on their knowledge of management and financial markets. He advises reading as much as possible to get a maximum amount of information on which to base an investment decision, and never to decide whether or not to invest simply because of the encouragement of others. "Ben Graham observed in *The Intelligent Investor* – Buffett's favourite investment book – that 'we have seen much more money made and kept by "ordinary people" who were temperamentally well suited for the investment process than by those who lacked this quality, even though they had an extensive knowledge of finance, accounting, and stock market lore'."[13]

In our view, it is not the analysts' skill that should be doubted, but rather the conceptual framework within which the analyses are conducted. As we noted to begin with, risk measures and some of the criteria used are perhaps not entirely suitable. Furthermore, the under- or overestimation of certain factors or events that can affect the price of securities, as well as the existence of behavioural biases – excess confidence, optimism or pessimism, for example – should be better taken into account.

The *Financial Times'* famous monkey, who picks stock by randomly throwing darts at a list, can sometimes make higher returns than those obtained using complex mathematical models. These **models** are usually very **sensitive** to the choice of **parameters**, which are very **difficult** to **estimate**. As stated earlier, it is difficult to get a precise, reliable result using estimations. In addition, these models are often based on **fragile hypotheses** that consequently limit their usefulness.

It may be time to consider that the **luck factor** can play an important part in investment decisions, and that other factors should be taken into account.

Our Advice

Above all, investors must keep in mind that an analysis has to be undertaken before making an investment decision, having collected as much information as possible. Besides the strategic analysis we have suggested, particular attention should be paid to a company's:

- business model;
- management;
- financial health (liquidity, level of indebtedness, rating);
- profits, dividends and associated ratios (P/E, P/B, etc.);
- free cash flow;
- stock movement;
- specific risks (political, regulatory, boycott, etc.).

---

[12] Taleb, p. 150.
[13] Pardoe, pp. 40–41.

8

Technical Analysis

Technical analysis is the **study** of price **charts** and various **indicators** derived from them, with the aim of predicting price movements.[1] It is based on three principles that we will now examine.

8.1 THE THREE FUNDAMENTAL PRINCIPLES OF TECHNICAL ANALYSIS

8.1.1 Prices reflect all available information

This assertion is the essential foundation of technical analysis, which claims that "**anything** that can possibly affect the price – fundamentally, politically, psychologically, or otherwise – is actually **reflected** in the **price** of that market",[2] without worrying about why prices rise or fall.

To begin with, these assertions show a certain **simplification** of **how markets work** and reduce the study of markets to the study of charts, which only formally reflect what has happened.

Moreover, prices may certainly incorporate all available market information, but can purely private information, particularly when it can be exploited before being made public (insider trading), really be regarded as available information? As we stated earlier, markets are not perfectly efficient; consequently, prices do **not perfectly** reflect all market information.

Finally, as we will see in more detail below, the market does **not always** incorporate all available information immediately because of the under- and overreaction of investors to information.

An interesting study on the under- and overreaction of financial analysts in post-crash periods highlights the following aspects. "The analysis of reactions to news mainly reveals a sharp decline in underreaction to extremely negative news. Overreaction to extremely positive news, more hesitant before the crash, also abates."[3] Therefore, this analysis indicates the existence of **underreaction** to **extremely negative news** and **overreaction** to **extremely positive news** in the pre-crash period.

---

[1] Taken from Murphy, p. X.
[2] Murphy, p. 2.
[3] Taken from Bessière and Kaestner.

Investors may also react to a lack of information, be tempted to react to rumours, or simply tell themselves stories to invent reasons to act.[4]

Evidently, the assertion that prices immediately reflect all available information is not always corroborated by the reality of the financial markets.

8.1.2   Prices move in trends

According to the second concept, prices move in trends and "a trend is more likely to continue than reverse [...] or a trend in motion will continue in the same direction until it reverses".[5] Therefore, it is advisable to surf the trend for as long as possible before its reversal.

Price movements are certainly a succession of increases and decreases, but do prices follow a **random path** or can their movements be predicted? We will try to answer this question in the next section, but let's stay for a moment with this idea of trends, as in our view it is an important concept.

A series of higher highs (closing prices for example) coupled with higher lows indicates a **bullish movement**. The market reaches new heights and the lower levels are gradually rising. Conversely, a series of lower lows and lower highs indicate a **bearish movement**. When movement is lateral or without any defined direction, it is referred to as "**sideways**".

Analysts usually define a **long-term** trend over a period of more than a year, an intermediate trend over a one to three-month period, and a **short-term** trend over a period of less than one month.

Alternations between bullish and bearish trends are called **market cycles** and are generally classified[6] according to their **duration**. Long-term or primary cycles last for two years or more. The seasonal cycle lasts one year. The intermediate or secondary cycle lasts for nine to 26 weeks. Finally, the four-week trading cycle is separated into two shorter cycles, alpha and beta, which last an average of two weeks each.

The **Kontradieff cycle** lasts about 54 years, during which the economy undergoes phases of growth and correction. There are four periods (seasons): spring, summer, autumn and winter and, according to some analysts, the winter that should have started some time around the year 2000 may have begun after the last peak in 2007. This winter cycle will last about fifty years.

Generally speaking, the primary and seasonal cycles determine the major trend of a market.

Following the three most significant high points and the three most significant low points, it is possible to draw the upper and lower lines of a **channel**, which can be used to identify

---

[4]Ibid.
[5]Murphy, p. 4.
[6]See Murphy, p. 359.

trend reversals. However, once a trend reversal is noticed, this means that we have already entered the new trend.

Other tools which help determine trends or trend reversals include chart patterns, such as the "head and shoulders", "cup and handle", "double or triple tops and bottoms" or "triangles", as well as several **indicators** such as the MACD, Bollinger bands, RSI or the stochastic oscillator.

A former trader who taught technical analysis for more that 10 years and became a major expert on Elliott waves said one day that, in his opinion, all these indicators should be forgotten in order to **focus** on what he believed was the essential aspect: **trends**. This concept, which we also see as essential, will be covered in more detail in the following sections.

As for **Elliott waves**, he said he would sometimes wake in the middle of the night, panicking, not knowing if we were in the 2nd or 3rd wave. The fact his wife thought he was going crazy combined with the difficulty of applying this theory finally led him to abandon the approach. However, at this stage it will be interesting to spend a moment looking into this theory.

i) Elliott Wave Theory[7]

Elliot Wave Theory, formulated by Ralph Nelson Elliott, describes the movement of financial markets. The starting point of the theory is that markets move in a **series** of **successive waves**, regardless of the scale of observation (from the minute to the very long term), in what can be termed a **fractal process**.

This methodology is largely inspired by the famous Dow Theory. It is built on a basic principle that is both simple and obvious: markets move according to trends (bullish or bearish), within which corrective phases (of varying lengths and significance) are interposed.

These trends and corrections are charted according to the following pattern: the trend in **five waves** and the **correction** (decline) in **three**. Around this basic principle are grafted precise rules governing the length and graphic patterns that these waves make. This fairly comprehensive theory incorporates all the chartist patterns and rules and the famous Fibonacci ratios, based on the golden ratio.

A market moves in **eight successive waves**. Waves 1, 3 and 5 are ascending waves, while waves 2 and 4 go against the bullish trend and are called corrective waves because they correct waves 1 and 3. Once the rise in 5 waves is over, a correction in 3 waves (a, b and c) begins (see Figure 8.1).

The influence of Charles Dow's theory is decisive here. Elliott was inspired by it, completing it to define the personality of the waves, especially the corrective wave. Prechter takes things even further, justifying the existence of these waves by the psychology of the different types of people involved in the market (buyers, sellers, traders, etc.). Each wave therefore has its own signature, which reflects the psychology of the moment.

---

[7]See also Murphy, p. 319ff.

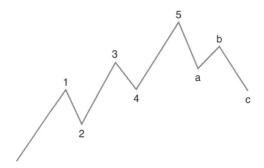

Figure 8.1   Graphical representation of the different Elliott waves.

Some assert that the Elliott wave model provides an indication of when to enter a particular market and when to exit, independently of the notion of profit or profitability.

However, as Murphy notes, "it is important to keep in mind that wave theory was originally meant to be applied to the stock market averages. It doesn't work as well in individual common stocks. It's quite possible that it doesn't work that well in some of the more thinly traded futures markets as well because mass psychology is one of the important foundations on which the theory rests."[8] It is most effective in the commodities markets, which are widely followed.

By applying Elliott Wave Theory to the stock market, some analysts believe that the major decline (wave A) took place after the peak of 2000, that the increase which followed until 2007 represented the ascending wave B, and that the new large decline (wave C) has just started and could last several decades.

Thus, **markets supposedly do not move randomly**, even if we allow for some degree of "freedom". By recognising the movements, investors can therefore position themselves appropriately and profit from the movement they have anticipated.

Events and news do not create the trend. On the contrary, everything is written in the collective unconscious. Whatever the time horizon or country, human psychology is immutable. It reproduces the same configurations in a recurring and fractal way.

This approach is very interesting, but the **difficulty** of **determining** the **movement** of the waves, and of the current wave, makes it somewhat difficult to use, with an overriding subjective factor in the analysis. As we have pointed out, investors seek a rather simpler method than this, and another model should be envisaged.

8.1.3   History repeats

This concept asserts that "the key to understanding the future lies in a study of the past, or that the **future** is just a **repetition** of the **past**".[9] Thus, the same errors are always

---

[8]Murphy, p. 340.
[9]Murphy, p. 5.

repeated (formation of speculative bubbles and crashes) by individuals who have not learnt the lessons of the past.

By adopting this clearly optimistic approach, we might believe that a time will come when the numerous **errors committed** in the past will be **assimilated** and we will have learned to act differently, more intelligently. Man evolves, sometimes against his will, but he evolves. Yet this can take time and asserting that history repeats itself constantly seems to us a somewhat exaggerated claim.

It was indicated earlier, and has been shown by many studies, that it is not possible to take advantage of past movements to predict future movements. Consequently, all these techniques, however tremendous they may seem, will not make it possible to generate excessive profits, and luck is an important explicative factor for those who would claim the contrary.

The problem lies essentially in the fact that **human nature likes order** and **structure**. It wants to see specific patterns in disordered price movements and formats the brain to detect them.

Moreover, even if a trading technique appears to work or give good results, its use will lead market players to increasingly anticipate the subsequent movement. It is somehow anticipated and known, as it is based on the trading technique already proven. Market players will therefore anticipate it more and more, leading to a kind of **self-destruction** of the technique over time.

As with a trading technique that had supposedly been found, everyone realises that history repeats, and will therefore predict the same movement that occurred last time that error was committed in the past.

However, we might imagine that there exists a secret trading technique that works, but is only used by a limited number of people. However, when we look at the list of the wealthiest individuals in the world, there is unfortunately not a single chartist, at least not for the moment.

8.1.4   Criticism of technical analysis

Some believe that technical analysis works because the majority of traders believe in it. They therefore create the trends that they foresee.

One criticism often directed at technical analysts is indeed that it is a **self-fulfilling** prophecy. Murphy, the great technical analysis expert, answers this criticism by stating that "it might be more appropriate to label it as a compliment. After all, for any forecasting technique to become so popular that it begins to influence events, it would have to be pretty good."[10]

However, it is not because a lot of people believe and use something that it is necessarily right. Before Australia was discovered, for example, everyone believed that swans were

---

[10]Murphy, p. 18.

only ever white because they had never seen any other colours, and white was therefore the norm. The discovery of a black swan invalidated this general belief derived from a very large number of observations of white swans.

8.2   CONCLUSION ON TECHNICAL ANALYSIS

All three basic concepts of technical analysis are truly debatable. This technique is essentially used by traders or speculators with a short-term view and a goal of **speculation** rather than an investment objective.

Many academic or empirical studies have shown that this approach, net of transaction costs, does no better than a "buy and hold strategy", i.e., holding assets over the long term with little portfolio rotation. The strategy of simply holding an index fund generates more money. Various tests have been done with different technical indicators, and it has also been shown that these are of no use for investors.[11]

Again, as Malkiel[12] notes, human nature likes order and the idea of **chance** is **hard** to **accept**. Taleb also adds that "our minds are wonderful explanation machines, capable of making sense out of almost anything, capable of mounting explanations for all manner of phenomena, and generally incapable of accepting the idea of unpredictability".[13]

So, **people seek models** and patterns in **random movements**. Joël de Rosnay said that "the best way to foresee the future is to invent it", and that is perhaps what people do. By developing models, they seek to predict, and perhaps invent, a kind of future, but the reality is sometimes not the one that was expected. The Chinese, known for being more gamblers than investors, may have the right idea in considering the stock market as a giant casino and luck as a decisive factor for the return on their investment.

Since information on companies appears randomly, prices must follow a random movement. This aspect will be looked at in more depth in the following chapters.

Finally, we will reiterate that **charts** only provide **information** on the **past** and, as noted by Warren Buffett, "if history revealed the path to riches, librarians would be rich".[14]

Nonetheless, **supports** and **resistances**[15] can indicate **important levels,** and breakouts from these thresholds can indeed provide valuable clues about future price movements. When a stock price moves within an interval without it being possible to meaningfully predict the next movement, investors should wait for more clarity. It is better to make a moderate but sure profit than to speculate on a profit that may indeed be higher, but is hypothetical.

---

[11] Malkiel, p. 135.
[12] Malkiel, p. 136.
[13] Taleb, p. 10.
[14] Pardoe, p. 133.
[15] Supports are previous low levels and resistances are previous peaks. Depending on price movements, these thresholds may be reversed (a former resistance becomes the new support, for example).

Our Advice

In our view, the fact that a certain number of market participants use technical analysis to make their investment decisions should be taken into account.

Accordingly, technical analysis can be **useful** for determining **trends** and **support** and **resistance** levels.

It should not, however, be used as the sole decision-making tool for investment. It is also useful for setting limit orders, which usually should not be placed on levels of support or resistance, but around these values.

9
Investment Approach Based on "Psychological Principles"

Instead of wasting time and energy calculating the intrinsic values of an asset or examining past price movements, another approach (the so-called Keynes approach) may be adopted, which involves analysing **investor behaviour** and their **optimism** and **pessimism**. This approach, based on psychological principles, is similar to behavioural finance, which will be studied in Chapter 21.

As Malkiel notes, the aim of the game is to buy securities before the crowd, whose conduct will cause a rise in securities prices, based on psychological principles. Initially, an investment is worth a certain price for the buyer, who expects to sell it to someone else at a higher price. In turn, the new buyer anticipates that other prospective buyers will assign it a higher value, and so on. The infatuation of the Internet years, and the speculative bubble it created, can in part be explained by this type of behaviour.

A **speculative bubble** is formed by the sharp upturn in a group of securities or a sector, driven by the **media** and sustained by new investors entering the market. This is usually accompanied by the **proliferation** of **publications** on the investment theme in newspapers and magazines.

However, according to Malkiel, the key factor for investing is not a company's social effect or technological impact, but its capacity to generate income and, especially, to make a profit.

Thus, the market always ends up self-correcting to reveal the **true** market **value** of a company, which is the expected value in the Warren Buffett approach.

This approach may seem risky to the extent that the market is governed by **irrational** behaviour. It is consequently very difficult to foresee behaviour, and to determine when it will change.

Part IV
Valuation of Financial Assets

Now we need to examine in more detail the ways of valuing the different assets for each of the classes we have presented.

10
Valuation of Money Market Investments

The value of a money market investment is fairly easy to evaluate as it essentially depends on the level of **short-term interest rates** and on the **quality** of the **borrower**.

The returns of a government bond with a fixed (short) maturity, or the LIBOR rate for the period considered, constitute reference values for money market returns, with necessary adjustments depending on the rating.

As we initially indicated, the **LIBOR** is the rate at which banks can borrow money on the interbank market. It is the rate offered to a bank that wants to borrow funds on this market.

The **fiduciary rate** is the rate at which investors can lend money to banks.[1] In this case, investors ask to lend a given amount for a certain period. This is therefore a rate "requested" by the investor.

The fiduciary rate will usually be lower than the LIBOR rate, and the size of the difference between the two rates will depend on the quality of the borrower as well as the need for a given currency at a certain maturity.

However, if the bank is in great need of cash and is in a difficult financial situation, the fiduciary rate may be higher than the LIBOR, as was the case for Irish banks in 2009.

Fiduciary investments are also a means of short-term financing for banks, to meet their cash flow needs.

As rates are fixed by the banks, investors can simply compare them for a given currency and maturity. They will invest with whichever bank satisfies their requirements in terms of **credit quality** (rating) and offers the best compensation.

They cannot compare a theoretical rate with a market rate, meaning that, in our opinion, investors should simply examine and compare the returns offered for this type of investment without any theoretical valuations.

The choice between the different types of money market investment (fiduciary deposit, money market fund, short-term bonds) is therefore the most important factor, without forgetting the need for proper diversification. Indeed, we indicated earlier that depending on the context, a fiduciary investment may prove more suitable than a money market fund or a short-term bond.

---

[1] A fiduciary investment is made by the bank in its own name, but on behalf and at the risk of the client.

Investors should finally compare the return offered by money market investments to that of other asset classes and, depending on the outlook for interest rates and the attractiveness of other assets, they will have to determine whether they should diversify their investments or focus on one or two asset classes.

Our Advice

For money market investments, we believe that the **degree of efficiency** is **high** due to the very high level of certainty about future cash flows (interest). Indeed, the information available and reflected is comprehensive.

The short-term rates are given by the market, and investors cannot really compare them to theoretical rates. They must therefore make a comparison between different borrowers.

11

Valuation of Bonds

By buying a bond, the holder will receive, in principle, a **fixed** and **regular income** (coupon) and if all goes as planned at maturity, obtain their final redemption. These elements can be regarded as financial flows.

To value a bond on a theoretical level, the most logical method is to calculate the **present value** of **future cash flows** using suitable rates, i.e., rates suited to the borrower's credit risk and to its term to maturity.

However, in **practice**, these rates are **hard to estimate** and, as with any estimation, are subject to a subjective analysis. For a known coupon and redemption amount, investors must make estimates about the movement of the different rates in order to determine an estimated theoretical price, which can then be compared with the market price. So the investment decision would have to rely on this basis.

It is easier to examine the market price and to study the **yield to maturity** in order to decide whether or not to invest in a bond, while obviously also considering the quality of the issuer. **Expectations** about future **inflation** and, above all, **interest rates** are far more important than calculating a theoretical price. For example, what is the point of buying a long-term bond at a fair price, or even at lower than the theoretical price, when interest rates have started to rise? Investors, in addition to seeing the price of their security fall, would be locked in to too low a rate for too long a period. They may for example have locked in a yield to maturity of 2% for five years, whereas a year or two later the yields rose to 3–4%. They would have been better off investing for a shorter period, then reinvesting in a year or two.

It is also useful to note that depending on supply and demand levels, aside from the size of the issue and liquidity factors, the difference between the purchase and sale price can be considerable. It would therefore be possible to find a theoretical price in between the two. Thus, investors should only consider the **market price**, as the calculation of theoretical prices is not really any help in making a decision.

They obviously must make a choice between the different types of bonds and issuers (sovereign or corporate) with their associated rating.

Investors finally have to compare the returns offered by bonds to those of other asset classes. However, though a government bond (country with strong finances) can be compared to a money market investment, a high yield bond should be compared to a riskier asset class.

In addition, depending on the outlook for interest rates and the attractiveness of other assets, investors will have to determine whether they should diversify their investments or focus on one or two asset classes.

We will finish this chapter with a short anecdote. A former bond trader worked for a while next to a young analyst fresh out of university, who spent all his time calculating the theoretical price of bonds and issuing recommendations or reservations when price differences appeared. One day, the trader said to him: "You know, investors buy and sell bonds according to their performance goals and usually focus on the price set by the market. In all my career, I have rarely seen an investor refuse to buy or sell a bond on the grounds that the listed price was different from its theoretical price. Your best calculator is the market." Today, he only analyses the market.

Our Advice

For bonds, we believe that the **degree of efficiency** is fairly **high** due to the generally high level of certainty about future cash flows (coupons). Information may however be less comprehensive and less freely available, meaning it is not as well reflected in prices.

The price of the bond is that listed by the market and investors must decide, according to a given maturity and the desired yield to maturity, if the corresponding price is attractive or not.

However, investors may, if desired, place a buy limit order based on a desired performance. With a view to sale, they must assess whether the capital gain generated compared to the original purchase price corresponds to their performance target.

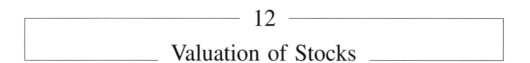

12
Valuation of Stocks

As we saw in the previous chapter, there are several ways of evaluating stock prices and, unlike other asset classes, it is important here to distinguish the stock price set by the market from the **intrinsic value**, which analysts seek to determine using fundamental analysis.

This distinction is important because, to quote Philip Fisher's paraphrase of Oscar Wilde, "the stock market is filled with individuals who know the price of everything, but the value of nothing".

In the following chapter, we will present three practical approaches that we believe are very useful for valuations in this asset class.

Our Advice

For stocks, the **degree of efficiency** is much **weaker**, because of greater uncertainty about future cash flows which, moreover, are only estimates. We believe that not all available information is reflected in prices and, furthermore, that information takes time to be reflected.

It is therefore worthwhile to analyse stocks as the market price often differs from the stock's true price (intrinsic value).

13
Valuation of Options

Although options are not regarded as an asset class, it is still worth mentioning the way in which they are valued in practice.

Studies[1] have highlighted considerable errors in option pricing. On the currency markets, where 15 million billion options were traded in 2001, a study showed that certain dollar-yen options were undervalued by 84% while other Swiss franc-dollar options were overvalued by 40%.

As Mandelbrot points out, "the most widespread **formula** was published in 1973 by Fisher **Black** and Myron **Scholes**, and we have known for many years that it is purely and simply false. Its **assumptions** are **unrealistic**. It assumes that price variations follow a bell curve, that volatility doesn't change over the option's life, that prices show no discontinuities, that taxes and commissions don't exist, and so on. Obviously, these simplifications facilitate mathematical calculations",[2] but it is clear that the valuation of options based on this formula is flawed and should be rejected, or at least adjusted.

In practice, adjustments are made, especially in terms of volatility. However, for this type of investment, investors must "rely" to some extent on the **market price** although it is not always correct.

---

[1]Taken from Mandelbrot, p. 295.
[2]Mandelbrot, p. 295.

14

Valuation of Real Estate[1]

There are various methods of valuing or appraising **direct real estate**.

The **sales comparison approach** gives an estimate of a property based on the price of comparable transactions. Although it is based on market prices, it is not suitable for heterogeneous goods and ignores differences from one country to another.

The **cost approach** is based on the so-called intrinsic value of the property, and is suitable for properties that suffer little depreciation and are subject to few transactions. However, it relies on a subjective estimate of the economic life of a property and of its residual useful life.

The **income approach**, and the **discounted cash flow (DCF)** method in particular, takes into account the property's characteristics and ability to generate income. This makes it suitable for real estate that generates regular income, and it has the advantage of being independent of accounting data. However, both future cash flows and residual value are difficult to estimate.

Naegeli's location class method[2] helps determine the relative share of land in relation to the total value of the property. The degree of the class varies according to the quality of the location, building density, attractiveness, infrastructure and market conditions.

Insurance value, replacement value or tax value are other property appraisal methods.

Finally, the **hedonic approach** entails valuing a property based on the principle that economic agents derive satisfaction from the characteristics of heterogeneous goods. Consequently, the surface, location, condition, age and maintenance are paramount attributes that will help determine an implicit price depending on each of these characteristics. A property with a certain characteristic will be worth more than one without it.

This method has the advantage of removing subjectivity from the appraisal process, but necessitates the implementation of a considerable database. In addition, it is only applicable to residential property.

This valuation technique is used in Switzerland and England for residential property and is, in our opinion, the best approach for real estate appraisal.

---

[1] See also Hoesli.
[2] This is a method used in Switzerland.

However, as indicated earlier, we are only considering **indirect real estate** as part of our analysis of portfolio construction. Investors should examine the prevailing conditions in a particular real estate market and determine the market outlook, including in terms of interest rates, to decide whether or not to invest in this asset class.

Price valuation becomes somewhat secondary, as once the decision to invest in this asset class has been made, valuation is performed indirectly through the fund. It is therefore strongly recommended to use an **expert** in the relevant real estate sector (or to invest in a specialised property fund) to determine the attractiveness of this asset class at a given time.

Investors may, however, study the various types of real estate indices to get an idea of recent price movements.

Securitised real estate indices are **poor indicators** of price movements, as indirect real estate behaves more like stocks than like direct real estate. Moreover, international indices do not take into account the differences that exist between countries.

The use of **hedonic indices** (for a consistent quality) seems the most suitable, in that they are based on transaction data and take into account the characteristics of different properties. This method is used, for example, to appraise residential properties in Switzerland, England and Sweden.

So-called **"valuation" indices** are established on the basis of periodic property appraisals by experts and are best suited for evaluating commercial real estate. However, they are prone to smoothing problems, i.e., attenuating variations in value over time.

Our Advice

In terms of future cash flow, real estate lies between stocks and bonds and, consequently, we qualify the **degree of efficiency** for this asset class as **moderate**.

We suggest performing analyses or consulting experts before investing. Investors should not rely directly on market prices, as they may be different from the intrinsic value of the property.

15
Valuation of Commodities and Metals

As mentioned previously, the price of both commodities and metals depends essentially on supply and demand conditions for the market in question, which are related to **economic cycles** and the economic climate.

As they do not generate income, this asset class is difficult to value using the Discounted Cash Flow method or a ratio-based approach.

A thorough analysis of **supply**, **demand**, **macroeconomic** and **climate conditions**, and even of **historical price movements**, must be undertaken in order to determine the outlook and consequent attractiveness of this asset class.

Once this study has been conducted, investors can decide whether or not to enter a particular market, and will simply pay the market price for a given commodity. The price outlook is therefore crucial.

In our opinion, when deciding whether to enter a market, it is as essential to evaluate the opportunity risk of the trade as it is to consider the commodity's price.

Our Advice

For commodities and metals, because of the absence of future cash flows, we qualify the **degree of efficiency** as **very low**. We consider that information is highly dispersed between different market participants and that it is not evenly reflected in prices.

Therefore, it is worth undertaking an analysis in order to profit from the various inefficiencies that may appear in these markets.

16

Conclusion on Valuation

In view of the above, we may ultimately wonder whether the valuation of a financial asset is really relevant, in that the market provides the price directly according to supply and demand.

As Mandelbrot notes, value is a slippery concept, and "if this value is constantly changing, how can it be of use to an investor or financial analyst weighing their decision to buy or sell? What is the point of a valuation model that requires new parameters for each new calculation?"[1]

Investors should not spend too much time valuing financial assets, but should **focus** instead on the **opportunity to invest** in one or several asset classes according to their attractiveness and outlook.

---

[1] Mandelbrot, p. 276.

Part V
Three Practical Approaches to Security Selection: Buffett, Graham and Lynch

Before continuing our analysis, we think it would be useful to mention three practical approaches to security selection.

17

Warren Buffett's Value Investing Approach

Warren Buffett's approach can be summarised as follows: "Despite these gyrations in the market prices of financial assets, many of them do have an underlying or fundamental economic value that are relatively stable and that can be measured with reasonable accuracy by a diligent and disciplined investor. In other words, the intrinsic value of the security is one thing; the current price at which it is trading is something else. Though value and price may, on any given day, be identical, they often diverge."[1] So Buffett compares the fundamental value of the asset in question with the price set by the market. His process of selection and analysis follows various principles that we will now describe.

First of all, "Buffett will only invest in **easy to understand, solid, enduring** businesses that have a simple explanation for their success. [. . .] Look for long-lasting companies with predictable business models."[2] He invests only in companies and industries he understands and with which he is comfortable.

His advice is to "buy stock in a great company, run by honest and capable people. Pay less for your share of that business than that share is actually worth in terms of its future earnings potential. Then hold on to that stock and wait for the market to confirm your assessment. [. . .] He puts his money in easy to understand, solid businesses with strong, enduring prospects and capable and ethical management."[3]

For Buffett, the **product** the company offers must be **enduring** and still exist in ten years' time. As he justly points out, "thirty years of performance makes for a great company. Three years does not."[4]

"Buffett avoids complex companies that are subject to dramatic change because of their uncertain futures. Earnings and cash flow are two of the pillars of a successful company."[5] He therefore recommends avoiding companies from developing industries, and buying securities issued by companies we understand, whose models and income growth are predictable.

He invites investors to look for companies with **strong barriers** to **entry**, i.e., those with a product or service that is:[6]

- needed or desired;
- not overly capital-intensive;

---

[1]Greenwald, Kahn, Sonkin and Van Biema, p. 3.
[2]Pardoe, p. 14.
[3]Pardoe, pp. 15–17.
[4]Pardoe, p. 65.
[5]Pardoe, p. 50.
[6]Taken from Pardoe, p. 56.

- seen by its customers as having no close substitute;
- not subject to price regulation.

Buffett pays particular attention to the company's management. He wants to know whether it acts in the **interests of shareholders** to create long-term value or, on the contrary, to get rich to the detriment of shareholders. With his company, Berkshire Hathaway, "Buffett makes money only when his shareholders make money. He treats shareholders as partners, and every decision he makes is made with the aim of improving shareholder value."[7]

He suggests **buying businesses, not stocks**, and he considers that while the price of a stock may be volatile, the price of a company is not. For Buffett, market downturns are buying opportunities and "most of Buffett's greatest investments were made [. . .] during bear markets when share prices of great businesses had plummeted".[8] Furthermore, he believes that a few good investments are enough, and there is no need to make a large number of purchases; "one good decision a year is a very high standard".[9]

Moreover, it is interesting to note that Buffett suggests **ignoring macroeconomic** factors and events, and focusing instead on those that affect the company and industry. He also recommends ignoring **stock forecasts** and **short-term** price **fluctuations**, and favouring strong companies likely to succeed independently of market movements. Buffett confesses "that he can't *begin* to predict the movement of the markets".[10]

He also recommends that investors "think 10 years, not 10 minutes. [. . .] Buffett's philosophy is based on patience and a long-term outlook."[11] So we can clearly see that he is an investor rather than a speculator seeking immediate profit. As for the stock market, he describes it as "a 'relocation center' – a means whereby money moves from the impatient to the patient".[12]

As he amusingly notes, "Wall Street is the only place where people go to in Rolls Royces to get advice from people who take the subway." Buffett does not believe in experts, technical analysis, or any advice on how to make money fast.

He is a proponent of **value investing**, a slow, laborious job focused on the long term, whose aim is to "seek out discrepancies between the value of a business and the price of small pieces of that business in the market".[13] However, this price difference must be significant to justify an investment.

Buffett therefore seeks to "determine the **discounted value** of the **cash** that can be taken out of the business during its remaining life".[14]

---

[7]Pardoe, p. 120.
[8]Pardoe, p. 95.
[9]Pardoe, p. 101.
[10]Pardoe, p. 156.
[11]Pardoe, pp. 35–36.
[12]Pardoe, p. 36.
[13]Pardoe, p. 133.
[14]Pardoe, p. 163.

As we might imagine, Buffett reads for several hours a day to get information on companies he is interested in (annual reports, articles, etc.), but does not waste time studying stock forecasts or financial theories based on formulas. The rest of the time he spends on the telephone and, especially, thinking about and focusing on what he believes is the essential notion: **value**.

Although this approach is very interesting, not all investors are able to allow themselves such a long time horizon. In addition, technological and social developments occur much more quickly than they used to. It has become difficult to guess whether a company's product will still be around in 10 years and if the company will still exist. Certainly, we admit that this may be the case with "traditional" companies but, for example, with the development of the Internet and free news websites, investing in a newspaper is perhaps a more risky bet today than it once was.

Buffett's approach may sometimes be too limited, but it does have the advantage of focusing on the value of a company, often one which operates in an industry temporarily neglected by investors.

If we look at recent investments Buffett made during the latest crisis, these seem to be focused on the banking and insurance industries, sectors abandoned by investors in the thick of the financial crisis. For Buffett, it is better to adopt a patient approach, to wait for a strong market correction and buy companies whose listing is clearly lower than their intrinsic value.

Now it will be interesting to look at the approach of Benjamin Graham,[15] regarded by many analysts, including Peter Lynch, as the father of modern financial analysis. Moreover, Warren Buffett holds that Graham influenced his life and his way of seeing and understanding the markets. Indeed, it was Graham who established the investment strategy based on the concepts of value and the margin of safety. The following points are taken from the famous book *The Intelligent Investor*.

---

[15] 1894–1976.

18
Benjamin Graham's Approach

One advantage of Graham's approach is its great simplicity, in that he distinguishes just **two types of investor**: the **defensive** investor and the **enterprising investor**.

The former seeks above all to **avoid errors** or **significant losses**, with a minimum of effort and time spent on frequent decisions. Furthermore, "the more the investor depends on his portfolio and the income therefrom, the more necessary it is for him to guard against the unexpected and the disconcerting in this part of his life. [. . .] The conservative investor should seek to mimimize his risks."[1] This type of investor will therefore seek both **security** and **freedom from bother** and must expect **lower profitability**.

The second type can spend more time **picking securities** and, therefore, make more investment decisions based on his or her **intelligence** and **skills**. He or she can therefore hope to achieve a **higher profitability**.

In terms of portfolio construction for both these types of investors, considering bonds and stocks, Graham recommends in general **never to invest more than 25% or less than 75%** in one or the other of these categories.

18.1   THE DEFENSIVE INVESTOR

According to Graham, the defensive investor should divide his or her funds between **high-grade** bonds and **common stocks**, with a **balanced** proportion of **50/50**.

The aim for this type of investor is to preserve this distribution as much as possible. He or she might reduce the proportion of common stock to 25% when the market reaches very high levels, and increase it to 50% following a long bear market, for example.

In terms of bonds, Graham believes that **government bonds** are the **best choice** and he recommends avoiding high coupon bonds that expose conservative investors to too much risk, ranging from declining value to default. Taking an additional risk for an increase in return of only 1% or 2% is not worth it. He also advises avoiding ordinary preferred stocks which are unsuitable for defensive investors.

Stocks, through their strong historical profitability, provide protection against the negative effects of inflation, that is, depreciation in investors' future purchasing power. Graham suggests simply following these **four rules**[2] for the selection of common stocks:

---

[1] Graham, pp. 56–57.
[2] Graham, p. 114.

1. Have an adequate though not excessive diversification (10 to a maximum of 30 different issues).
2. Each stock selected should belong to **large, preeminent** and conservatively financed companies, such as the leaders in a given industry.
3. Each company selected should have a **long record** of **continuous dividend payments**.
4. The investor should impose a **maximum price** for his stocks, in relation to its average earnings over the last seven years. He suggests a limit of 25 times the average earnings, and no more than 20 times those of the last 12 months.

18.2   THE ENTERPRISING INVESTOR

Like the defensive investor, the enterprising investor should also distribute his or her funds between common stocks and high-grade bonds. However, he or she may consider **foreign stocks, ordinary preferred stocks** or so-called **secondary stocks** (not the industry leaders) but only when they are available at a discounted price (no more than two thirds of their estimated value). Furthermore, he suggests avoiding an investment policy based on growth stocks, due to their tendency to fluctuate sharply.

Graham also believes that the approach which consists in buying low and selling high – the **market timing** strategy – is akin to **speculation** and "the average investor cannot deal successfully with price movements by endeavoring to forecast them".[3] He notes, however, that all **bull markets** have shared certain characteristics:[4]

- a historically high price level;
- high P/E ratios;
- low dividend yields compared to bond yields;
- much speculation on margin;
- many new common-stock issues of poor quality.

We will cover market timing in the following section, but these points were worth introducing at this stage of our analysis.

A 50/50 split is also recommended but with a significant margin of 25% to 75% for the stock component. Regarding **stocks**, Graham recommends investing in **three fields**:[5]

1. The relatively unpopular large company
   The enterprising investor should first of all focus on large companies that have become temporarily unpopular, that have the financial ability and brain power to carry them through a temporary crisis and back to a successful position. The use of qualitative or quantitative filters is also recommended.
2. Purchase of bargain issues
   Graham considers an issue to be a "bargain" when its value calculated using discounted future cash flows is at least 50% higher than the price.
3. Special situations, or "workouts"
   This refers to taking advantage of opportunities that appear during corporate restructuring or reorganisation of debt. Markets tend to undervalue companies engaged in the process of

---

[3]Graham, p. 192.
[4]Graham, p. 193.
[5]Graham, p. 163.

reorganisation or in complicated legal proceedings. Nonetheless, this is an unusual field that will only interest a small minority of enterprising investors. Graham also recommends maintaining a balance between the two asset categories. The stock position should be reduced during bull markets, and the bond component increased accordingly. Conversely, during bear markets, it is better to buy stocks than bonds.

As opposed to the speculator who aims uniquely to anticipate market movements, "price fluctuations have only one significant meaning for the true investor. They provide him with an opportunity to buy wisely when prices fall sharply and to sell wisely when they advance a great deal. At other times he will do better if he forgets about the stock market and pays attention to his dividend returns and to the operating results of his companies."[6]

He even believes that it is completely impossible to forecast bond price movements. In his opinion, "the investor must choose between long-term and short-term bond investments on the basis chiefly of his personal preferences".[7]

18.3 SECURITY ANALYSIS

18.3.1 Bond selection

For Graham, "the chief criterion used for corporate bonds is the number of times that total interest charges have been covered by available earnings".[8] The ratio, which obviously is not fixed over time, will depend on the industry in question and minimum coverage is recommended.

18.3.2 Stock selection

For Graham, an investment decision involves comparing the price of a stock to its estimated value according to analysis. He is obviously a proponent of value investing.

In addition, he developed an interesting list of **seven criteria** for determining whether to include a stock in a **defensive investor's** portfolio.

1. Adequate size (avoid overly small companies)
2. A sufficiently strong financial condition
3. Uninterrupted dividend payments for the last 20 years
4. No losses for the last seven years
5. Increase in per-share earnings of at least 33% in the past 10 years
6. Current price no more than one and a half times book value
7. Current price should not exceed 15 times average earnings of the past three years.

For the portfolio of an **enterprising investor**, Graham suggests using other, less stringent selection **criteria**.

---

[6]Graham, p. 205.
[7]Graham, p. 210.
[8]Graham, p. 283.

1. Financial condition
   - current assets worth at least one and a half times current liabilities, and
   - debt not more than 110% of net current assets (for industrial companies)
2. Earnings stability (no deficit in the last five years)
3. Dividend record (some current dividend)
4. Earnings growth.

18.4   THE MARGIN OF SAFETY CONCEPT

For Graham, the margin of safety, or **difference** between the **intrinsic value** and the **current price**, represents the **margin of error** for any investor.

This difference between value and price should ideally "be about half, or at least no less than a third of the fundamental value".[9]

This margin will depend on the purchase price: it will be greater if the price paid is low, and lower if it is high. However, he admits that even with such a margin, an individual stock can suffer heavily, and the best means of protection remains diversification.

Before concluding with this approach, it is interesting to note that this school of thought pays no attention to the betas of stock, or to the models of Sharpe or Markowitz, or to the covariance of returns between securities, and focuses solely on the value of a company and its stock price. Yet it is still far from enjoying unanimous support.

---

[9]Greenwald, Kahn, Sonkin and Van Biema, p. 26.

19
Peter Lynch's Approach

Peter Lynch was fund manager of Magellan from 1985 to 1992 and never experienced a negative performance during this period. As well as combining the various elements that we have discussed in relation to Buffett and Graham, Lynch has developed some very interesting avenues. Moreover, he is highly sceptical about the value of academic theories of finance, and has strong doubts regarding the efficient market hypothesis. According to Lynch, it is impossible to forecast market movements and he only believes in "great businesses" (under-valued and/or under-appreciated companies).

For Lynch, "stocks are relatively predictable over twenty years. As to whether they're going to be higher or lower in two to three years, you might as well flip a coin to decide." Here his analysis is similar to that of Malkiel, which we will discuss in the following sections. Furthermore, according to Lynch, "the best companies always end up succeeding, the mediocre ones failing, and their respective investors being compensated accordingly".[1]

By advising to invest only in what is **simple** and what we **know**, Lynch echoes Warren Buffett's approach, but looks above all for what he calls "**tenbaggers**", a stock whose value increases by ten times its purchase price. According to Lynch, there are plenty of these in the world around us and for a small investor's portfolio, one tenbagger is enough to make all the difference in terms of performance. Unlike for the portfolio of a large fund, which must select many tenbaggers to make any difference.

Lynch spends hundreds of hours analysing companies and speaking with CEOs and financial analysts but, above all, he recommends keeping an eye on the world around you to identify **investment opportunities**, if possible **before anyone else**. We can spot them in our workplace, at the mall, during a trip or in the course of conversation. These unique opportunities can be discovered months or even years before analysts examine and begin to recommend them. Lynch suggests that investors be **curious** and **observe** what's going on around them in order to find investment opportunities. "Take advantage of the valuable, fundamental information from your job that may not reach the professionals for months or years."[2]

He tells of how he discovered Hanes, makers of *L'eggs* stockings, thanks to his wife and her friends who use the product. After a little research, Lynch invested for the Magellan fund and his initial investment increased six-fold. The analysts did not start to study this company until they noticed the significant increase in its stock price.

---

[1]Lynch, Prologue, X.
[2]Lynch, p. 163.

As he summarises perfectly, the aim is to discover investment opportunities before Wall Street. Indeed, a financial analyst will only pay attention to a security once its price has undergone substantial movement.

However, finding a company is just the first step; the next step is obviously to analyse it. You might find an interesting opportunity in an industry, but you still need to choose the right company. Lynch recommends investing in stocks rather than in the market. He focuses solely on companies, or **individual stocks**, and favours relatively small businesses that offer greater growth prospects than large multinationals.

Finally, he recommends investing "at least as much time and effort in choosing a new stock as you would in choosing a new refrigerator".[3]

19.1   STOCK CATEGORIES

The first step is to classify the stock in one of the **six categories** that Lynch has established,[4] although companies may move from one category to another over time. Furthermore, companies have three growth phases and it is important to determine if the company in question is changing phase.

Firstly, there is the start-up phase, then the rapid expansion phase where the company is moving into new markets, and finally the mature (saturation) phase where growth becomes difficult. Here are the different categories.

19.1.1   Slow growers

Slow growth companies develop **slowly**, more or less at the same rate as the progression of GNP (gross national product).

A slow growth stock can generally be recognised by the **regular** and **generous dividend** paid to its shareholders. Electricity companies, for example, belong to this category.

When considering this type of stock, it is important to ascertain whether dividends are paid regularly and if they grow over time.

19.1.2   The stalwarts

These stocks are faster than slow growth stocks and can reach an annual growth in earnings of 10% to 12%. Companies like Coca-Cola, Bristol Myers, Procter & Gamble and Colgate Palmolive belong to this category. They have little chance of going bankrupt, but it is important to verify their long-term growth rate.

---

[3]Lynch, p. 164.
[4]Lynch, p. 61ff.

The potential profit on these stocks depends mainly on when they are purchased and at what price. The P/E ratio is decisive in indicating to investors whether or not they are overpaying for the stock.

For example, an investor who has held a Procter & Gamble stock since 1963 has only quadrupled his or her initial investment. For such a long holding period, the risks taken have not really paid off. The **holding period** is a very important issue that we will cover later on.

For Lynch, in the case of stalwarts, it is better to make a return quickly. They are bought with an **expected gain** of **30% to 50%**. Once sold, similar stock that has not yet been recognised should be sought in replacement.

During a crisis, people travel less, put off buying a new car, buy fewer clothes, eat out less often, but continue to buy as much cereal and the same amount of dog food. That is why companies like Kellogg's or Nestlé, for example, are candidates worth including in a portfolio.

19.1.3   The fast growers

Fast growing companies develop fast, sometimes at an annual rate of 20% to 30%. Lynch holds them for as long as their **earnings** are **increasing**, their **expansion** continues, and no obstacle is encountered.

The growth rate of earnings is obviously essential for this type of stock, but it is especially necessary to compare the P/E ratio to the earnings growth rate to see if the two curves move in parallel.

When analysing a product or service, it is also crucial to determine the share of sales in total turnover.

It should be emphasised that this type of stock does not have to belong to a fast-growing industry, as room to continue developing is more decisive for the growth of a company. For example, the hotel industry has an annual growth of almost 2%, while Marriott has developed strongly over the last few years, increasing its market share to 20%.

It is also useful to look at whether the company has been able to **replicate** its **success** in other cities or countries, thereby demonstrating its capacity for expansion.

However, if this stock becomes too important, its growth capacity will be limited. So it is best to look for companies with high growth potential, and sell them before this potential is exhausted.

19.1.4   Cyclicals

A cyclical stock is a company in which sales and profits rise and fall regularly and in a somewhat predictable pattern. In a cyclical industry, business grows, then slows and grows again, then slows once more and so on. At the end of a recession and in a vigorous economy, these are the stocks that appreciate.

Inventories and the relation between **supply** and **demand** for the products the company sells are the decisive factors in achieving adequate positioning in the business cycle in question.

Automotive companies, airlines, tyre manufacturers, steel producers and chemical companies are cyclical stocks. As most of these companies are reputed multinationals, we often tend to put them in the stalwart category, but the cyclical character of the industry is critical.

19.1.5   Turnarounds

These companies are **not growing**, but in the event of a recovery, they can move back up very quickly. Lynch distinguishes **four types** of turnarounds.

First of all, there are those that are **subsidised**, whose future depends entirely on a loan guaranteed by the government. Then there are those that must resolve one or more **unanticipated problems**, such as operational accidents that will take time to repair. The extent of such a company's losses and debts must be carefully studied.

Next, there are **perfectly good companies within** bankrupt companies that will be able, after separation, to take off on their own to the delight of investors. There is also **restructuring**, which lets the company rid itself of unprofitable subsidiaries in order to concentrate on its core business.

Whatever the type of company in difficulty, the amount of its **liquid assets** and its **debt level** are the essential factors in analysing its future capacity for recovery. The way in which the company intends to go about this must also be examined, taking into account the outlook for the sector.

19.1.6   The asset plays

By "asset plays", Lynch means a company that's sitting on a **treasure** that you know about, but that Wall Street has overlooked.

The assets may be in the form of a large pile of **cash** (the famous "war chest") or **real estate**, such as land or housing stock managed in parallel with the company's business. You also find these asset plays in companies operating in the metal, oil, newspaper and pharmaceutical industries and television stations. Companies' losses may also represent value. Indeed, a company in serious financial trouble may, for example, benefit from a tax credit, meaning that future profits will be exempt from taxation.

The aim is therefore to identify the existence of these **hidden assets**, and then try to estimate their value, taking the company's debt into account. Finally, investors must consider whether the company is vulnerable to takeover by a third party.

19.2   THE PERFECT COMPANY ACCORDING TO LYNCH

Above all, Peter Lynch appreciates **simplicity** and always asks himself if "any idiot can run this business". He also looks for other characteristics in a company, and has compiled a list of **13 factors** to help select them.

a) The perfect company has a dull, or even better, ridiculous name

For Lynch, the more boring the name, the better.

b) The perfect company does something dull

In his opinion, "[a] company that does boring things is almost as good as a company that has a boring name, and both together is terrific".[5]

c) The perfect company does something disagreeable

The ideal business is one that makes people shrug, retch or turn away in disgust. He gives the example of a company engaged in washing greasy auto parts.

d) The perfect company is a spin-off

The result of the separation of a division or business unit from a parent company, that then takes its independence, often offers investors exciting and lucrative opportunities.

As Lynch rightly notes, parent companies do not want to let their subsidiaries go just to see them getting into trouble, as this may bring them negative publicity. Spin-offs usually have strong balance sheets and are well prepared to deal successfully with their new independence.

e) The institutions don't own it, and the analysts don't follow it

For Lynch, the lower the percentage of shares held by institutions, the better. The idea is to find a company that no analyst has visited, or that they admit knowing nothing about. As we said earlier, the goal is to discover the company before Wall Street does.

f) Look out for toxic waste and/or the Mafia

According to Lynch, there is no more perfect industry than waste management, and some others such as hotel and casino management, reputed to be "influenced" by the Mafia, which may have great prospects. Rumours about the Mafia allegedly controlling these industries have kept many investors at bay, but Lynch suggests keeping things in perspective; the fact is that hotels and casinos usually appear on recommendation lists.

g) There is something depressing about the perfect company

Besides the boring or disagreeable nature of a business, being depressing is another key factor for Lynch. He gives the example of Service Corporation International, which is in the funeral business. The company became a "20-bagger" (twenty times the initial investment) before Wall Street even began to pay it any attention. Since then, it has performed worse than the market.

---

[5]Lynch, p. 77.

h) The perfect company operates in a no-growth industry

Investors usually prefer to invest in a high growth industry, where there is noise and move-ment, but Lynch far prefers a no-growth (or low-growth) industry where there will be little competition. There is no need to worry about potential rivals or to enter a price war, because nobody else is interested. The company has a free rein to continue to grow and gain market share.

i) The perfect company has a niche

Exclusive licence is obviously the ideal situation, as the company that enjoys these rights can freely increase its prices and, consequently, its profits. Managing a quarry is one example of such a licence, as are pharmaceutical and chemical companies that hold a patent giving them the right to manufacture and sell a unique drug for a given period.

j) People have to keep buying the perfect company's product

As Lynch puts it, it is better to invest in a company that makes medicines, soft drinks, razor blades or cigarettes than in a toy manufacturer whose products are often only bought once.

Regular sales are essential for ensuring stability, if not growth, of profits in the future.

However, there are also companies that Lynch recommends avoiding, such as hot stocks in a hot industry, those with the best advertising or those that all investors hear about and end up buying simply because everyone else does.

k) The perfect company is a user of technology

It is better to invest in companies that use technology (scanners, for example) to reduce their costs and increase their profits, than in companies that make that technology (scanner manufacturers) and whose products are likely to be made obsolete or outdated by competing products.

l) The insiders are buying the perfect company's stock

The best sign of a company's success is to see its executives and managers investing in its equity.

However, it should be emphasised that *sales* of stock are not necessarily revealing and investors should be very cautious about attempting to draw conclusions. Managers may sell their shares simply to generate the cash to buy a house or send their children to university. Therefore, it is more representative to see insiders buying shares – driven by the desire to participate in the company's growth – than selling, which can be motivated by any number of reasons. There is only one reason for managers to invest in their company: the feeling that the stock is undervalued relative to the company's growth potential.

m) The perfect company is buying back shares

Finally, a company buying back its own shares is a positive sign for Lynch and, more importantly, for investors, because it represents the reward offered by the company to its shareholders.

However, instead of undertaking this kind of buyback or a dividend payout, sometimes companies decide to make often expensive acquisitions unrelated to their core business, which then weigh heavily on their balance sheets and their ability to generate earnings growth.

As Lynch says, "If a company must acquire something, I'd prefer it to be a related business, but acquisitions in general make me nervous. There's a strong tendency for companies that are flush with cash and feeling powerful to overpay for acquisitions, expect too much from them, and then mismanage them. I'd rather see a vigorous buyback of shares, which is the purest synergy of all."[6]

19.3   EARNINGS AND EARNINGS GROWTH

When buying a company's shares, investors are actually buying the **growth** of **future earnings**. For Lynch, as part of security analysis, it is essential to begin by comparing the earnings line to the price line. These two lines usually move in tandem and although one may seem to stray from the other a little, they always end up coming back together.

Therefore, comparing the price line with the earnings line helps quickly determine whether a stock is overpriced.

Comparing the P/E of the stock with that of its industry is the next step, making it possible to **rule out** stock with a **very high P/E ratio**. The P/E can also be regarded as a measure of the number of years necessary to recover the amount initially invested.

The problem, however, is that present earnings only help to evaluate the current stock price, but it is information about future earnings that investors seek.

According to Lynch, although it is impossible to predict future earnings, it is possible to determine whether a company can make them **grow**. It has **five ways** of doing this:

1. reducing costs;
2. raising prices;
3. if possible, expanding into new markets (but will it work elsewhere?);
4. selling more products in old markets;
5. closing or getting rid of a losing operation.

---

[6]Lynch, p. 97.

Investors should focus on these factors to evaluate the company's ability to grow their earnings in the future. They should also find as much information as possible about the company, to understand exactly how it goes about generating profits and thereby analyse its potential success.

For a **slow growing stock**, dividend stability and growth over time are the essential factors in determining attractiveness.

For a **stalwart**, the analysis of the P/E ratio and the stock price will be decisive. It is also worth considering whether an event may accelerate growth, and if so, which event.

When looking at a **fast grower**, the question is obviously for how long and by what means the company can continue to grow at this speed. The number of new shops opened, for example, and the development of market share are relevant factors for analysis.

When considering a **cyclical stock**, industry conditions, inventories, prices and the capacity of production facilities are decisive factors.

In the case of an **asset play**, you need to find out the value of the assets.

Finally, for **turnarounds**, investors should consider how the company is going to go about improving its situation, and if the measures envisaged are likely to pay off in the future.

It is also useful to recall that **stockholders** are able to get information directly from companies and their head office. As such, Lynch believes that "nice earnings and a cheap head office are a good combination. [...] Other unfavourable signs include fine old furniture, trompe-l'oeil tapestries, and wood-panelling."[7]

Finally, it is possible to analyse an industry simply by looking around you. A (partial) analysis of the automobile industry can be carried out, for example, in parking lots of ski resorts, malls or other leisure spots.

19.4 SELECTION CRITERIA

Most of this information can be found in companies' **annual reports**. However, Lynch recommends spending no more than a few minutes reading them. In his opinion, "the cheaper the paper, the more valuable the information".[8] He recommends focusing instead on the following criteria.

19.4.1 The sales percentage

When we examine a company, the first thing we observe is the products and services it offers. Independently of the profitability itself of a product, it is essential to determine the

---

[7]Lynch, p. 126.
[8]Lynch, p. 130.

impact of the **product** in question on the company's **sales** and earnings. For example, a product may sell very well but represent a negligible share in the company's sales and, therefore, have little impact on its earnings.

19.4.2   The P/E ratio

For Lynch, the P/E ratio of a company valued at its fair price is equivalent to its growth rate. It is therefore necessary to find out the **growth rate** and **compare** it to the **P/E ratio**. If the P/E ratio is lower than the growth rate, the investor may have found a good stock.

According to Lynch, **book value** often has little to do with the true value of a company. Moreover, the closer an investor is to a finished product, the harder it is to predict its resale value.

19.4.3   Liquid assets

Examination of a company's balance sheet will show the amount of cash as well as a figure which includes its marketable securities, which together give the overall **cash position**. The higher this is, the more prosperous the company.

It is essential for a potential investor to know whether or not a company has **considerable liquid assets**.

Subtracting long-term debt from cash and cash equivalents gives the company's net cash position. By then dividing this value by the number of shares in circulation, we get **net cash per share**. By comparing this number to the market share price, investors can determine the value of the company's growth potential and of the "true" P/E ratio. In addition, this value can also be interpreted as the lower threshold of the share.

Lynch uses Ford as an example. He estimated net cash per share at US$16.30. With a market price at the time (early 1988) of US$38, Lynch considered the share to be worth US$21.70 (38 − 16.30). The P/E ratio of 5.4 (US$38/7 per share) given initially in fact came down to 3.1 (21.70/7).

19.4.4   Debt

The balance sheet gives us the amount of **short-term** and **long-term debt**.

When long-term debt is higher than cash and equivalents, the financial situation of the company is deteriorating. Conversely, the reduction of debt and increase in cash and equivalents is a good sign.

It is interesting to note that Lynch ignores short-term debt, considering that the value of the company's other assets is enough to cover this debt.

This factor is crucial for companies in recovery or in the start-up phase, as it will determine which ones will survive and which will go bankrupt. Furthermore, the **kind** of **debt** is also important. Bank debt, which is due on demand of the bank, puts the company in a worse position than funded debt, which is not due as long as the interest is being paid.

19.4.5   Dividends

As mentioned previously, **stability**, that is, the existence itself of a dividend over time, as well as its **growth**, is an important criterion for stock selection. The dividend is the first part of a stock's return.

For Lynch, **share repurchases** by the company are **positive**, while acquisitions made by forgoing dividend payments to shareholders generally have a negative impact on share price movement. However, for companies seeking fast growth, dividends are often reinvested, and it is better to favour these stocks above traditionally generous companies without any real growth prospects or outlook.

19.4.6   Hidden assets

Companies that own **natural resources** such as land, forests, oil or precious metals often present assets in their balance sheets at their purchase price although they are worth much more on the market. Moreover, some assets amortised over time disappear from the balance sheet. Investors must take these undervaluations into account.

19.4.7   Cash flow

In general, cash flow is the money a company makes by selling its products or services (revenues), taking account of costs incurred in its activities.

Lynch prefers **companies** that have little or no investment expenses, i.e., those that have a **high free cash flow** (cash flow after deduction of capital expenditures).

19.4.8   Inventories

It is also important to analyse inventories and to find out if they are piling up. Growing inventories can lead companies to lower their prices to liquidate them (not to mention the price of storage), which implies a drop in profits. On the other hand, the **depletion** of inventories is a **good sign** for the company and consequently for investors.

19.4.9   Growth rate

For Lynch, as noted earlier, a company's earnings growth rate is the most relevant rate in terms of investment, and should be compared to price movement.

19.4.10   Gross profits

Finally, Lynch examines gross profits, which represent the company's **profit minus costs**, including interest but **before taxes**.

By dividing the company's sales by its gross profit, we get the profit margin before taxes that should be compared to that of the industry in question.

19.5   CONCLUSION ON PETER LYNCH'S APPROACH

Peter Lynch believes that the **end of the year** usually provides the best opportunities to buy. Opportunities also present themselves during the **drops** and freefalls that occur every two, three or four years, but buying at these times is not for the faint-hearted.

A very interesting approach to stock valuation is suggested above, which will be incorporated into the discussion that is to follow. It is worth bearing in mind that "the market, like stocks, can, in the short term, move in the opposite direction from the fundamentals",[9] but "in the long term, the direction and sustainability of profits will prevail".[10] Moreover, he believes it is impossible to predict market movements over one or two years.

Lynch criticises all those experts who recommend that their clients systematically sell their positions as soon as they have doubled their initial investment. The problem is that they will never find a "tenbagger" that way. He indicates that he has never been able to predict which stocks would see their price growing five- or ten-fold, but he held on to them for as long as their story remained intact.

Finally, **valuation models** are very **sensitive** to **parameters** and ultimately only provide estimates. Furthermore, as Lynch reveals, "we all read the same papers and listen to the same economists. We all come from the same homogeneous mould. Few of us have left the beaten track."[11] The right direction is therefore off this beaten track, and lies in adopting a new, unconventional and even surprising approach.

The idea of value advocated by Buffett and Lynch should be definitively assimilated by any investor, as the selection itself of value is essential in any investment decision.

---

[9]Lynch, p, 204.
[10]Lynch. p. 212.
[11]Lynch, p. 12.

Part VI
Behavioural Finance

Theories based on the Capital Asset Pricing Model (CAPM) and on the efficient market hypothesis assume that **individuals** act rationally and predictably. Whereas in **reality**, they often seem to **behave irrationally**.

We human beings think that we are logical, but research has shown that **information** is systematically **analysed unconsciously** in the parts of the brain related to emotion. It would therefore seem that **decisions** are based on **emotion**.

As Taleb justly points out, "we react to a piece of information not on its logical merit, but on the basis of which framework surrounds it, and how it registers with our social-emotional system".[1]

Lynch is also shocked "to see the speed at which an investor's feeling can change when the reality hasn't".[2]

Each individual perceives risk differently. Individual risk preferences are not solely determined by deviations from the mean, but depend significantly on the objectives set or on gains and losses made in relation to a certain benchmark or reference point.

---

[1]Taleb, p. 53.
[2]Lynch, p. 37.

20
Investors in Behavioural Finance

"Prospect theory", developed by Kahneman and Tversky,[1] defines a **value function** to describe the irrational behaviour of investors. Investors use gains and losses, i.e., variations in their wealth over time, as a reference. This function has the following **three characteristics**.

Firstly, investors are **risk averse** when it comes to **gains** and **more open to risk** when pertaining to **losses**. This is often reflected in investors' tendency to sell winning securities (to book and secure the profit) and to hold losing securities (to try to "redeem" themselves and recover their loss as quickly as possible).[2] Recent examples of traders such as Nick Leeson (from the bankrupt Barings Bank) or Jérôme Kerviel (Société Générale) illustrate this willingness to take more risks to try to recover losses sustained on a position as quickly as possible – positions which were highly speculative in these two cases.

Secondly, investors **hate losses** more than they love gains. In other words, these researchers have shown that the aversion to losses is much stronger than the satisfaction derived from gains. Losing one dollar is two and a half times more painful that the satisfaction derived from a dollar.

Thirdly, investors perceive gains and losses in relation to their **subjective reference point**, such as the 0% threshold, the inflation rate or a defined minimum return.

Moreover, it seems that investors **deform probabilities**, that is, they **overestimate low probabilities** (distribution tails) and **underestimate high probabilities**, biasing their perception of the risks associated with the decisions they make. The occurrence of highly improbable events is frequently overestimated, often based on personal experiences.

Furthermore, as Taleb notes, "what we see is not necessarily all that is there. History hides Black Swans from us and gives us a mistaken idea about the odds of these events."[3]

So as we can see, investors do not always act rationally and various aspects of human nature influence the way we invest. It is essential to understand these irrational mechanisms because, as Malkiel states,[4] "we are often our own worst enemy when it comes to investing".

---

[1] See Kahneman and Tversky, 1979.
[2] Note however that Prospect Theory does not alone explain the so-called "disposition" effect (see Vlcek and Hens, 2005).
[3] Taleb, p. 50.
[4] Malkiel, p. 237.

Investors are not always conscious of the risks taken when they make investment decisions, and can therefore act in an irrational manner. There are several **psychological biases** that can lead investors to select and treat information with bias, and particularly to under- or overestimate the risks taken.

21

Heuristics and Cognitive Biases

In order to facilitate analysis and information processing, individuals use **practical, simple rules**, often drawn from experience or analogies, called heuristics or "rules of thumb". These rules help us to make choices and decisions. However, they can be subject to **errors of judgement** called cognitive biases.

We would now like to take a look at these heuristics and cognitive biases,[1] which we have classified into three categories.

21.1 INFORMATION SELECTION

The first category concerns biases in the selection of information, demonstrating that individuals prefer **information** that is **readily available, precise, chosen** by those we believe are **well informed** and, finally, that is **consistent** with our **view**.

21.1.1 Availability heuristic

This bias describes the tendency of individuals to judge the relevance of a piece of **information** by its **availability**. It also represents the **strength of association** that can influence investor decisions. The more we read comments on a subject, the more we believe them. So, from an individual's standpoint, the fact that a certain piece of information is more readily available increases the probability that it will happen.

Moreover, this bias often causes investors to overreact to news.

21.1.2 Herding

This concept relates to investors' tendency to be influenced by what the crowd says and thinks. In a context of uncertainty, when information is asymmetrical, they tend to believe that **others** are **better informed**, which causes **mimicry**.

Furthermore, as it can cost time and money to acquire and analyse information, it is both tempting and easy to follow others, or those we believe know best.

---

[1] See also Hens and Bachmann, and Kahneman, Slovic and Tversky, 1982.

21.1.3   Ambiguity aversion

Investors prefer **precise information** to vague information (*Ellsberg Paradox*) and they do not like situations where they are uncertain of the probability distribution of future returns.

However, this bias is reduced by **experience**. Inexperienced investors see a lot of ambiguity in risky investments whereas experienced investors have more precise convictions.

21.1.4   Wishful thinking

This way of thinking leads to **interpreting things** as we would **like** them to be, rather than as they really are.

Investors' convictions can therefore justify their investment decisions. They make their choices according to their perception of reality, retaining certain information and excluding other information.

21.2   INFORMATION PROCESSING

The second category concerns the biases related to information processing, which lead individuals to allocate probabilities of different scenarios being realised according to a certain value system. This is usually based on generalities, similarities, models or processes, or on excessive confidence. These biases particularly affect investors' consciousness of risk.

21.2.1   Representation bias

This is a bias that may lead investors to estimate probabilities based on their pre-existing beliefs, for example, by applying a given probability to a situation they believe to be similar but which in reality is not.

This can also lead them to believe that the results reached within small samples are representative of results that would be obtained in an entire population.

Investors tend to **look for similarities**, or what they believe is most representative, when making a decision, which causes a risk of underestimating the probability that this is not the case.

21.2.2   Confirmation bias

We often establish **generalities** based on **observed facts**. For example, the fact of seeing white swans does not confirm that black swans don't exist. However, in seeing a black swan, it is possible to assert that all swans are not white.

"We have a natural tendency to look for instances that confirm our story and our vision of the world."[2]

---

[2]Taleb, p. 55.

21.2.3   Narrative fallacy

Human nature tends to try to establish causal relationships in events it observes, seeking explanations and logical links at any cost.

In other words, we often look for a **relationship** of **cause and effect** in events that we observe, even though the cause is perhaps fortuitous in many cases.

21.2.4   Gambler's fallacy

Individuals maintain the illusion of having control over situations over which they in fact have no influence whatsoever. They tend to look for logical sequences in random processes.

They believe that a random walk process, such as tossing a coin, is in fact subject to mean reversion, i.e., that it will follow a cycle. For example, once we are "at the top", we will have to "come back down"; or, after landing on "tails" 10 times, "heads" should turn up, while the probabilities are actually the same for each throw. They therefore **underestimate** the **frequency** of **repetitions**. Studies have shown that the movement of stock prices does not follow mean reversion.[3]

Similarly, they are likely to overvalue a losing security which "should come back up" and to observe trends when there aren't any.

21.2.5   Anchoring

Anchoring is the tendency to be **influenced** by an **arbitrary reference** when evaluating a quantity. For example, mentioning a figure will lead an individual to use that figure as a reference when giving a reply. Expert opinions and forecasts constitute such "anchors" for investors, who are likely to refer to them when making decisions.

21.2.6   Framing

The **way information** is **presented** influences decision-making, causing biased decisions (splitting bias) and allocation that disregards risk. A factor is given more weight in decision-making simply because it is presented in more detail.

Investors may decide only to consider the total (aggregation effect) or to look at each part separately (segregation effect).

21.2.7   Probability matching

For typically binary choices (buy or sell), investors tend to decide according to the probabilities they associate with each scenario, looking for patterns in random processes.

They make decisions based on probabilities they assign to the different results, but which do not always correspond in reality. For example, for ten throws of a coin, if heads appears

---

[3] See Kim, Nelson and Startz, 1991.

6 times (60%) and tails 4 times (40%), an investor will decided to bet on heads, believing that heads has a greater chance of appearing, even though the probabilities for each new throw are identical.

21.2.8 Wearing blinkers

"We focus on a few **well-defined sources** of **uncertainty**, on too specific a list of Black Swans (at the expense of the others that do not easily come to mind)."[4] In other words, we often tend to concentrate on scenarios with variable probabilities, but without thinking of improbable events that may indeed occur. Human nature is somehow not programmed for these highly improbable events (the "nevers") that are therefore often discounted.

To illustrate this, it is interesting to look at the difference between the risks that had been anticipated by a Las Vegas casino and the unexpected losses that actually occurred.[5]

First of all, the casino lost about 100 million dollars when an irreplaceable performer from its main show was attacked by a tiger (the show, *Siegfried and Roy*, had been a major Las Vegas attraction). The tiger had been reared by this trainer and even slept in his bedroom. Until the attack, no one suspected that it would turn against its master. In scenario analyses, the casino had even conceived of the animal jumping into the crowd, but nobody had imagined an eventual tiger attack on its trainer.

Second, a disgruntled contractor was injured during the construction of a hotel annex and attempted to blow up the casino by placing dynamite around the underground foundations. Fortunately, he was discovered in time, but the casino was only insured against construction problems.

Third, for years an employee hid the forms that he was supposed to send to the Internal Revenue Service declaring any gambler's profit which exceeded a given amount. The casino, accused of tax fraud, almost lost its licence and ended up having to pay a colossal fine, and this, despite the surveillance systems and procedures intended to monitor employees.

Fourth, the casino owner's daughter was kidnapped, which caused him to dip into the casino coffers in order to pay the ransom, a risk which obviously had not been anticipated.

The casino had spent hundreds of millions of dollars on gambling theory and high-tech surveillance systems while the bulk of their risks came from outside these models.

21.2.9 Overconfidence bias

This bias describes investors' tendency to be **overconfident** in terms of their **predictions** and their **own judgements**.

Individuals are willing to take more risks than they can in fact withstand. So, the risk of being on the wrong side – "Miscalibration bias" – is often underestimated because of overconfidence. This also results in their underreaction to market news.

---

[4]Taleb, p. 50.
[5]Example taken from Taleb, pp. 129–130.

Investors tend to exaggerate their **own skills** and to reject the role of **luck**, thereby exaggerating their ability to control events.

As Taleb summarises, "we attribute our successes to our skills, and our failures to external events outside our control, namely to randomness".[6]

Investors are also convinced they can beat the market. They speculate more than they should and carry out too many transactions.

Furthermore, we often believe we have better knowledge when we have access to more information, but more information does not necessarily mean more knowledge.

Investors also have a selective memory of success. They remember successful investments and forget mediocre results, thereby reinforcing their overconfidence.

21.2.10   Illusion of control

When a situation involving chance replicates a situation requiring skill, individuals behave as if they could control the outcome of an uncontrollable event. For instance, when they invest in the stock market for themselves online, investors **feel as if** they are in **control** of their assets, while the market in fact remains unpredictable.

We might well wonder if an investor ultimately controls anything by holding a company's stock in his or her portfolio. We will leave the question open but, in our opinion, the only way of retaining a considerable level of control, and perhaps the only way of making money, is by owning the production facilities. There is no denying that most of the wealthy people in this world own their own company.

Supporters of a team bet more money on that team. Similarly, employees who hold stock in the company they work for have a more optimistic vision of the stock price. This optimism bias belongs to the same family of biases as the illusion of control.

21.3   THE USE OF ASSETS

The third category covers various irrational human behaviours in terms of the use of assets, which can affect the process of portfolio construction and security selection.

21.3.1   Mental accounting

Investors tend to **divide** their assets into **different categories**, and they allocate different degrees of utility to each class. They then make separate choices for each of their mental accounts.

---

[6]Taleb, p. 152.

This approach has the advantage of simplifying decision-making. However, by separating the different assets, we lose sight of the whole and the potential benefits of diversification (positive effect of a weak correlation between different asset classes, etc.).

21.3.2 Disposition effect

As we noted earlier, investors often **hold onto** their **losing assets for too long** due to their lower risk aversion regarding losses. But in doing so, they lose the opportunity of a potential gain in selling a losing security and investing in another which may make a significant gain. Because for the moment it is only a paper loss, and hasn't yet been realised, investors prefer keeping the security in the hope of a price rebound, although they could sell and reinvest in something more profitable.

On the other hand, investors tend to **sell** assets that have made a gain **too quickly** due to their greater aversion to risk as far as gains are concerned. This tendency can be explained by the fear of regretting one's choice in the future ("I should have sold"), or by the belief in a mean reversion process that would push the price back down once a rise has been registered.

21.3.3 House money effect

This effect, which is the opposite of the disposition effect, describes the **tendency** for investors to **increase the proportion of risky assets in the event of a gain**. They consider the gain already realised as a safety cushion allowing them to take more risks.

The dominant effect will depend essentially on the individual's aversion to losses and risk.

21.3.4 Endowment effect

This is the **difficulty of parting with an asset that was pleasant to buy and hold**. The maximum price paid by an individual to acquire an asset will be lower than the minimum compensation that will motivate him or her to part with this asset. The difficulty of parting with losing securities is a similar bias.

21.3.5 Home bias

Investors often prefer investing in assets from their **country of residence** rather than in foreign assets. They have a **preference** for familiar situations because they feel better informed.

21.3.6 No go's

Investors sometimes have **individual, ethical and religious preferences** that limit their investment universe, such as, for instance, an unwillingness to invest in the tobacco or arms industries.

21.3.7 Sunk costs

Investors are sometimes attached to **past investments** and, because they don't like to admit their bad investments, they may keep them for too long at a loss. This reflects the disposition effect we mentioned earlier.

21.3.8   Lack of control

Investors don't like assets they have **no control** over. This bias may explain the reticence of some clients to invest in hedge funds, as they can't imagine investing in a kind of "black box" they don't understand and, more importantly, cannot control. However, it is debatable whether buying stock in a large multinational gives them any greater control.

21.3.9   Pride and regret

Depending on past decisions and the success or otherwise of buying a given asset, **regret** can play an important role in future decision-making. A bad investment experience in an asset can lead to it no longer being considered in the future.

In the specific case of the relationship between a client and advisor, if the investment decision seems positive, the client will attribute it to his or her own skills, whereas if it turns out negative, the client will protect his or her ego by blaming the advisor.

Our Advice

It is well and truly worth being conscious of these different behavioural biases that can be involved in decision-making, both in terms of the selection and processing of information.

It is necessary to format our brains, which are used to reasoning rationally, so that they also take these irrational components into account.

A better understanding of these biases helps to keep things in perspective and reduces our dependence on them.

22

Investment Approach Based on Behavioural Finance

Psychological biases are certainly **interesting opportunities** to consider, but the exploitation of an anomaly which has started to be widely recognised is likely, bit by bit, to self-destruct over time (the January effect, for example[1]).

We are now going to look at a particular investment strategy that specifically aims to exploit these biases.

22.1 MOMENTUM STRATEGY

We mentioned earlier that investors seek above all to know whether it is better at a given moment to stay out of the market, or better to invest. The key word in this sentence gives a clue to one solution: moment. The so-called momentum strategy is worth looking into here.

Richard Driehaus, regarded as the father of this strategy, believes that we can make the maximum amount of money by buying high and selling even higher.

Momentum, or the relative continuity in returns from securities, is the **tendency for securities having performed well (badly) in the past to perform well (badly) in the future**. Momentum strategy involves buying stocks that have generated high positive returns over the last three to 12 months and selling those that generated a negative return over the same period.

In 2001, Narasimhan Jegadeesh and Sheridan Titman[2] assessed the profitability of momentum strategies for various sample periods (1965–1989, 1965–1997, 1990–1997). The study showed that these strategies maintained a consistent level of profitability. They also demonstrated that this strategy generates a return of 1% per month for the following three to 12 months. Winning stocks for the last three to 12 months have a strong chance of still being winning stocks over the subsequent three to 12 months. The effectiveness of this selection rule, obtained using American market data, has been validated on other international financial markets, particularly by Professor Rouwenhorst[3] who came to the same conclusion.

---

[1] The "clean-out" of positions from portfolios in December for tax reasons causes security prices to fall at the end of the year, and then rebound in January when reincorporated into portfolios.
[2] Jegadeesh and Titman.
[3] Rouwenhorst.

This investment strategy consists in buying, at the start of each period, portfolios of the best performing securities and selling the worst performing, with the position being held for k months (k = 3, 6, 9, 12).

The momentum effect reaches its **maximum** when the **formation period** of the portfolios equals **12 months** and the **holding period six months**.

Portfolios with the best performance histories generate the best actual performances, whether the historical performance is calculated over the last six or 12 months. The best strategy is therefore to use the historical performances for the last six or 12 months with a holding period of between six and nine months maximum.

Performances generated by momentum strategies have obviously piqued the curiosity of researchers, and two approaches have been developed in an attempt to justify this phenomenon.

The first is the **rational approach**, which considers that momentum investors bear a **high risk** by adopting this strategy and the high returns represent the appropriate compensation for this risk.

Seasonal effects may also explain the strategy's success. If a stock has performed averagely and the end of the year is near, investors may well decide to sell it for tax reasons,[4] causing its price to fall. Once the tax incentive has passed, the price moves back up.

The second is the **behavioural approach**, which holds that investors adopting this strategy are in fact exploiting **behavioural biases** in the interpretation of information, such as mimicry, under- and overreaction to news, and the overestimation of oneself and one's own judgement.

In a study[5] carried out in 2006 on momentum strategy profits, it was shown that profits are predominantly due to investors' **underreaction** to information. The study also showed that these profits can be attributed to **delayed overreaction** and not to compensation for a high level of risk.

This phenomenon can therefore be explained by certain behavioural biases, namely: conservative bias, representativeness bias and self-attribution bias.

The **conservative bias** results from investor tendency to under-weight recent information compared to prior information. In addition, the **representativeness bias** incites individuals to perceive trends where there are none. Individuals tend, for events that occur infrequently, such as stock transactions, to overestimate the probability that the event will reoccur in the future, especially when they have observed it recently.

Because of the **self-attribution bias**, investors overweight information that confirms their first evaluation and underweight information that is inconsistent with it. Consequently, their

---

[4]Sustaining losses in order to decrease capital gains to be declared for the year.
[5]Boujelbène Abbes, Boulgebène and Bouri.

estimations increase in strength with time, which produces a momentum effect, like a kind of delayed overreaction.

Assuming that small firms have a slower information diffusion process, the authors conclude that profits from using the momentum strategy are larger for these small firms.

By picking stocks according to their historical performance, it is possible to generate abnormal profitability. The actual performances decrease logically with the holding period. Holding these stocks for over nine months reduces the profitability we can gain from this strategy.

In conclusion, it would seem that the returns from the momentum strategy are not due to compensation for higher risk. In the end, the results obtained confirm the delayed over-reaction of investors to information.

If we observe a momentum effect on the stock market in the short term (one to two years), there is, on the other hand, a reversal effect in the long term (three to five years), because the securities that made significant gains over the last three to five years tend to produce lower than average returns over the subsequent three to five years. So it is dangerous to choose securities that have been performing very well for the last five years. The wisest bet is stock that has produced excellent returns over the last 12 months (when kept for only one year), but that has experienced the worst results in its group over a longer horizon (at least three years). Investors should be aware of some **mean reversion** over time.

The momentum approach would appear to be advantageous and is simple to implement, as it uses little data. However, the exploitation of this anomaly has started to be used excessively by the financial industry, as are all anomalies in the financial markets that result in higher than normal returns.

In our opinion, it is too early to judge the relevance of this approach, but it is worth retaining the idea of a holding period and an observation period.

23
Criticism of Behavioural Finance

Professor Fama suggests[1] that even though there are anomalies that can't be explained by modern (traditional) financial theory, market efficiency should not be totally abandoned in favour of behavioural finance. He notes that most anomalies can be regarded as short-term events due to chance that are corrected over time.

So the markets can be efficient even if many market players are irrational. Furthermore, the behaviours described are typically observed in individuals, while there are other players on the markets who are more rational and perhaps more important (in terms of size), such as institutional investors. We might wonder which group has a bigger impact on prices.

Nonetheless, it is important to be conscious of these psychological biases and of the irrational behaviour of investors. Malkiel recommends resisting the temptation to make too many transactions, and considers the buy and hold strategy with a diversified market portfolio to be the most suitable approach. However, he also says that the ideal holding period for securities is for ever,[2] while this is not necessarily the case for most investors.

---

[1] See Investopedia: Behavioural Finance.
[2] Malkiel, p. 281.

Part VII
Forecasting Market Movements

It is hard enough to forecast the weather, with few parameters to take into account. Considering the extensive number of variables acting on the markets, it is even more difficult to make forecasts. As S. Goldwyn justly states, "Forecasts are difficult to make, especially those about future."

Many analysts try to predict market movements, but none manages to get it right consistently.

A **random movement** is a movement that is not predefined or programmed, whose future development is utterly unrelated to its past or present position. It has **no memory** and changes entirely at random. But perhaps there is a certain "structured" order in such an apparently random process which, ideally, could be modelled? A statistical approach based on probabilities is the first path to explore.

24

Investment Approach Based on Probabilities

We can roughly summarise market movements by saying that they represent a succession of upturns and downturns over time, although the size of these movements will vary.

The **probabilities** of an upwards or downwards movement are **not** always **equal** and, depending on the context, the probability of an upturn can be higher or lower than that of a downturn. Furthermore, the size of upwards movements can differ from the size of downward movements, which has a significant impact on profit. Profit, of course, depends not only on the *occurrence* of a rise or fall, but also on the *size* of the rise. The size of an upturn or downturn will necessarily have a direct impact on results.

For the reasons outlined in the first part of this book, we do not believe that the use of probabilities to determine the possibilities and size of an upturn or downturn is an appropriate means of forecasting future prices. Different scenarios are possible to estimate by probabilities, but there is no way of asserting which scenario *will* occur because all the others, due simply to the fact they exist, may also occur. The **estimated probabilities** themselves are based on **historical data**.

So the financial models developed by Markowitz, Sharpe and Black-Scholes are not really suitable; not only do they use the concept of volatility as a measure of risk, but they also assume that price changes are practically continuous. However, as we have already pointed out, prices jump, soar suddenly or collapse, thereby discrediting the assumptions underlying these models.

Mathematics is supposed to provide precise answers but, in our opinion, the usefulness of this discipline in stock market investing is limited. We believe that investments depend more on convictions than on the application of elaborate formulas.

Our Advice

We believe that forecasting future market movements on a statistical basis should be avoided.

Although there are, admittedly, different probabilities associated with the various scenarios that we expect, any of these may occur, not to mention those we haven't thought of but may also occur. Therefore, this approach does not appear suitable for forecasting market movements.

25

Random Walk Theory

Does this mean that the markets follow a purely random movement?

The academic world holds that past prices cannot reliably indicate their future movements. Prices change randomly and are therefore unpredictable. As we stated earlier, random walk theory is based on the efficient market hypothesis, and the best investment strategy under this approach is the **buy and hold**. Any attempt at beating the market in the long term is doomed.

In light of all the conclusions we've come to in the previous chapters, it would seem difficult to forecast market movements and, consequently, to make higher returns than the market. However, the rather limiting buy and hold strategy neglects an important point: prices follow trends, they do not follow a random walk. According to Mandelbrot, they even have a kind of memory.

In which case, the objective is not to beat the market but simply to perform at least as well as the market in the periods where investors should invest, i.e., in bull markets. This obviously implies that there are periods in which investors *shouldn't* invest. Which brings us to the idea of market timing.

Our Advice

We believe that the markets do not follow a random walk, that instead they move in trends. Therefore, a so-called buy and hold strategy that involves keeping positions in a portfolio "for life" is unsuitable for private investors.

26

Market Timing

Market timing involves investing, or being **invested**, in **bull** markets and **getting out** or staying out of **bear** markets, which obviously assumes that investors have correctly predicted these movements.

It is true that "with market timing, you run the risk of not being invested on the stock market's best days. Although the trading days that contribute strongly to an increase in returns are rare, they do play a major role in overall performance. Which should make us wary of market timing."[1] However, the days of severe market decline contribute perhaps more significantly to overall performance, and it is specifically these declines that should be avoided.

According to a study[2] of daily returns on different stock markets between 1990 and 2006, the average annual performance of the Swiss market was 9.4%. Someone who had not been invested on only the 20 worst days would have made an average annual return of 15.9%. On the other hand, someone who had not been invested on only the 20 best trading days would have made the meagre return of 3.6%. Over an observation period of 17 years, 20 days corresponds to 0.004% of all trading days.

Market timing might seem practically impossible to carry out, but the main thing this study teaches us is that **it is better to avoid the bad trading days** (15.9% performance, or an annual performance 69% higher than average) than to endure them (3.6% performance only, or an annual performance of 161% below average). Table 26.1 is even more explicit on

Table 26.1 Impact of market corrections on initial investments and necessary recovery

Initial value	Loss in %	Value after the loss	% rebound to recover initial level
100	−10%	90	11%
100	−20%	80	25%
100	−30%	70	43%
100	−40%	60	67%
100	−50%	50	100%
100	−60%	40	150%
100	−70%	30	233%
100	−80%	20	400%

---

[1] Künzi.
[2] See Künzi article, ibid.

this point, as it shows the size of the necessary recovery according to the magnitude of correction endured.

The difficulty of applying a market timing strategy should not however lead us to adopt a simple buy and hold approach. The goal is not to "buy as low as possible and sell at the top of the market, but to buy and sell at the right time".[3] Investors would then be likely to suffer **market fluctuations** over time, and these can be very violent with extended **recovery periods** (Table 26.2).

Table 26.2   Time necessary to recover the initial lever depending on the market growth afterwards

Initial value	Loss in %	Value after the loss	% rebound to recover initial level	Time necessary to recover (years & months)		
				10% p.a.	5% p.a.	2% p.a.
100	−10%	90	11%	1Y & 2m	2Y & 2m	5Y & 4m
100	−20%	80	25%	2Y & 5m	4Y & 7m	11Y & 4m
100	−30%	70	43%	3Y & 9m	7Y & 4m	18Y & 1m
100	−40%	60	67%	5Y & 5m	10Y & 6m	25Y & 10m
100	−50%	50	100%	7Y & 4m	14 & 3m	35Y & 1m
100	−60%	40	150%	9Y & 8m	18Y & 10m	46Y & 4m
100	−70%	30	233%	12Y & 8m	24Y & 9m	60Y & 10m
100	−80%	20	400%	16Y & 11m	33Y	81Y & 4m

Over a 10-year period from the start of 1999 to the end of 2008, someone who invested their capital in stocks would have lost money and ended the period worse off than someone who had invested in government bonds. Therefore, they were not remunerated for the risks taken. Although exceptional returns did occur over short periods, considering the period overall, the result is fairly disappointing – worrying even – especially for investors with a relatively long time horizon.

Turning to the European market, the return on the DJ EuroStoxx50 index for this period was −26.77%, while the government bonds index reached +58.76%. You can imagine the return that could have been made by carefully choosing when to invest in stocks and, more importantly, avoiding strong correction phases.

It is also apparent that the recovery periods are very long, lasting years, while the correction periods are shorter and much more violent. In our view, it is better to avoid the worst trading days than to endure them while benefiting from the best days. Active management is crucial.

However, as Malkiel[4] notes regarding the American market, his observation period of 54 years included 36 bull years, three years where the market did nothing and 15 bear years. In his opinion, the buy and hold approach is the one that works the best, but how many investors can allow themselves such a long time horizon? Pension funds probably, but even some of these were required to take corrective measures after the large market decline of 2008.

---

[3]Lefèvre, p. 71.
[4]Malkiel, p. 172.

It is worth noting that Malkiel[5] himself says that for a time horizon of 10 years or less, it is impossible to predict returns. Investors must therefore be willing to accept market fluctuations, and potentially to lose capital.

In terms of institutional management, Swensen believes that market timing "voluntarily deviates the portfolio from the objectives of its long-term policy, exposing the institution to risks that it could easily avoid. Because the asset allocation policy is the principal means by which investors express their risk and return preferences, a good manager will try to minimise deviations from these objectives."[6]

Before continuing our analysis, it is again worth demonstrating the impact of seasonality on performance according to holding period or, in a way, to market timing.

An investor who systematically buys the Dow Jones index on 31 October and sells it on 30 April – following the old adage "sell in May and go away" – achieves a much better performance than an investor who buys on 30 April and sells on 31 October. The former achieves a performance of 6000% for the period 1945–2008, while the latter has to be content with a performance of 9% (see Figure 26.1).

So is it possible to forecast market movements by any means whatsoever, even if we can't achieve perfect market timing? We saw in an earlier chapter that neither technical analysis nor fundamental analysis allows market movements to be predicted perfectly. Therefore, the solution has to be sought elsewhere; we suggest taking at look at an approach based on macroeconomic factors.

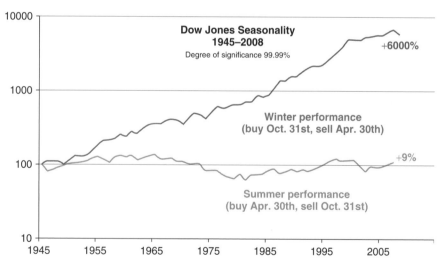

Figure 26.1   Performance of the Dow Jones index "purchase October 31st – sale April 30th" vs Performance same index "purchase April 30th – sale October 31th" on the period 1945–2008. *Source*: Dominicé & Co.

[5]Malkiel, p. 328.
[6]Swensen, p. 104.

Our Advice

A buy and hold strategy is unsuitable for private investors. It can however be justified for pension funds with very long investment horizons.

Markets move in trends and the most important thing is to avoid (strong) bear phases rather than enduring them over time.

Although perfect market timing is impossible, **active management** or ideally **proactive** management should be considered.

27

Macroeconomic Investment Approach

The pertinence of a **macroeconomic approach** may be studied by looking in particular at the model proposed by Peter Navarro – namely, **macrowave investing**.

According to Navarro, by adopting this approach investors can better **anticipate** market **trends**, and they must never invest against a trend.[1] It is therefore essential to study general market conditions before buying a position, because it is the large market movements that will make the difference.[2]

The sectors to favour and those to avoid can be determined using various macroeconomic news and indicators. In his view, even natural disasters and wars represent macroeconomic opportunities.

Before we start presenting Navarro's analysis, we first need to look at the main **macroeconomic forces** in the market and the various indicators used to measure them. It is recommended to follow the development of these indicators to determine the real improvement or deterioration of the economy. Sometimes, no precise conclusion may be reached. In this situation, it is better to wait for more clarity and certainty about the direction the market will take. A data publication alone is insufficient and it must always be examined in context.

Furthermore, it is preferable to focus on **leading indicators** (see below) that provide signs as to what is to come, rather than lagging indicators, which only change direction once economic conditions have already changed.

Below is a list of these leading indicators[3] (Table 27.1) and their meaning for investors. There is also an index of leading economic indicators that is worth following.

This index includes several economic components whose variations can be used to predict changes in the economy for the coming months. According to the definition given by the OECD,[4] the leading indicators help forecast turning points (peaks and troughs) between expansions and slowdowns of economic activity.

---

[1]Here he is obviously referring to the chartist adage "Trend is your friend".
[2]Lefèvre, p. 58.
[3]Taken from Navarro, p. 156.
[4]Taken from www.oecd.org.

Table 27.1 Table of leading indicators and related comments

Leading indicators	Comments
Average work week	More overtime precedes an expansion and less a recession.
Unemployment	The number of job seekers increases when the economy starts entering a recession and drops with the recovery.
Percentage of companies receiving slower deliveries	Slower deliveries means business is booming; faster deliveries signal an economic weakening.
New manufacturing orders for consumer goods	As orders increase, production soon follows. As they fall, there's trouble ahead.
New building permits	This industry is the first to react to rises and falls in interest rates.
Consumer confidence index	Growing consumer confidence is followed by economic growth; when confidence falls, the GDP goes with it.
New orders for industrial investment	Historically, the market peaks months before a recession and troughs before the recovery begins.
The money supply	More money means lower interest rates and therefore more investments.
The interest rate spread (10-year bond less Fed funds rate)	When short-term interest rates exceed long-term interest rates, this inverted yield curve signals recession.

Sources

In the United States, the Leading Economic Index (LEI) is published monthly by the Conference Board and may be found at www.conference-board.org. The various components of the index can be found there. Index calculations are also performed for other countries or regions, such as the LEI for the euro area.

The OECD also establishes composite leading indicators for its member countries and groups of countries, such as the euro area (www.oecd.org – statistics, leading indicators). An increase of over 100 indicates expansion and a decrease of over 100 a slowdown.

In the United States, the **Fed reports** (Federal Reserve Bank – American central bank) are also an **important source** of information. The Beige Book, which is published eight times a year, reflects discussions on regional economic conditions prepared by each Federal Reserve Bank. It contains comments that tend to predict and forecast changes over the subsequent months or quarters. There are also two documents prepared for the members of the Federal Open Market Committee (FOCM), namely the Green Book, which provides forecasts on the American economy, and the Blue Book, which undertakes an analysis of national monetary policy.

In Europe, the European Central Bank (ECB) also publishes **monthly reports** (the Statistics Pocket Book and the Monthly Bulletin) containing a selection of macroeconomic indicators for the members of the European Union, as well as comparisons between the euro area, the United States and Japan.

To ensure a firm understanding of the concepts that are to follow, we will first briefly outline the different types of state intervention aimed at guaranteeing or stimulating a certain level of production and employment and, consequently, economic growth.

27.1   STATE INTERVENTIONS[5]

The type of state intervention will depend first of all on the political affiliation of the ruling party and the dominant school of thought in terms of macroeconomics. For example, in the United States, the Democrats are generally Keynesian, and favour an active fiscal and monetary policy. On the other hand, the Republicans are more divided, and tend to discourage this kind of intervention. Now let's examine the various approaches, focusing essentially on what has happened historically in the United States.

The **classical**, so-called **non-interventionist economic approach**, influenced predominantly by the economist Adam Smith, considers the problem of unemployment to be a natural part of the economic cycle. According to this approach, unemployment self-corrects over time and therefore there is no call for the government to intervene in the free market to correct it.

The 1929 financial crisis and the subsequent Great Depression in the United States led John Maynard Keynes to reject the notion of self-correction. He asserted that the only means of recovering from this severe recession and revitalising the economy was state intervention in the form of an appropriate **tax** or **fiscal policy**. This approach implies a fiscal policy that aims to **reduce taxes** and **increase public spending**. Keynes' approach was adopted by President Roosevelt, particularly through his ambitious public works programme of the 1930s, subsequently supported by the boom of the 1940s with the Second World War. The 1964 tax cut was also based on this approach and contributed to the strong prosperity the US experienced in the decades that followed.

However, in the 1970s, the United States experienced stagflation – a period of recession or economic stagnation combined with inflation. Keynes' interventionism to reduce unemployment in fact created inflation, and the actions to reduce inflation had a negative effect on growth, thereby aggravating the recession. According to **monetarism**, the approach defended by Milton Friedman, inflation and recession actually depend on the growth rate of the money supply. The government printing too much money causes inflation, and not enough leads to recession. There is a so-called "natural" rate of unemployment according to this approach

[5] Taken from Navarro, pp. 23–39.

and the only way to curb inflation is to increase the rate of unemployment above the natural rate, which amounts to creating a recession. From 1979, former Fed president Paul Volcker adopted a contractionary monetary policy, raising interest rates to over 20% to control the double-figure inflation rates that the country had been experiencing for the last few years.

In 1980, Ronald Reagan proposed a simultaneous tax cut, increase in tax revenues and acceleration of economic growth. He believed that by adopting an approach based on supply, the tax cuts would allow citizens to work more and invest more, thereby generating stronger growth and more tax revenues for the State. Unfortunately, this did not happen and the American deficit worsened.

During the Bush presidency a **new approach** emerged: so-called **neoclassical economics**, which are based on **rational expectations**. If expectations are formulated rationally, then all available information – including the effects of an active fiscal policy – is taken into account, and government measures may become ineffective specifically because they are anticipated by market players. More stable policies focused on the long term are therefore preferable, instead of considering short-term reactions.

As we noted earlier, the chosen approach depends heavily on the government in power and the school of thought it decides to follow. However, it is essential for investors to be familiar with the type of intervention that will be chosen as its consequences will vary for each industry. We will now look in more depth at tax and fiscal policy, then monetary policy.

27.1.1   Tax and fiscal policy

There are two means for a government to **stimulate** its country's **economic activity** and seek full employment.

First, it may envisage an **increase** in **public spending**, allowing the State to make investments in order to support private companies and promote their competitiveness. State support for education, training and technological development allows companies to create greater added value on the products and services offered, and therefore become more competitive internationally. This tool is most appropriate in the event of a crisis in supply, i.e., on the corporate side. In a way, in times of economic crisis, government spending is substituted for the decline in household consumption and private investment, thereby ensuring a sufficient level of growth.

Second, a **tax cut** may be considered by the State to revive household consumption. This tax stimulus is intended to increase consumers' disposable income, inciting them to step up their consumption. However, depending on the extent of the economic crisis, the unemployment rate and the expectations of the various players involved, consumers may simply save their disposable income and postpone their purchases. Furthermore, depending on the level of competitiveness of their products and services and of their currency, consumers may look increasingly to cheaper foreign products. This approach is best suited to a crisis in demand, the State hoping to stimulate consumer spending, but the disadvantages just outlined cannot be discounted.

In both cases, these government actions lead to an **increase** in **public deficit**. Careful policy-making is therefore required to reduce debt if the economic conditions are favourable or increase it in the event of a recession. In theory of course, an increase in the public deficit should be temporary, because if the measure is effective, economic activity should increase – as should the tax base – even with lower tax rates. Often, however, this effect remains theoretical. In addition, a high level of public debt in some States can limit the possibilities of taking on debt in the future.

In general, the government has **two tools** available to finance its deficit. It can **issue bonds** to raise capital on the market, or it can print money. In practice, the Central Bank will buy government bonds before they arrive on the market, following what is known as an **accommodative policy**. This approach is fairly positive in the short term for stocks and negative for the currency. For bonds, it has an adverse effect in that the probable return of inflation is likely to impact negatively on prices.

27.1.2 Monetary policy

Monetary policy is usually conducted by the Central Bank, which controls the **amount** of **money** in circulation.

As we mentioned earlier, it can either follow an **expansionary monetary policy** to stimulate the economy, or a **contractionary monetary policy** to avoid an overheated economy and excessive inflation. It has two main means of doing this. There are also other kinds of intervention possible for central banks but we won't go into further detail on these here.

Firstly, it can perform **open market operations** by buying government securities for an expansionary policy (an intended fall in interest rates) and selling government securities for a contractionary policy (an intended rise in interest rates).

It can also **set interest rates**. In practice, in the United States for instance, there are two distinct rates: the discount rate, which is the interest rate that the Fed applies to banks that want to lend it money, and the Federal funds rate, which is the rate that banks use among themselves when lending each other money. A drop in these rates allows banks to borrow money at a lower cost, creating an expansion of the money supply. Conversely, a rise in these rates makes it more expensive for banks to borrow, causing a contraction in the money supply.

27.1.3 The appropriate policy

In general, **fiscal** policy is the preferred instrument when the economy has fallen into a **strong recession** or a **depression**. A **monetary** policy is preferable when the government is trying to fight **inflation** or a **slight recession**.

27.2   THE MAJOR MACROECONOMIC FORCES

For the first three of these forces, we recommend above all following the **calendar** of **macroeconomic events** and **publications**, which can usually be found in the business and finance section of the major daily newspapers and on the websites of governmental organisations.

Sources

For the United States, a calendar of the main economic indicators can be found on the following websites:

www.economicindicators.gov
www.bloomberg.com/markets/ecalendar/index.html

The calendar of euro-indicators, containing a link to the publication calendar of the national statistics institutes, can be found on the Eurostat website under the following link:

epp.eurostat.ec.europa.eu/portal/page/portal/releasecalendars/newsreleases

See also a selection of the main European economic indicators at:

epp.eurostat.ec.europa.eu/portal/page/portal/euroindicators/peeis

The statistics on the OECD website provide a series of monthly economic indicators:

stats.oecd.org

There are other websites that provide the macroeconomic calendar for the week or months to come, some of which are more focused on one country or region in particular:

www.boursorama.com/infos/statistiques/accueil_indicateurs.html

---

27.2.1   Inflation

As we indicated at the start of this book, inflation can be defined as a rise in the **general level of prices**, with the essential consequence of a **decrease** in consumer **purchasing power** in the future. Conversely, **deflation** can be defined as the fall in the general level of prices.

It is referred to as **monetary inflation** when **too much money** is issued by the State, leading to a price rise. According to the quantity theory of money modelled by Irving Fisher, any increase in money supply which exceeds the increase in gross domestic product (GDP hereafter) mechanically drives up the general level of prices in the medium term. Too weak a demand for money, due, for example, to high savings, can lead to the same result. This assertion is based on the following equation and assumes that the velocity of money, which measures the tendency to spend money, is stable over time:

$$\text{Money Supply} * \text{Velocity} = \text{Price} * \text{Transactions}$$

$$[\text{or } (\text{Price} * \text{Transactions}) = \text{GDP}]$$

However, it seems that the velocity of money is not always stable, that it actually changes over time. Furthermore, a rise in the household savings rate reflects a tendency to spend less, which has the effect of lowering this velocity. Lower velocity therefore makes it possible to limit price rises.

Consequently, monetary growth is not in itself sufficient to cause inflation, which will depend on changes in velocity and GDP growth. Finally, when a central bank increases the money supply, the final destination of the money is key in determining whether it has indeed been integrated into the system. Following the subprime crisis and the intervention of the Fed – which injected colossal amounts of money – it became apparent that a very large part of the sums made available to banks had not been "redistributed" to companies and private individuals, but had rather been kept by the banks.[6]

Furthermore, if we include the demographic component, growth is likely to be much more modest than in the past because of the expected growth of the inactive population (the elderly) and attendant decrease in the working population. However, if growth remains sufficient in the future to "absorb" this ageing population, the problem will become more political than economic.

In the event of **strong economic growth** (where demand for products or services exceeds supply), inflation can also be stimulated by **demand**, in turn causing prices to rise and creating **demand-pull inflation**. It can also be caused by **wage increases** when wages rise too quickly relative to economic growth.

When the **production costs** of products or services, especially related to raw materials, increase significantly, this is reflected in the final price paid by consumers. This is referred to as **cost-push inflation**.

The type of inflation is critical, as it will determine the policy adopted by the Central Bank. This will be more reactive (interest rate hike) when faced with demand-pull inflation, which carries a risk of overheating, and more reserved in the case of inflation related to increases in energy or commodity prices, for example. In the event of cost-push inflation appearing in a context of (pre-)recession, an interest rate hike would exacerbate the slowdown, further reducing a consumer demand already weakened by rising energy or raw material prices. When faced with the last type of inflation, namely that related to wage increases, the Central Bank will undertake strong measures to fight it. This form of inflation may take longer to bring under control than demand-pull inflation.

When inflation starts to rise or is likely to rise in the future, the Central Bank can adopt a so-called **monetary tightening** policy, which involves a rise in **short-term interest rates**.

This aims to "slow down" growth to avoid the economy overheating, i.e., excessively fast growth with no control over price increases or, consequently, inflation. However, this interest rate rise is likely to reduce both consumption and, in the event of currency appreciation, exports.

---

[6]In the form of cash and cash equivalents such as T-bills.

In general, rising inflation can be controlled by an interest rate hike, but this incurs the risk of a future economic slowdown. As we mentioned earlier, an increase in interest rates is negative for stocks. For bonds, such a rise will push prices down, but as investors will shy away from stocks, the attractiveness of this asset class will help raise prices. The final net effect is therefore difficult to determine.

Conversely, when inflation is under control or growth slows down, the Central Bank must follow this trend. If the risk of economic slowdown is significant, a drop in interest rates may be considered to stimulate the economy. As such, it can adopt a so-called **expansionary monetary policy**, which involves a **drop** in **short-term interest rates**. This measure aims to promote growth to boost the economy, but carries the risk of higher prices and therefore inflation in the future. At this stage, it is worth noting that the objectives of central banks differ according to the country. For instance, the objective of sustaining growth is much more important in the United States than in Europe.

These **short-term interest rates**, reflected by the money market, are therefore influenced by the Central Bank's policy in terms of **inflation**, as well as expected **growth**.

Long-term interest rates, usually represented by 10-year or even 30-year government bond yields, are influenced by the future **financing needs** and **capacities** of public and private agents. So if these long-term financing needs are expected to rise, long-term rates will also rise, and if these needs are expected to decrease, long-term rates will fall.

The presence of moderate inflation is not a negative factor, as long as the economy is enjoying a reasonable level of growth. The worst-case scenario that any Central Bank seeks to avoid is **stagflation**, i.e., inflation without economic growth.

A little short-term deflation is not negative either, but **prolonged deflation** such as that experienced in Japan can have **severe consequences** on the economy. As deflation leads to further deflation, consumers seeing prices fall tend to postpone their consumption in anticipation of further price reductions. This phenomenon obviously does nothing to help economic recovery, rather aggravating the recession.

This is why central banks with the sole objective of price stability have a positive inflation objective. As inflation rates may vary, an objective of 0% would be too risky as a situation of deflation could occur frequently.

There are **various indicators** for measuring inflation.

a) Consumer Price Index – CPI

This measures **inflation** at the **consumer** level, but some indexes, like the core CPI, disregard food and energy prices in order to evaluate the type of inflation more accurately (demand-pull or cost-push). This is an important indicator for bonds and stocks.

b) Producer Price Index – PPI

This indicator reflects **production costs**, especially for finished products. The core PPI index does not include food and energy, and is best suited for evaluating the type of inflation. However, it is important to consider the effects of seasonality. This is often considered as a leading indicator of the CPI, and therefore of expected inflation.

c) Employment Cost Index – ECI

This index measures the third form of inflation, namely **wage inflation**, and tracks wage development. The existence of wage inflation can provoke a future rise in interest rates.

d) Average hourly earnings

This index is also used to measure the third form of inflation, but we must be careful not to draw premature conclusions from it. An increase may simply be the result of an increase in overtime, while base wages remain the same. Or, the increase may be explained by a change in the composition of the workforce, which has become better qualified and therefore better paid. Finally, the various job-related benefits are not taken into account; only the nominal increase is considered. The previous indicator is more reliable because it takes into account both the nominal increase and the various workers' benefits and compensation.

Sources

In the United States, the CPI (Consumer Price Index) and the PPI (Producer Price Index) are published monthly by the Bureau of Labor Statistics. The ECI (Employment Cost Index) is published quarterly. The Current Employment Statistics (CES) provide information on average hourly earnings.

www.bls.gov/cpi; www.bls.gov/ppi; www.bls.gov/ncs/ect; www.bls.gov/ces

In Europe, the Harmonised Index of Consumer Prices (HICP), the Industrial Producer Price Index and the Labour Cost Index are available on the Eurostat website:

epp.eurostat.ec.europa.eu/portal/page/portal/euroindicators/peeis

This website's database also provides information on labour costs by country:

epp.eurostat.ec.europa.eu/portal/page/portal/statistics/search_database

---

27.2.2 Economic growth

As we have seen, economic growth is essential for a country to ensure its prosperity, an optimal level of production and full employment. It is **measured** by the growth of **Gross Domestic Product (GDP)**, which changes over time and is one of the most closely followed indicators. Other types of indicator do exist for evaluating growth.

It is important to compare growth rates between countries, as a country's demand for imports depends essentially on its revenues. For example, if growth is stronger in the United States than in Germany, demand for imports of German products will grow, at the same time creating an increase in the US balance of trade deficit.

a) GDP growth

GDP measures the **total value** of **wealth produced** by a country over a given period, i.e., the total value of goods and services produced domestically. Practically, this value is calculated by adding all the **expenditures** made by different production factors: private consumption (C), gross investment (I), government spending (G) and the balance of trade (eX − i), i.e., the difference between exports (eX) and imports (i). This gives the following formula:

$$GDP = C + I + G + (eX - i)$$

As such, the Investments/GDP ratio constitutes an indicator of future growth potential. Meanwhile, the Debt to GDP ratio indicates a country's level of debt.

As we have already pointed out, growth brings with it the risk of inflation, which can lead to possible interest rate hikes to curb inflation. Conversely, low growth indicates a risk of economic slowdown or even recession. This may lead to an interest rate cut to stimulate the economy, which in turn carries the risk of inflation in the medium or long term.

GDP indicates the growth of a country and is published **quarterly**. Two consecutive quarters of negative growth correspond to the economic definition of a recession.

Sources

In the United States, GDP is provided by the Bureau of Economic Analysis (BEA), which also gives information on the balance of payments, the current account balance and the trade deficit.

   www.bea.gov

In Europe, the GDP of the euro area and of member countries, as well as the balance of trade and current account, can be found on the Eurostat website:

   epp.eurostat.ec.europa.eu/portal/page/portal/euroindicators/peeis

---

Real GDP is more pertinent as it measures growth while excluding the influence of inflation, i.e., it is adjusted for price changes. As it appears quarterly, the GDP report is quite volatile and subject to revision. It comes out later than other indicators, so it is better to focus on consumption and investments, two of its major components. However, it completely ignores undeclared work, thereby underestimating a country's real level of activity.

When examining GDP, it is also interesting to study two types of deficit that may occur, as well as the current account balance.

i) The current account balance and the trade deficit

The **Gross National Product (GNP)** represents the total value of goods and services produced by the citizens of the country in question. The formula is virtually identical to the one described above, the difference being the addition of net income from abroad (income receipts from the rest of the world – income payments to the rest of the world).

$$GNP = C + I + G + (eX - i) + \text{net income from abroad}$$

The **current account balance** is obtained by adding the **balance of trade** for goods and services (eX – i) and the **net income from abroad**.[7]

The current account balance (CA) is also obtained by adding net private savings (S – I) and net public savings or fiscal balance (T – G).

$$CA = (S - I) + (T - G)$$

A current account **surplus** means that the country invests abroad and it can consequently **lend** to other countries. The domestic **currency** is usually **strong** and interest rates low.

A current account **deficit** means that the country spends more than it produces and it may finance its consumption by **borrowing** abroad. In this case, there is a **risk** of currency **devaluation**. A negative domestic savings rate also implies a current account deficit. Unfortunately, an interest rate hike to stimulate savings or attract foreign investors is likely to have a negative impact on stocks and bonds.

As we saw above, the balance of trade (eX – i) is a component of the GDP calculation.

A trade **surplus** means that **exports** exceed **imports**, with a positive impact on growth.

The reverse is true of a trade **deficit** (**imports** exceed **exports**). A trade deficit may lead to a weakening of the domestic currency to stimulate exports, but as foreign holders of securities denominated in that currency will seek to avoid a depreciation of their investments, they may sell these assets, pushing the stock market down. This will result in increased pressure on the currency. Investors in the domestic market are likely to follow the movement, and if the Central Bank decides to sustain its currency through an interest rate hike it risks worsening the situation even further.

The Trade Balance Report provides the level of imports and exports for a country and indicates whether there is a trade surplus or deficit. The total deficit is somewhat secondary to changes in exports or imports. Import and export prices are also an important source of information on this point.

Depending on the cause of increases or decreases in imports and exports, market reactions will differ.

---

[7]The current account balance also includes a fourth item entitled "net unilateral transfers".

The **deficit** may be explained by an **increase in imports** due to strong domestic growth compared to other countries. In this case, such a scenario will have little impact on the stock market. Depending on the outlook for inflation however, the bond market may suffer.

On the other hand, the deficit may come from a **decrease** in **exports** due to a **recession** in other countries. In this case, the stock market is likely to suffer, especially in export-oriented industries. Meanwhile, the bond market prefers this scenario, which puts downward pressure on interest rates to stimulate exports.

When the deficit results from a decline in exports due to an **interest rate hike** initiated by the Central Bank, neither the stock market nor the bond market will react favourably. However, the final reaction will depend on measures taken by foreign governments to maintain their currency or otherwise.

ii) Budget deficit

We spoke in the first section of the consequences of fiscal policy on the budget, particularly on the increase in its deficit. This deficit should be compared to GDP to measure the country's capacity to produce and thereby pay off its debt. It is therefore a **relative measure**, which should be compared with other countries. Note that a chronic budget deficit is dangerous for the economy and is not encouraging to the stock and bond markets.

To **finance** its **expenditure**, a State has **three options**. First, it can **raise taxes**, but this measure is often unpopular, especially during an election campaign period.

Second, it can **borrow** on the **market** by issuing bonds. The quality of public finances will essentially determine the rate it can offer on the market. Occasionally, this rate may be equal or even superior to that offered by corporate bonds, showing in fact a government issue of poorer quality.

Finally, the State can obtain funds from the Central Bank, which can intervene by adopting a so-called **"accommodative" policy**, i.e., buying the government bonds before they hit the market. In a way, this kind of operation amounts to creating money, but the increase in supply can cause inflation. Once again, a potential interest rate rise is never well received by the stock and bond markets.

So attention should be paid to the development of the deficit; it's important to study the budget report showing the level of budget deficit. This appears every month, but suffers from effects of seasonality due, for instance, to quarterly payments by taxpayers. As monthly fluctuations can be considerable, it is better to examine a given month compared to the same month of the previous year.

Sources

The Budget of the United States Government can be found at:

www.gpoaccess.gov/usbudget/index.html

For Europe, the deficit and gross debt of public administrations are available on the Eurostat website:

epp.eurostat.ec.europa.eu/portal/page/portal/euroindicators/peeis

The so-called "structural" deficit, which exists even in a context of full employment, is distinct from the "cyclical" deficit, which is linked to a situation of recession and is easier to fight using appropriate monetary or fiscal policies.

b) Consumption indicators

Household consumption represents nearly **two thirds of GDP**. Its development is therefore a strong determinant of GDP growth. As such, three indicators are worth examining.

i) Retail sales report

This is one of the most important monthly indicators, and can have a strong impact on the markets. It reflects the level of **consumer spending** (sales of all retail goods) and influences economic growth. Increased sales are therefore a positive sign, but with a potential inflation risk that may be controlled by future interest rate hikes. Conversely, if sales are down, there is a risk of economic slowdown or recession which must be monitored.

This is one of the most important leading indicators, which falls when the economy starts to enter a recession, and is the first to rise when the economy takes off again. It is also important to examine whether the changes in consumption affect all industries, or certain sectors in particular.

It is better to evaluate this indicator excluding car sales, which usually represent a large percentage of sales and can suffer from considerable seasonal fluctuations.

This indicator can also be very volatile and does not include spending on services.

Sources

The Advance Monthly Sales for Retail and Food Services is available on the US Department of Commerce website:

www.commerce.gov/category/tags/economics (latest Retail sales report)

For Europe, the volume of retail sales can be found on the Eurostat website:

epp.eurostat.ec.europa.eu/portal/page/portal/euroindicators/peeis

---

ii) Personal income and expenditures

Changes in **disposable income** and **household consumption** will determine future consumer demand, and therefore have an impact on growth. If disposable income is rising, people will usually spend more money. If it's falling, they tend to save. In the past, the United States had a very low savings rate (between 1% and 2% over the last three years), but this rate is currently rising for American households. In 2009, it sat at almost 4% – high for the US but relatively low when compared to 17% in France,[8] the rate calculated for the third quarter of 2009.

---

[8] See the article from L'expansion, "le taux d'épargne des ménages va rester très élevé en 2010" (30 December 2009).

> **Sources**
>
> In the United States, Personal Income and Outlays is published monthly by the Bureau of Economic Analysis (BEA):
>
> www.bea.gov
>
> In Europe, total household consumption is available on the Eurostat website:
>
> epp.eurostat.ec.europa.eu/portal/page/portal/euroindicators/peeis

iii) Consumer Confidence Index – CCI

The confidence indices evaluate the **expectations** and **feelings** of **households** vis-à-vis their **future consumption**, thereby constituting a leading indicator on growth, as long as the changes are significant.

As we noted earlier, there is a link between consumer confidence and actual consumption. If confidence is high, consumption is very likely to increase, thereby generating growth. Conversely, if confidence is weak, consumption is likely to be limited or postponed, causing an economic slowdown.

> **Sources**
>
> The CCI (Consumer Confidence Index) is published monthly by the Conference Board and can be found on their website:
>
> www.conference-board.org/economics/ConsumerConfidence.cfm
>
> The ESI (Economic Sentiment Indicator) for the European Union and the euro area is published by the Directorate General for Economic and Financial Affairs (DG ECFIN) and is available on the following website:
>
> ec.europa.eu/economy_finance/db_indicators/surveys/index_en.htm

c) Corporate indicators

Investments represent nearly 20% of GDP and, as with consumption, an increase in investments contributes to GDP growth.

i) Purchasing Managers' Index – PMI

In the United States, the Institute of Supply Management (ISM) publishes a monthly report on manufacturing (ISM Manufacturing Report on Business) and another on services (ISM Non-Manufacturing Report on Business). The latter is more recent, having been created in 1998, and is consequently less closely followed by the markets.

The most important indicator to reflect the condition of the United States' manufacturing industry is the composite Purchasing Managers' Index (PMI), which is organised into five categories (each worth 20%):

- new orders;

- production;
- employment;
- suppliers' deliveries;
- inventories.

When it falls under 50, the index indicates a recession, especially if the trend continues over several months. A level of above 50 shows economic growth.

Sources

These reports and the Purchasing Managers' Index are available on the website of the Institute for Supply Management:

www.ism.ws/ISMReport

In Europe, the PMI is provided by Markit and the reports can be found on their website:

www.markiteconomics.com/MarkitFiles/Pages/PressCenter.aspx

---

ii) Factory Orders and Durable Goods Report

This indicator helps measure the level of factory orders and durable goods, and therefore corporate demand, which in principle will have a subsequent impact on sales and corporate earnings.

Sources

In the United States, the Factory Orders Report, which is published every two months, and the monthly Durable Goods Report are provided by the US Census Bureau and are available on their website:

www.census.gov/indicator/www/m3/index.htm
www.census.gov/indicator/www.m3/adv/

In Europe, new industrial orders can be found on the Eurostat website:

epp.eurostat.ec.europa.eu/portal/page/portal/euroindicators/peeis

---

iii) Industrial production and capacity utilisation

This report gives an overview of the country's industrial production, particularly the capacity utilisation of factories. Levels of above 82–85% tend to predict future price hikes and shortages on the supply side. A level of below 80% tends to indicate a slowdown of the economy and a possible recession.

Sources

In the United States, this report is published monthly by the Board of Governors, Federal Reserve Board:

www.federalreserve.gov/release/g17/current/default.htm

> In Europe, the report on industrial production is available on the Eurostat website:
>
> epp.eurostat.ec.europa.eu/portal/page/portal/euroindicators/peeis
>
> The current level of capacity utilisation can be obtained at:
>
> epp.eurostat.ec.europa.eu/portal/page/portal/euroindicators/data/main_tables

d) Other indicators

It is also worth studying the **international trade** situation, by examining the development of the Baltic Dry Index (BDI), which is an index of shipping prices for various dry bulk cargoes such as grains, ores or metals. It is calculated on an average of prices for 24 global shipping routes.

> **Sources**
>
> This index is provided by the Baltic Exchange in London, but access must be paid for. The address of their website is:
>
> www.balticexchange.com
>
> It is also communicated by financial information services such as Bloomberg or Reuters.

27.2.3 Recession

By definition, a country has entered a recession when it has undergone **two consecutive quarters** of **negative growth**. It is important to detect the signs of a major economic slowdown as early as possible.

When a recession is expected or is taking place, and there are no inflationary pressures, bond prices may rise in anticipation of rate cuts to combat them. Stocks will tend to weaken in anticipation of a decline in future results, but it is important to select industries carefully, choosing those best prepared to withstand or even take advantage of the crisis.

Besides the indicators related to growth presented above, there are several **indicators** used to determine whether or not the economy is entering a recession.

a) Initial Jobless Claims Report and Employment Situation

The Initial Jobless Claims Report indicates the number of newly unemployed on a weekly basis. The Employment Situation, published monthly, gives the unemployment rate, the number of jobs created on nonfarm payrolls (manufacturing, business, government agencies), and other factors such as the average work week. An increase in overtime is often a preliminary stage before hiring new workers. On the contrary, a reduction in overtime may presage future redundancies.

The total number of unemployed persons represents the country's unemployment rate and therefore the level of economic activity. It is closely monitored by politicians, especially at election time.

If unemployment is rising, the risk of economic slowdown, or even recession, is significant. Consequently, an interest rate cut is possible to stimulate the economy. A high figure may be positive in that it can sometimes mark the end of a crisis.

Waning unemployment points to growth, but this can carry a risk of overheating and inflation. An increase in interest rates to control inflation is therefore possible.

To assess the risks of inflation and recession accurately, it is nonetheless important to compare this rate with the so-called "natural" unemployment rate. Investors should also carefully examine whether the job creation or losses are affecting the economy in general or only certain sectors. In the United States, a variation of less than 30 000 in the number of jobless is regarded as statistically insignificant.

Sources

For the United States, the Jobless Claims Report is published by the US Department of Labor and is available on their website:

www.dol.gov/opa/media/press/eta/main.htm

The Employment Situation, published by the Bureau of Labor Statistics, can be found on their website:

www.bls.gov/news.release/empsit.toc.htm

For Europe, the unemployment rate and other employment data are available on the Eurostat website:

epp.eurostat.ec.europa.eu/portal/page/portal/euroindicators/peeis

---

b) Existing Home Sales Report and New Home Sales Report

The Existing Home Sales Report appears at the end of every month for the developments of the previous month. It is strongly related to mortgage interest rates and therefore reacts quickly to any changes in these rates. The report also gives the housing inventory and median prices, but includes no detailed information on the type of housing. A low inventory can be an early sign that construction is likely to increase.

The New Home Sales Report depends on demand, and usually starts to rise when the economy is coming out of a recession. This indicator also helps measure growth. This is because individuals who buy land to build their house on will subsequently spend money to furnish it, landscape the garden, etc., generating private consumption expenditure with a positive effect on growth.

So both these reports provide information on the level of growth or economic slowdown in the country, but because their publication is delayed relative to the construction of new homes, they cannot be considered as leading indicators. Although more focused on the housing market, they also help determine the overall macroeconomic perspective.

Increased sales or high figures are positive for the economy and indicate growth. Furthermore, if housing prices rise, homeowners and landlords can take on more debt to consume (buy) more. However, this situation brings with it the risk of inflation, which can lead to possible interest rate hikes to curb inflation.

Conversely, if sales are down or the figures are low, there is a risk of economic slowdown or recession. A lowering of interest rates is possible in the future, but this will also depend on inflation. If prices drop, homeowners and landlords will take on less debt and therefore consume less.

Sources

In the United States, the Existing Home Sales Report is published monthly by the National Association of Realtors and is available on their website:

www.realtor.org/research.nsf/pages/EHSdata

The New Home Sales Report is published by the US Census Bureau and can be found on their website:

www.census.gov/const/www/newresales.index.html

---

c) Housing Starts and Building Permits

This monthly indicator is also regarded as one of the **important leading indicators**, as it usually falls when the economy starts to enter a recession, and is the first to climb when the economy takes off.

However, the impact on the markets will depend on the condition the economy is in when the monthly report is published. If the economy is expanding and inflation is a concern, an increase in construction will be seen as fairly negative because of this inflation risk. On the other hand, in a context of economic slowdown or recession, such an increase will be greeted as positive.

Sources

In the United States, this indicator is published by the US Census Bureau and can be found on their website:

www.census.gov/const/www/newreconstindex.html

In Europe, the production and construction index is available on the Eurostat website:

epp.eurostat.ec.europa.eu/portal/page/portal/euroindicators/peeis

d) Confidence indices

Confidence indices such as the Consumer Confidence Index (CCI) or the index provided by the University of Michigan give an indication of consumer **expectations** and **sentiment** about their **consumption**.

There is a strong link between consumer confidence and actual consumption. If confidence is high, consumption is very likely to increase, thereby generating growth. However, as we stated earlier, this can create a risk of inflation, making an interest rate hike possible in the future.

Conversely, if confidence is weak, consumption is likely to be limited or postponed, causing an economic slowdown. Consequently, an interest rate cut is possible to stimulate growth.

Other confidence indices also exist, such as the ZEW index, which gauges the sentiment of German investors. It measures the confidence of financial analysts and investors about the outlook for inflation, interest rates, stock indexes, currencies, oil and corporate profits over the next six months. A positive index means that sentiment is improving, while an index of below zero indicates a deterioration.

There are also confidence indices for industry – the German Ifo index, for example – that give an idea of expectations and sentiment about the development of the business climate and future growth.

Sources

The MCSI (University of Michigan Consumer Sentiment Index) is published monthly and can be found at:

   www.customers.reuters.com/community/university/default.aspx

In Germany, the ZEW index (*Zentrum für europäische Wirtschaftsforschung*) is provided on a monthly basis by the German Centre for European Economic Research, which also calculates the monthly Ifo index on the economic climate:

   www.zew.de/en/publikationen/Konjunkturerwartungen/Konjunkturerwartungen.php3

   www.Cesifo-group.de/portal/page/portal/ifoHome/a-winfo/d1index

---

27.2.4 Productivity and technological change

Another of the market's most closely followed indices is the increase in worker productivity. By productivity, we mean the relation between production and the resources used to achieve it.

An increase in productivity makes it possible to **produce more for less**, which can lead companies to lower their prices and become more competitive on the market. This will stimulate consumer demand for the goods that have become cheaper (improved purchasing power).

Improved productivity also leads to **lower unit labour costs**, and a consequent increase in company profits. Companies can therefore make new investments to ensure their development, stimulating demand for goods and services. The same is true for the State which, due to increased tax revenues, can increase public spending and particularly investments.

Finally, companies may decide to **distribute** this **surplus** to their **employees** by raising wages. This will result in an increase in their purchasing power and a boost to consumption of goods and services.

As we can see, increased productivity has a **positive impact** on **growth**. However, greater efficiency does not necessarily lead to new jobs. The immediate impact is difficult to estimate, but in the long term, increased productivity is usually positive for employment.

The report on productivity and costs only appears on a quarterly basis and is published later than GDP.

Sources

Besides the economic calendars, reports on productivity are available on the Bureau of Labor Statistics and OECD websites:

www.bls.gov.news.release/prod2.toc.htm
www.oecd.org (Statistics portal – Productivity)

Furthermore, the **technology used** by a company influences its productivity. As such, technological change is one of the most important factors influencing long-term stock prices. A company that has missed a technological shift is doomed to disappear, as it will be unable to adapt to the new market conditions.

These can be linked to the **incorporation** of **new technologies** that lower production costs or that favour the use of cheaper raw materials. Companies that manage to become less dependent on crude oil in a given sector will therefore be better positioned. If we look at transport, for example, the sector to benefit the most from the context of rising oil prices will be rail. This sector already enjoyed strong growth in 2008 when oil prices reached historic highs.

Thus, it is crucial for investors to keep track of technological advances and to examine how they are integrated by companies, which must offer products and services adapted to their time and their customers. For example, the last company to manufacture typewriters (Smith-Corona) went bankrupt, its products having become obsolete.

27.2.5 Regulations and taxes

Finally, **government statements** or **decisions** can have a devastating impact on securities. Decisions to liberalise or privatise, to regulate, control or subsidise, can affect industries and especially companies.

Sources

Regularly reading the newspapers (paper or online) is a good way to stay informed and be better able to anticipate changes of potential significance for certain sectors, or those that may affect businesses.

27.3 SECTORIAL ANALYSIS[9]

It is important to know the various sectors and industries well in order to determine the impact that **macroeconomic events** can have on them.

Different industrial sectors react to differing degrees – and sometimes in opposite ways – to good and bad macroeconomic news. According to Navarro, you have to think in terms of sectors to profit from the opportunities these events provide. The same goes for the stock, bond and money markets, which react differently to macroeconomic news and can therefore develop in opposite directions.

So investors should first ensure they are familiar with the main sectors of the economy, then identify the strongest and weakest companies within these sectors. Then they need to reflect on how each sector reacts to different types of macroeconomic news.

To begin with, it is necessary to examine the **type of customer** by sector, namely **consumers** (households), **companies** or the **government**.

In general, the computer and leisure sectors depend on sales to consumers. The consumer confidence index, retail sales and personal income are the indicators to follow.

The chemical and paper sectors depend more on industrial buyers. An indicator like the industrial production and capacity utilisation rate is more relevant here.

Finally, the main customers of the defence and aerospace sectors are governments, meaning that any news on the State budget must be scrutinised with great care.

Next, it is necessary to find out if, in the production process, the sector tends to use **workers**, **machines** or **oil**, or a **combination** of two or all of these.

---

[9]Navarro, pp. 65–79.

In this respect, the retail sales sector is regarded as **labour intensive**, which means it is more sensitive to the rise and fall of unemployment rates and to wage inflation. Utilities – companies providing public services such as water, electricity and gas – are seen as **capital intensive** and are very sensitive to interest rate fluctuations. Finally, the transport sector is **fuel intensive** and reacts to fluctuations in energy and oil prices.

Some sectors are "**cyclical**", such as the auto industry, construction and transport, which react more strongly to economic slowdowns or recessions than so-called "**non-cyclical**" sectors such as health, pharmaceuticals or food. For macroeconomic investors, this distinction helps determine which sectors to sell or avoid in the event of a slowdown and which to buy when the economy is taking off.

Finally, the agricultural, electronics, industrial equipment, computer and pharmaceutical industries are export-oriented, while financial services and health care are less dependent on exports. Export dependent sectors react more strongly to the balance of trade and currency fluctuations.

As we noted above, it is also necessary to keep up to date politically to determine the risks related to new **regulations** as early as possible, especially in sectors such as energy, pharmaceuticals, or the chemical and defence industries.

The **climate** can also influence sales and therefore corporate margins. The return of rain to Brazil after a period of drought will help lower coffee prices, allowing a company like Starbucks to increase its margins. On the other hand, a flood can destroy crops, this time pushing prices up.

27.4   PETER NAVARRO'S APPROACH

For Navarro, market risk represents the purest kind of **macroeconomic risk**. In order to minimise this risk, macroeconomic investors must be capable of going long, short or flat, i.e., knowing whether to be a buyer, seller, or neutral, and must never go against a trend.

With regard to sector risk or company risk, it is useful to follow the events likely to affect them. According to Navarro, sector risk represents 50% to 80% of the price movement of a security and depends specifically on the macro and microeconomic forces acting on a given sector.

Company risk, or specific risk, can be related to management, unfavourable regulations or bad news. Risk related to regulations is particularly marked in the drug, tobacco and agriculture sectors. Diversification, particularly using a tracker fund, helps minimise this risk. A study of the fundamentals, such as growth in per-share earnings, the P/E ratio or technical levels (near to a support or resistance), helps limit it. It is also important to examine the calendar of earnings announcements, which is often a risky period for trading a stock.

27.4.1 Trends[10] and stock picking

Although it is certainly important to be familiar with the different industries and sectors of the economy, this is not enough. Investors must be able to determine, using various indicators, the **general market trend** and that of the **individual sectors**, in order to identify the strong and weak sectors and those which may soon gain in strength or deteriorate.

As we pointed out earlier, "Trend is your friend" and you should never invest against a trend. In order to determine the market trend, the following indicators can be used (the example refers to the American market).

a) S&P Futures

These are an excellent indicator of the market direction. If they are rising, the markets are usually rising, and vice versa.

b) TICK and TRIN

In the case of the US market, TICK gives the difference between the number of stocks rising (upticking) and those falling (downticking). So a positive TICK indicates a bull market.

The TRIN incorporates the relative volume of advancing issues and the relative volume of declining issues, using the following calculation. A TRIN lower that 1 is a sign of a bull market.

$$\text{TRIN} = \frac{\text{Number of advancing issues/Volume of advancing issues}}{\text{Number of declining issues/Volume of declining issues}}$$

TICK and TRIN must be pointing in the same direction to confirm a market trend, as mixed signals don't really allow a trend to be ascertained clearly.

Next, trends for the different sectors should be established. A study of the sector indices and trackers helps detect which sectors are advancing and which are declining. Before trading a stock, it is essential to examine the sector's situation, as the price movement of an individual stock depends for over 50% on the movement of the sector it belongs to.

Simply investing in a market **index** certainly reduces risks thanks to large diversification, but it also **limits potential gain**. Investment in a particular sector helps avoid excessive concentration, but a part of the capital invested will suffer fluctuations due to the **weak companies** in the sector, thereby affecting the potential profit. So it is more appropriate to favour strong, solid stocks in the chosen sector during a bullish trend.

---

[10]Taken from Navarro, pp. 81–90.

Finally, when evaluating the trend, it is also important to follow the news and the calendar of macroeconomic indicators. Reading the newspapers regularly and attentively helps minimise the risk associated with fluctuations due to announcements or political decisions affecting the sector. It can be useful to construct different scenarios according to the level of the indicator, which can then be compared to the estimates, and to evaluate the potential consequences on different sectors.

Regarding **individual stocks**, a **fundamental analysis** is carried out first, followed by a **technical analysis** to refine the market timing.[11] Stocks that successfully pass the fundamental and technical analysis tests are finally selected to make up the stock basket for the sector in question.

It is advisable to proceed in this way, as even a stock which seems attractive from a technical or fundamental point of view won't be able to do much in a generally bearish market or sector. So the technical and fundamental analysis must be taken into account, along with the macroeconomic context.

27.4.2 Sector rotation

Peter Navarro also suggests looking at **economic cycles** and investing in different sectors according to the phase in which we find ourselves in the cycle. Table 27.2[12] shows the sectors and phases of the cycle during which it is best to invest. The choice of sector is the easy part; determining the phase of the cycle is more complicated.

To understand this table better, it is worth starting from the top market situation – phase 5, and then studying the cycle's development.[13]

In a top market situation, the economy is growing strongly but runs the risk of overheating. The Central Bank has already raised interest rates several times to bring it under control and avoid excessive inflation. The unemployment rate is usually very low, retail sales are exploding and consumer confidence is in great shape. Energy prices continue to rise. At this stage, inflation is a major worry and this is the moment (early bear) for investors to start turning to more defensive and non-cyclical sectors.

As interest rates are too high, the economy slows down and starts entering a recession, with a drop in production and confidence and rising unemployment. The Central Bank starts to lower interest rates, investments decline and industry is waiting for better days to start investing again. Investors first begin (approaching late bear) moving toward the utilities sector, which is capital intensive and sensitive to interest rates. Falling energy prices also benefit this sector.

When interest rates are at their lowest, the cyclical and financial sectors will be favoured (late bear) as they benefit particularly from low interest rates.

---

[11]It is also possible to undertake the technical analysis first, then the fundamental analysis.
[12]Taken from Navarro, p. 190.
[13]Taken from Navarro, pp. 175–177.

Table 27.2 The most suitable sectors according to market cycles

Market phase	Category	Best sectors within the category
1. Early bull	Transport	Rail
		Shipping
2. Early to middle bull	Technology	Computers
		Electronics
		Semi-conductors
3. Middle to late bull	Capital goods	Electrical equipment
		Heavy-duty trucks
		Machinery and machine tools
		Manufacturing
		Pollution control
4. Late bull	Basic industries and materials	Aluminium
		Chemicals
		Containers
		Metals
		Paper and forest products
		Steel
5. Late bull to top market	Energy	Oil
		Natural gas
		Coal
6. Early bear	Consumer non-cyclicals and health care	Beverages
		Cosmetics
		Food
		Health
		Drugs
		Tobacco
7. Approaching late bear	Utilities	Electricity
		Gas
		Telecommunications
8. Late bear	Financials and consumer cyclicals	Automobile
		Banks
		Real estate financing
		Housing
		Real estate
		Retail sales

The economy will then start to take off and the transport sector will become attractive in this new phase (early bull). Production will start to increase, as will sales.

Investments in new factories or equipment won't be made until the following phase (early to middle bull) with an increase in new orders. The technology sector will benefit first, then (middle to late bull) the sectors that will take advantage of the increase in demand for machines and equipment.

The economy is now working at full speed, with virtually full employment and many hours of overtime being worked. This phase (late bull) is the moment to turn to the industrial sector, which benefits from increased demand for aluminium, steel, chemicals and paper.

The Central Bank is starting to raise interest rates to avoid excessive inflation, and it is usually at this point (late bull to market top) that demand for energy explodes. The energy sector is therefore to be favoured.

The Central Bank continues to raise interest rates and energy prices keep climbing, which is beginning to weigh on the economy. The market reaches its summit (market top). The indicators start to deteriorate and the cycle comes to an end.

27.5   CRITICISM OF THE MACROECONOMIC APPROACH

By anticipating certain factors, based on current, historical and estimated data, analysts propose forecasts for the development of securities, markets and currencies.

This approach only considers **objective data** and disregards the **psychology** of the individuals behind each of these factors. An analysis that takes behavioural aspects into account would be desirable, but we understand that this is a difficult exercise as its role is precisely to focus on the fundamentals, i.e., the tangible aspects.

Peter Lynch, the guru of the Magellan fund, one day declared:[14] "If you spend more than 14 minutes a year worrying about the market, you've wasted 12 minutes", underlining the lack of reliability of macroeconomic forecasts.

Indeed, in practice, analysts often make mistakes, or rather the results that occur differ from the suggested scenario. Not because their analyses were wrong in substance, but simply because they fail to take into account other factors, particularly the current market trend in the broadest sense of the term, which includes investor psychology.

Our Advice

We believe that the **macroeconomic context** must be considered, and that it is essential to keep a close eye on the various **indicators** we have presented above.

We favour a so-called **top-down approach**, i.e., determining first of all the general market trend, then the trend of the different sectors and industries, before finally selecting individual securities. A combination of fundamental and technical analyses is then necessary.

However, human psychology is complex and macroeconomic, fundamental or technical analyses are not enough on their own. Nonetheless, these approaches should be combined within the framework of a more all-encompassing model that we will present in the following chapter.

---

[14]Taken from Navarro, p. 69.

Part VIII
Modelling Market Movements

We turn now to the modelling of market movements. How relevant is this modelling? Is it possible to implement a model to forecast these movements?

We mentioned earlier the possibility of order appearing in the midst of apparent disorder. This is the view advanced by mathematician Benoit Mandelbrot, the father of the **fractal approach**.

A fractal is a geometric shape that can be divided into several parts, each of which is a reduced-sized copy of the whole. In other words, a fractal object is an object in which each part is also a fractal object. The whole can therefore be "deduced" from each of the parts of which it is composed. As such, order emerges from what seems initially to be disorder, implying the non-existence of random movement. The idea is to try to identify **regularity within irregularity**.

An analysis of each fractal and its development will therefore help understand and, in a way, anticipate the following fractal object, or even the whole.

In finance, if we break down market movements, we can see that they represent a series of upswings and downturns. Each movement is a fractal and together these upwards and downwards movements give the general movement of the whole, or the market.

Each movement should therefore make it possible to explain the following movement, or even to infer the movement of the whole.

According to Mandelbrot, the traditional tools currently used in the finance industry do not work and their underlying assumptions are incorrect. Indeed, in his opinion, price variations are practically never continuous, but make trivial or substantial jumps. They are neither independent nor stationary, nor do they marry the proportions of the famous bell curve of normal distribution. Finally, he does not believe that the efficient market hypothesis has been verified in practice.

In his study on cotton prices, Mandelbrot observed obvious **correlations** between **past** and **future prices**, and asserted that there are also long-term correlations. Based on the analysis of the growth rings of trees, he established that correlations fall more slowly than expected, so slowly in fact that they never seem to disappear completely.[1]

A new path he explored is that of the **multifractal model**. This model, in the scholar's view, uses little data to provide a large amount of information, unlike other financial models.

---

[1]Taken from Mandelbrot, p. 205.

It is based on fundamental, long-lasting facts about how the market works. This model is economic and imitates the market.

Examining price fluctuations, he noted that they develop in irregular trends. Price variations are clearly concentrated according to their size. He distinguished first the big variations, which are concentrated and quick, followed by smaller, slower variations. So, over shorter periods, prices fluctuate more strongly, while over longer periods they tend to stabilise.

According to Mandelbrot, market **timing** is **essential**, as large **gains** and **losses** are concentrated in **short intervals** of time.

This concentration can be extremely useful for avoiding the risk of loss or, on the contrary, profiting from market movements depending on the type of variation. It would therefore be worth designing an index to predict stock market storms with a time horizon long enough to prepare for them, similar to seismic warning centres. "**You cannot beat the market [...] but you can sidestep its worst punches**",[2] and it is stock market crashes that destroy the investor, not the small downturns.

Given our previous conclusions, we cannot but share this approach and agree with his analysis, but in a somewhat adapted form.

Each movement is the result of a multitude of factors that produce increases or decreases. The number of factors is very high, and also extremely varied (interest rates, inflation, political decisions, indicators, corporate earnings announcements, human behaviour and psychological factors, etc.). Faced with this large variety of factors, we could first consider conducting a multiple linear regression to determine which of these significantly influence price developments. Thus, using data on each of these so-called explicative factors, the model would indicate an increase or decrease. Besides the very large number of explicative factors, conducting such a regression would involve a gargantuan database, super computers and, most importantly, a very strong assumption: the explicative factors found would be the only ones to explain the model.

However, it would seem that these factors develop randomly, and their occurrence comes as a surprise to the market, which must then immediately incorporate the newly available information, eventually leading to an increase or decrease. Furthermore, the model – which would only obtain data on a given explicative factor at the last moment – would have to be able to provide the direction of the movement in a fraction of a second in order to allow proper positioning on the market.

Finally, we could consider entering expected data for the factors with different probability scenarios, but this brings us back to the debate over whether using a probability distribution is coherent. Unless of course these expected data are unbiased data on future values. In other words, insider trading on the whole range of factors would be the only way to predict the market's development before it happened. On the individual, national or even worldwide scale, this approach is hardly conceivable.

---

[2]Mandelbrot, p. 274.

By applying the fractal approach to these different factors, we can consider that each of these in fact follows a certain order, and does not develop randomly. Each factor would be a fractal of the "final" fractal object that is the market. Determining a **trend** per factor would therefore be the way to go.

Furthermore, we said earlier that an upswing or downturn is the result of the market integrating a newly available piece of information (or factor). But is the factor integrated immediately? In other words, is the market efficient? We have already concluded in the negative.

Mandelbrot does not believe in market efficiency either, and many empirical studies demonstrate the existence of biases that result in each new piece of information taking some time to be reflected in prices. We obviously agree.

At this stage of our analysis, it is worth recalling that the bulk of our reasoning applies to the individual. All the financial theories that are based on an overly mathematical or probabilistic approach forget that behind the market, behind each factor and company and finally each investor, lie human beings.

Unfortunately, the crisis of 1929 failed to teach us enough lessons from the past; history does tend to repeat and human greed has changed little – if at all – over the centuries. **Human psychology** remains constant. Already at the time, trader Jesse Livermore said in relation to the crisis of 1929 that man **tends** to **forget the past**, and therefore to lose his memory of past financial crises. The generation that has lived through the crises of 2001 and 2008 should fear that this memory be lost with the next generations.

Fortunately, we have been studying human behaviour for much longer than finance, so it's not surprising that we are led to look for a solution in the realm of behavioural finance. We believe the ideal model to be a "human" one, which is both simple and comprehensive.

We need to find a model or approach that provides the investor with an answer to a simple question: **should I enter (stay in) or exit the market?** The answer to this question must be independent of expected return. Indeed, we have already established that the final return will depend specifically on the moment at which the investor enters and exits the market. So despite an attractive historical – and therefore expected – return, there are times at which it is appropriate to invest in order to participate in bull trends, and other times at which it is better not to be involved in the market. A good manager should know when it's time to invest and when it's preferable to stay in cash or bonds. As such, portfolio management consists in **managing risks**, not expected returns.

Depending on the chosen degree of risk, it is ultimately the **decision** to **enter** or **exit** the market at a given moment that constitutes the risk taken by the investor. Investors also appreciate simplicity and ease of use, making the concept of entry and exit attractive.

Let's make an amusing analogy with a lover of barbecued sausages. Despite the delicious taste of barbecued sausages, this person is not going to have a barbecue if it's raining or looks like rain. You would have to be stupid to have a barbecue in the rain on the pretext that the sausages are delicious. Similarly, you have to wonder what could justify staying in an established or expected bear market, even if the expected returns on stocks are high, when it would be so much wiser to avoid the stock market for a while and stay in cash.

Each movement takes into account a range of different information at a given time. This includes not only so-called "objective" information, but also "subjective" information: the psychology of financial players.

The suggested approach has to identify trends for investors and, especially, take into consideration both objective and subjective factors (the psychology of individuals).

28

Suggested Investment Approach

In the light of all the preceding analyses and our conclusions, we are now going to outline an investment approach capable of helping investors identify trends and, more importantly, define the moments at which it is wise to enter (stay in) or exit the market.

The approach presented below was devised after reading the following introductory lines from the *Theory of Speculation* by Louis Jean-Baptiste Bachelier:

> "The determination of these movements is subordinated to an infinite number of factors: it is therefore impossible to hope for mathematical forecasts. Conflicting opinions about these variations are such that any one time, buyers believe in an upswing and sellers in a downturn."

The second half of this statement forms an important part of our approach, because it indicates how price movement will be determined by the **degree of conviction** of one category of investors compared to another. If there are more investors who believe in an upswing, prices will be pushed up rather than down, as those who expect a downturn will exert less influence.

Mandelbrot proposed a multifractal model, and the term "multi" is essential here too as it will form the basis of the approach we suggest: the **multi-force approach**.

The price of a stock can move upwards, downwards, or remain stable. Various "elements" will influence the price in a given environment, which itself is constantly changing.

Given that strong correction periods tend to be concentrated, the first step is to design a sort of stock market thermometer, or **concentration of activity indicator**, equivalent to a Richter scale of stock market activity. The idea is to examine current volatility and compare it to historical volatility.

The second step will be to determine the **forces** that push prices **up**, those that push them **down** and those that have no influence on prices. The **resulting force** will be the decisive one, which will exert pressure in the final direction.

In our opinion, it is worth distinguishing major trends from "waves", or short-term bullish or bearish movements, which do not help work out the general direction of the market.

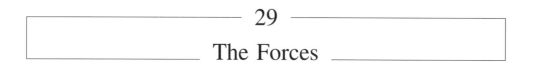

29

The Forces

Amongst the various forces, and in the light of all that we have discussed so far, we will include:

29.1 THE MACROECONOMIC FORCE

Investors must consider, using a series of indicators, if the **macroeconomic environment** is conducive to investment or not.

29.2 THE FUNDAMENTAL FORCE

Taking **fundamental analysis** into account may seem surprising for some, but as we have noted, the market represents a whole range of individuals following different objectives and buying and selling securities for different reasons. Price movements therefore also depend on a Fundamental Force.

The **fundamentals** of a particular sector, the search for **intrinsic value** and the analysis of the various relevant **ratios** will help determine this force.

29.3 THE TECHNICAL FORCE

For the reasons mentioned above, **technical analysis** should also be taken into account. Its results will determine the Technical Force. Some investors or traders act solely on the basis of expected trends or patterns, such as the "head and shoulders", "cup", or "double tops" and "double bottoms". This aspect cannot be ignored, and must be incorporated into the model.

Others believe that prices follow a mean regression process, and invest accordingly. In practice therefore, moving averages are extremely commonly used technical indicators. We believe that speculation, which is mainly present in the short term, is essentially accounted for in this force.

29.4   THE BEHAVIOURAL FORCE

Psychological biases obviously must be included, and are perhaps the model's main force.

As we have already stated several times, behind the market and prices lie human beings, who are usually irrational and are subject to various emotions; they make subjective decisions that must be integrated into the process of price formation and development.

An investor's experience and sensitivity to the different forces will obviously play a part in the process of analysis.

29.5   THE LUCK FORCE

This force does exist and will always exist, but it can never be determined. In our view, it is not a major force, but it does exert an immeasurable pressure on prices. Investors must be conscious of this; as Louis Pasteur said, "chance favours only the prepared mind".

30

The Forces' Strength

To begin with, it is necessary to study each of these forces and then their potential strength. The **resulting final force** can then be determined, which will allow investors to make their choice: buy, sell or hold their security or position in a particular asset class.

It is obviously possible that for a given situation, certain forces produce opposite pressures. Therefore, it is important to determine which has a dominant effect on the others. It is also possible that no dominant force can be determined. In this case, it is better to wait for more clarity or visibility of the markets before making an investment decision.

31
The Beauty of the Approach

An analysis of the different forces can be carried out using indicators or indices that we might qualify as objective, but with a subjective impact in terms of the conclusions they give.

On the other hand, calculating the strength of a force requires a far greater dose of subjectivity, as there is ultimately no rule of measurement. An investor's experience will help determine this strength, as will discussions and exchanging ideas with peers.

The beauty of the suggested approach lies precisely in the fact that it is ultimately **human**: it doesn't rely on a black box where figures are entered in one side so it can spit a numerical result out the other. In this sense, this new investment approach provides a truly simple and comprehensive analysis framework.

To reach conclusions, our "model" employs the financial reflection of the human brain to the highest degree. Indeed, there is no better filter for the analysis of irrational behavioural factors than a brain that can adopt both a rational and an irrational mode of thinking. Machines do not have this ability, and any attempt to model or rationalise the irrational will only produce an imperfect model of the human brain.

As Copernicus noted long ago, "mathematics are for mathematicians". At the beginning of our analysis, we asserted that statistical laws are not really adapted to finance. It may be time to assert that the laws of human nature necessarily apply to that which man has created: the financial markets.

Part IX
Portfolio Construction and Management

Finally, we have come to the point where we can propose a strategy of portfolio construction and management that is tailored to the principles outlined so far in this book.

In our opinion, there should be as many different portfolios as there are investors. Each investor is unique and, through his or her objectives, has a sensitivity to risk and losses and a time horizon all of his or her own. Thus, we favour an approach that allows **tailor-made asset allocation** for each client.

This approach must also be **flexible** – not relying on a fixed distribution between asset classes over time. In this respect, it is interesting to note that "an investor who from February 1988 to February 2009 had invested 100 dollars in stocks, including reinvested dividends, and 100 dollars in U.S. Treasury bonds, would have got almost the same return from each".[1] It is debatable whether the investor in stocks was adequately compensated for the risks taken and the variation his or her capital underwent over this period.

This observation, made by two independent analysts, shows that a passive buy and hold strategy in stocks isn't always very effective, and therefore appears unsuitable. These days, a more active and dynamic management approach is necessary.

Finally, the return/volatility relationship is also worth questioning. Indeed, it has been demonstrated[2] in a very interesting example that the more volatile an investment, the lower its compounded return. In other words, a more volatile asset is not necessarily or systematically more profitable than a less volatile asset.

---

[1] Rodet and Giacoletto.
[2] On this point, see Ian Martin's article in Agefi.

32

Modern Portfolio Theory According to Markowitz

Harry Markowitz was awarded the Nobel Prize in Economics in 1954 for his work, particularly his demonstration of the concepts of diversification and correlation. The analysis you are now reading would not have been possible without his research, but it must be said that for many years now his principles have constituted the basis of modern financial theory without anyone really seeking to question them.

Within the framework of modern portfolio theory, Markowitz designed a so-called **efficient portfolio** that minimises risk for a given return thanks to **diversification** and **low correlation** between assets. Each security is described using two parameters: expected return and risk.

By combining different assets that are not perfectly correlated, risk can be reduced, even to the point of becoming lower than that of the least risky of securities. The lower the correlation, the more the portfolio's risk can be reduced.

The problem with this theory is that it is based on **volatility** as the **only measure of risk**. But, as we have already seen, volatility is not an appropriate measure of risk and normal distribution is unsuited to stock market price fluctuations. Extreme events are much more common than a theoretical distribution would have us believe. Interestingly, Markowitz himself remarked that the bell curve wasn't necessarily the best way to measure risk. Furthermore, the **number of calculations** required is **very high**, especially in terms of correlations.

The correlation factor can also be criticised for the fact that in practice, all securities are positively correlated. Following the market corrections that occurred in 1987, 2001 or in late 2008, the proportion of a portfolio held in stocks was more relevant than the correlations between different stocks, because in a market that has begun a sharp correction phase, all stocks drop at once.

Nonetheless, it can be worthwhile using very weakly correlated stocks to decrease risk. Yes, but which risk? If we consider that stocks are inherently risky assets, the correlation criterion becomes less relevant. The variety of stocks held helps diversify a portfolio, but is a portfolio made up essentially of stocks really less risky?

The concept of **diversification**, however, is important, as it helps reduce the **specific risk** that we talked about earlier. According to studies, the benefits of diversification apply from as little as 30 securities. At 60 securities, it is practically eliminated. International diversification is also an advantage, as is diversification between different asset classes.

Diversification certainly helps reduce specific risk, but it in no way eliminates **market risk**, which remains present no matter what. As we have seen, this market risk is not limited to volatility, but incorporates a large number of underlying risks. We might even wonder if investors are really conscious of all the risks they are taking.

It is interesting to note that Warren Buffett recommends, on the contrary, concentrating your investments. In his view, "if you've found the right stock, why buy only a little?"[1] When putting together a stock portfolio, he advises **including no more than 10 different stocks**. In his opinion, "diversification can increase your chances of subpar returns".[2]

Meanwhile, Peter Lynch says that "there's no point in diversifying into unknown firms, just for the sake of diversifying".[3] For small portfolios, he suggests holding between three and ten stocks.

Indeed, small positions don't add much value to a portfolio and once we've decided to invest in a particular sector or stock, the **position** should be **substantial**. We agree with Buffett on this point, and believe that over-diversification can impact negatively on a portfolio's performance. Obviously, in the event of a market downturn, it is better to be diversified. But as we said earlier, a sharp correction will make all stocks fall, independently of their correlation and their diversification in a given portfolio.

Our Advice

For two reasons – use of the volatility criterion as a measure of risk and the large number of calculations required to determine an efficient portfolio – we believe that Markowitz's initial approach is somewhat outdated, and that other paths should be explored.

Richard Michaud, in his criticism of mean-variance optimisation, says that this "significantly overweights (underweights) those securities that have large (small) estimated returns, negative (positive) correlations and small (large) variances. These securities are, of course, the ones most likely to have large estimation errors."[4]

Before continuing our analysis, it would be useful to present the approach of Chief Investment Officer at Yale University David Swensen. He and his team manage the university's endowment fund of over 20 billion dollars. The annual performance of this institutional portfolio over the last 20 years has risen to nearly 16%.

---

[1] Pardoe, p. 72.
[2] Pardoe, p. 75.
[3] Lynch, p. 169.
[4] Taken from Swensen, pp. 139–140.

32.1   DAVID SWENSEN'S APPROACH

In light of the above criticisms, Swensen suggests adjusting the financial markets' historical data, and then starting the optimisation process. He relies on observations dating back to 1925, and uses the input shown in Table 32.1 for the quantitative model.[5]

Table 32.1   Expected return and standard deviation for the different asset classes

Asset classes	Expected return	Standard deviation
US bonds	2%	10%
US equity	6%	20%
Developed equity	8%	20%
Emerging equity	6%	25%
Absolute return	6%	10%
Private equity	12%	30%
Real assets	6%	15%
Cash	0%	5%

Source: Yale University Investments Office

In terms of correlations, he suggests the correlation matrix in Table 32.2.[6]

Table 32.2   Correlation matrix between different asset classes

	U.S. bonds	U.S. equity	Developed equity	Emerging equity	Absolute return	Private equity	Real assets	Cash
US bonds	1.00							
US equity	0.40	1.00						
Developed equity	0.70	0.25	1.00					
Emerging equity	0.60	0.20	0.75	1.00				
Absolute return	0.30	0.15	0.25	0.20	1.00			
Private equity	0.70	0.15	0.60	0.25	0.20	1.00		
Real assets	0.20	0.20	0.10	0.15	0.15	0.30	1.00	
Cash	0.10	0.50	0.00	0.00	0.35	0.00	0.30	1.00

Source: Yale University Investments Office

With constraints on withdrawals and purchasing power in particular, on 30 June 2006, Yale University had the asset allocation shown in see Table 32.3.

He suggests using **mean-variance optimisation** analysis with **modified, forward-looking data** and constraints in terms of maximum weighting, in order that no asset class dominate the portfolio. Once the results have been obtained, he recommends respecting strategic allocation policies strictly through regular rebalancing.

---

[5]Taken from Swensen, p. 147.
[6]Swensen, p. 157.

Table 32.3   Asset allocation for Yale
University's portfolio on 30.06.2006

Asset classes	Weight
US bonds	4%
US equity	12%
Foreign equity	15%
Absolute return	25%
Private equity	17%
Real assets	27%
Cash	0%

Source: Yale University Investments Office

This approach may be appropriate for **institutional management**, but it doesn't necessarily suit private investors who generally have shorter investment time horizons.

33
The Capital Asset Pricing Model (CAPM)

William F. Sharpe, a great admirer of Markowitz, went to see the professor in 1960 to ask him to supervise his thesis and to suggest that Markowitz simplify his portfolio model.

According to Sharpe, if all investors are looking for efficient portfolios, they will all ultimately want the same one: the famous market portfolio. It's the market itself that would, in a manner of speaking, conduct Markowitz's fastidious calculations to determine this market portfolio.

For Sharpe, all investors should hold a **risk-free asset** and this **market portfolio**. The only difference between investors lies in the **proportions** held in these two positions.

This approach has the advantage of considerably reducing the number of calculations, and of pricing any individual security, by determining the expected return of an asset according to its risk, measured by beta. By analogy, a high beta means high volatility and therefore more risk. All that is required therefore is to make a global market forecast, and to calculate the beta for each stock, which will ultimately determine the extent of the stock's movement compared to the market. This approach led to Sharpe's Capital Asset Pricing Model.

However, given that all the **factors** are **estimated**, especially the returns, it is hardly feasible to reach a precise result. The model relies on an estimate reached using other estimates, which must then be compared to a market price often determined in an irrational manner in inefficient markets. Consequently, we have a hard time understanding how the use of this approach can be justified for valuing securities and constructing a portfolio.

Moreover, besides the difficulty of knowing exactly which market or index is supposed to represent the market portfolio best, this approach pays no heed to the fact that each investor is unique, with different targets and perceptions in terms of risk.

Nonetheless, the idea of a market portfolio helped define passive management and, more importantly, allowed a new approach to portfolio construction to be developed, to which we will now turn.

Our Advice

We concluded in the first chapter that beta was not an appropriate measure of risk. As such, any portfolio construction that relies on this concept should be rejected.

There are "improved" variants of the CAPM that include other factors, such as the "multi-factor CAPM" or "Arbitrage Portfolio Theory", but these models are based on the same concept and therefore should also be rejected.

34

The Minimum Variance Portfolio

Passive management involves investing in a market index or an instrument that replicates this index (a tracker fund for example) with a view to achieving a **performance identical** to the **index**. If the market is efficient and the CAPM holds, then the weights given by the market are supposed to be optimal. However, as we have already pointed out, index weighting by market capitalisation does not necessarily attribute optimal weights to different securities. Therefore the market portfolio is not necessarily efficient.

In practice, it also appears that the observed market portfolio (*ex post*) differs from the expected market portfolio (*ex ante*) in terms of risk and return. But is there a portfolio that can deliver a higher performance than the index for a lower risk?

The market portfolio, or market index, served as a basis of comparison for studies by Haugen and Baker, who demonstrated the **minimum variance anomaly** in 1991. They proved that there is a portfolio – called the minimum variance portfolio – that makes a higher return for a lower risk than the benchmark index (Wilshire 5000 index in the study).

This portfolio is therefore an **improved version** of the **market portfolio,** thanks to both the choice of stocks and the weights assigned to them, which improve the composition of the benchmark index and, more importantly, its performance.

Some studies[1] show that an equally weighted portfolio can do better than a minimum variance portfolio, but it is important to remember that the **objective** is to **minimise variance** by concentrating on risk management rather than on expected returns. Close attention should be paid to constraints regarding maximum weight, as well as the frequency with which positions are reviewed.

Unigestion, a pioneer of minimum variance portfolio construction and management, selects stocks within the original investment universe using various criteria and a whole series of filters (financial health, liquidity, specific risk). They believe the universe should include a sufficient number of stocks/sectors to guarantee proper portfolio diversification. The aim is to pick stocks with the lowest volatility and little correlation between them. First, the minimum variance portfolio is defined using constrained optimisation. This quantitative approach is then validated qualitatively by the management team. It also has the advantage of focusing solely on risk management, without incorporating expected return criteria.

---

[1] See Behr, Güttler and Miebs, and Prof. Martellini's comments in the FT of 15 September 2008.

Table 34.1 Minimum variance strategy performances

Performances as of 31.12.2010	Performance			Risk 3 years*				Max. Drawdown (since 1998, weekly basis)
	2010	3 years	5 years	Volatility	Tracking Error	Correlation	Beta	
Strategy Minimum Variance Europe (EUR)	13.00%	−2.57%	3.52%	15.80%	10.64%	0.94	0.61	−43.41%
DJ Europe Stoxx 600 TRI	11.61%	−5.99%	0.54%	24.08%				−57.55%
Strategy Minimum Variance Japan (JPY)	0.45%	−8.16%	−4.57%	20.02%	12.28%	0.93	0.65	−42.81%
MSCI Japan TR Net	0.57%	−14.26%	−9.50%	28.41%				−59.70%
Strategy Minimum Variance World (USD)	13.12%	−1.31%	3.92%	15.41%	12.30%	0.93	0.56	−40.07%
MSCI AC World TR Net	12.67%	−4.29%	3.44%	25.44%				−56.50%
Strategy Minimum Variance US (USD)	13.24%	−1.80%	2.55%	19.09%	8.38%	0.95	0.76	−44.20%
S&P500 Total Return Index	15.06%	−2.86%	2.29%	23.97%				−52.79%
Strategy Minimum Variance Emerging Markets (USD)	21.62%	6.40%	14.21%	23.04%	13.19%	0.96	0.65	−50.28%
MSCI Emerging Markets TR Net	18.88%	−0.32%	12.78%	34.22%				−62.52%

Performances are net of fees. Past performances are not an indication for future performances.

*On a weekly basis.

Unigestion has specialised in stock management, and is able to successfully outperform the market index over the long term with less volatility, as shown by Table 34.1.[2]

However, the minimum variance portfolio is subject to market fluctuations and produces negative performances during market corrections. Because of its lower volatility, these **negative performances** are **not as bad** as those of the market. This portfolio obviously participates in **bull markets**, but to a **lesser** extent. Given these characteristics, it nonetheless manages to generate a better performance over time, demonstrating that it is always better to avoid or minimise losses, as we have stated several times.

Our Advice

In our opinion, given that index weighting is not always optimal, this approach is an attractive form of improved passive management, bordering on active management.

However, the main disadvantage is that this portfolio is invested 100% in stocks, leaving little room for flexibility.

---

[2] Taken from the Unigestion Newsletter, 2010.

35
Value-at-Risk (VaR)

We also concluded in the first chapter that VaR was not an appropriate measure of risk. As such, any portfolio construction that relies on this concept should also be rejected. However, VaR does have the advantage of focusing more on the possibility of losses, and therefore on the truly negative consequence of risk materialising (capital loss).

Before continuing our analysis and suggesting a new approach to portfolio construction, it is worth looking into how banks construct portfolios in practice.

36

Discretionary Mandates

In practice, the efficient frontier, beta or VaR concepts are used to construct and manage portfolios. Furthermore, funds practising active management are often included in portfolios and, as Swensen notes, "as size is the enemy of performance, more established managers with greater funds under management tend to produce less eye-catching results".[1] J. Lerner of Harvard Business School and A. Schoar of MIT's Sloan School even assert that the more spectacular the growth, the more severe is the drop in performance.

In the framework of so-called benchmarked strategies, a market benchmark is used to measure performance against a market or a composite market index. When the management team achieves a positive performance higher than the benchmark, or if it manages to limit a drop to say −15% while the market has made a negative performance of −20%, the target of outperforming the benchmark is reached.

However, this strategy does not always ensure the market is outperformed, and as Swensen says regarding bonds and domestic stocks, "after deduction of all fees, the average manager produces market-like returns".[2] He recommends avoiding active management in markets regarded as efficient (bonds) or to undertake it with the utmost caution and realistic expectations. He sees fairly illiquid markets as offering more investment opportunities for active management.

As we indicated in the previous section, the returns offered by cash, or simply the inflation rate, are often regarded by investors as the benchmark. In addition, there is often a lack of flexibility in terms of investment in different asset classes, with the originally defined percentages being fixed or allowing few variations.

Furthermore, **behavioural finance** is not sufficiently taken into account. Investors tend to be conservative during bear markets and dynamic during bull periods. In other words, they are very sensitive to losses and always prefer to avoid them.

In our opinion, more consideration of the investor's benchmark (0%, inflation rate, money market rate, etc.) and more **flexibility** should be integrated into portfolio construction. Total flexibility (0–100%), or at least more flexibility within each asset class, should be envisaged. Finally, an asset class should be invested in according to its **attractiveness** at the given time.

Volatility as a measure of risk is still too often taken into account in portfolio construction. However, as we have said, stocks are risky assets, for which risk can be regarded as the

---

[1] Swensen, p. 115.
[2] Swensen, p. 108.

decision to enter or exit the market (or a risky asset). There is a classification of the various risky assets, but an approach based on volatility no longer seems suitable.

Management profiles are sometimes too numerous and the management fee structure poorly adapted. In terms of management costs, management fees, which represent a certain percentage of the assets, are distinct from transaction fees related to the amount of the purchases and sales in the portfolio. These fees diminish the portfolio's final performance. An "all in" fee is a more equitable solution for investors, because a single rate applies regardless of the total number of transactions. Another interesting approach is to charge a management fee covering the minimum operational and administrative management costs, and performance-related fees when performance exceeds a certain level (the LIBOR, for example).

Finally, excessive use of investment funds often has the disadvantage of over-diversification, payment of fees on several levels and the possibility to exit only at NAV (net asset value).

With regard to bull and bear movements – periods of over- and under-performance of investment funds over time – it is better to use index or tracker funds that offer better flexibility (exit and entry at the market price), the possibility of placing stop loss orders and, especially, lower management costs. However, as we will see further on (point 38.2.9 a), both the degree of inefficiency of the asset class being considered and market trends should be taken into account.

37

The Dollar-cost Averaging Approach

This investment method consists in investing the **same amount** at **regular intervals** over a long period, making it possible to buy in both market upswings and downturns and avoid market timing.

In other words, in a bear context, investors lower the average cost per share at each investment, ultimately **reducing** their **average purchase cost**. The following example in Table 37.1 illustrates this approach.

This approach is worthwhile for creating a position, because it enables this to be done in several goes, thereby reducing the average acquisition price. Besides the fees involved with these regular purchases, which can be especially significant for small amounts, investors must regularly have funds available and be able to consider a relatively long investment time horizon. However, for this investment period, they must be willing to endure fluctuations that may be very high, and will affect their entire position – making the average purchase price secondary. Indeed, by following this approach, market exposure increases with each new investment.

As we mentioned earlier, it is better to avoid the stock market at certain times and invest at others. The minimum purchase price is when the market dips, and investors should then buy more, even in absolute terms, as subsequent purchases made at a higher price will just increase their average purchase price.

Moreover, depending on the desired degree of exposure to stocks, this approach cannot be used indefinitely, as the stock percentage may quickly be reached.

Finally, buying a position is only one step, and it is just as important to know how to sell and take the profit according to the target return.

We will simply retain the fact that a position can be created in several stages, but continued investment does not seem appropriate.

Table 37.1 Example of a "Dollar-cost Averaging" approach

	Period 1	Period 2	Period 3	Period 4	Total	Average price	Average cost
Investment	100	100	100	100	400		
Stock price	25	50	20	50		36.3	30.8
Quality	4	2	5	2	13		

38

Our Portfolio Construction Method

We mentioned earlier that it is a good idea first of all to determine the maximum losses that investors are willing to suffer, i.e., to define their proportion of risky assets. In other words, investors must contemplate how much of their assets they can risk losing in the future if they decide to invest. This component may be expressed either as an amount of money or as a percentage of their portfolio. Then, depending on the attractiveness of the asset class at the time of analysis, investments will be made.

Interestingly, Zaker[1] proposes a similar approach for hedge funds. During asset allocation, he suggests defining which share of the portfolio can be illiquid, which amounts to deciding on the share of hedge funds on the basis that this type of investment lacks liquidity. Moreover, depending on market conditions, some strategies will be more suitable than others, which underlines the fact that the attractiveness of an investment varies over time, and depends on the moment that we are performing the analysis.

We suggest taking things one step further by including an illiquid component (hedge fund component) within each asset class according to its strategy. Thus, a long-short equity fund should be accommodated in the equity component, and a convertible arbitrage fund in the bond component.

Before presenting our portfolio construction and management method, it is worth mentioning the flexible approach of de Rotschild's Quam fund, with management that "can vary between 0% and 100% in each classic asset class. [...] The observation period goes from 3 to 6 months, while the management horizon is 15 days. [...]. The fund doesn't avoid risk but controls it."[2] Our management strategy promotes such flexibility, while taking into account the observation and holding periods mentioned previously.

38.1 BASIC PRINCIPLES OF PORTFOLIO CONSTRUCTION

Investors' portfolios should be constructed according to their **specific objectives** and **needs**, and obviously their **risk profile**, i.e., after having determined the share of their holdings they are prepared to risk.

Allocation between the various **asset classes** will then be carried out by combining several analyses. Next, depending on market conditions, the **attractiveness** of one or more asset classes will be determined. This analysis must be performed dynamically, so that changes in

---

[1] See presentation and article by Zaker.
[2] Garessus, *Le Temps*.

market conditions can be taken into account, and, more importantly, in an entirely flexible manner to allow for adaptation to these conditions.

This allocation is much more important than the diversification ensured within each asset class. In addition, negative or weak correlations have a positive effect on the portfolio, because they help reduce the portfolio's risk and improve its return.

So the first step is deciding, for each asset class, whether or not it should be included. The next step is to make choices within the selected asset classes.

Finally, it is useful to include transaction costs, fees associated with the investment such as custodial fees, and ultimately tax, which may have a significant impact on performance.

In terms of portfolio management, we should also bear in mind these simple rules:

- always trade a small number of securities that you know well;
- respect the existence of cycles (trends);
- be patient;
- take advantage of a few opportunities a year.

Before presenting our approach, we would like to look at Peter Navarro's rules for investing.

38.1.1   10 rules for protecting your capital

In his book, Navarro[3] recommends the following 10 rules to help investors protect their capital and trade on the markets effectively.

a) Cut your losses

It is essential to know how to cut your losses when the situation deteriorates, in order to limit them and especially to reduce the investor's opportunity costs. It is better to sell a security, even for a small loss, and reinvest the capital in another security with better prospects, which can not only recover the original losses but generate gains.

b) Set intelligent stop losses

It is also important to decide on the level of losses you are willing to accept and to set stop losses accordingly. You can use a mental stop loss, but you have to have the discipline to sell once the limit is passed. This solution does leave a little more time to evaluate the situation, but the investor has to follow the stock attentively every day. This type of order can also be set directly on the market at a defined level, but we recommend respecting the following rules:

- leave enough room for the stock to fluctuate;
- do not set stop losses near important technical levels (supports, resistances);
- avoid round numbers, such as 10, 20 or 100.

---

[3]Navarro, pp. 92–106.

c) Let your profits run

Equally as important as knowing how to cut your losses is knowing how to let your profits run without liquidating too early. This isn't easy in practice, and setting a return target for the position held will help.

d) Never, ever, let a big winner become a loser

To lock in profits, or at least most of them, the stop loss price must be constantly redefined according to the stock price movement.

e) Never average down on a loser

As the saying goes, don't catch a falling knife. Similarly, it is unwise to increase your capital on a stock that keeps losing value with the excuse that the price is going down. It's best to pick another stock with a better outlook.

f) Don't churn your portfolio

The number of trades should be limited. At times, when there is no defined market direction or too much uncertainty above its development, it can be wiser to do nothing.

g) Use market orders to capture the price movement in a trending market

In a market with a defined trend, it's better to use market orders to avoid having to follow the market and modify your order after each unsuccessful attempt.

h) Use limit orders to capture the spread[4] in a trading range market

Limit orders, on the other hand, can be used in a market with no clear trend.

i) Never use a market order before the opening bell or with a new IPO

As prices can swing wildly just after opening or before an Initial Public Offering (IPO), it is not advisable to set orders at these moments.

j) Choose the right broker

Depending on the prices and commissions offered, it can sometimes be necessary to change brokers.

38.1.2   The 12 rules of risk management

Navarro[5] also suggests following 12 basic rules in terms of risk management.

---

[4]Difference between the ask and bid price.
[5]Taken from Navarro, pp. 108–122.

a) Watch the macroeconomic event calendar very carefully

It is essential to keep up with the calendar of macroeconomic events, such as central bank decisions on interest rate levels or the publication of the price index, to minimise risks of potential reversals or excessive price fluctuations following these announcements.

The impact of a macroeconomic event will depend on the context in which the information is released and whether it will attract the market's attention. A rising unemployment rate during an economic boom will have less impact than during an economic slowdown or early recession.

b) When in doubt, go flat

When macroeconomic signals are equivocal and the market direction is hard to ascertain, it is better to wait for more clarity and, for example, invest in money market instruments.

c) Beware the earnings announcement trap

Before any transaction, it is crucial to consider the announcement period for quarterly corporate results. Companies announce their earnings at the end of each quarter, and depending on their fit with estimates, prices may fluctuate strongly.

A Wall Street adage says "buy the rumour, sell the news". Indeed, a rumour of better-than-expected results can push the stock price up, driven first by traders, then by the general public jumping on the bandwagon. Some traders already start exiting at this point. When the results announced are higher than the consensus estimate, the stock rises even more, driven by the general public, but sometimes it drops sharply afterwards because of another expected result which was not reached. Earnings can be lower, equal to or higher than expected, but it is important to differentiate between the consensus estimate and the so-called "whisper number".

The consensus estimate is based on subjective judgements by analysts who are covering the stock and receive estimates from the company, which often tries to be cautious. This estimate is therefore biased, and can be circumvented by referring instead to the "whisper number". This includes a much broader panel of opinions and provides a better basis for evaluating earnings. Navarro suggests using websites like www.Whispernumber or www.Earningswhispers.com.

The stock price may also fluctuate before the event, so that once the announcement is made, if it meets expectations, the price will remain steady.

d) Always trade in liquid stocks

Adequate liquidity makes it possible to enter and exit a position very quickly, thereby reducing downside risk potentially suffered by the seller. Navarro recommends never trading a stock that has an average daily volume below 500 000 shares.

e) Trade enough volume

The weight of a position in a portfolio will depend on each investor, who has to determine the losses he or she is willing to undergo, but it should not exceed 10% of invested capital, or 20% at the most.

f) Make sure your trades are not highly correlated

It is important to ensure diversification between different weakly correlated industries to minimise the portfolio's risk. Several highly correlated positions concentrate risk.

g) Match price volatility to your risk

Although Navarro associates the level of risk with the level of volatility, this is mainly to suggest placing stop loss orders with regard to this volatility so as not set them too close to a stock's normal margin of fluctuation.

h) Manage your entry and exit risk

It is often better to buy a position in several goes, which gives time for the expected direction to be confirmed. It is also wise to book your profits in several goes, to profit from a possible market rise.

i) Beware of trading on margin

When using leverage, it is essential to place stop loss orders to limit losses, and to determine acceptable losses based on capital that is really available, i.e., not borrowed.

j) Analyse your trades

It is crucial to be able to analyse your trades, especially your losers, so as not to repeat the same errors twice (market order before the opening bell, stop loss not set or set too close to the price, stock bought before an earnings announcement or some macroeconomic news, etc.).

k) Do your research

Before each trade, you have to do your homework. First, you need to be familiar with the different industries, their leaders and followers. Then it's important to identify how macroeconomic events (according to the calendar) affect the stocks, while bearing in mind their technical characteristics (volumes, spreads, fluctuation margins, moving averages, etc.). Finally, a fundamental analysis should be carried out.

l) Ignore hot tips and other free advice

Navarro recommends ignoring analysts – who rarely advise selling stock because of the eternal conflict of interest between the analyst and their employer – and friends' advice, but to make decisions based on your own judgement.

38.2   THE PORTFOLIO CONSTRUCTION PROCESS

The following approach can ultimately be summarised as a process in **nine steps**, which should be reviewed regularly (at least once a year).

38.2.1   The investor's life objectives

The first step is to determine the investor's goals, taking into account not only his or her **professional** and **personal projects** but also his or her **cultural, social** and **religious** background.

38.2.2   The investor's life cycle and investment time horizon

The second step is to identify the investor's current stage of life:

- accumulation (asset accumulation and ability to generate future income);
- consolidation (income exceeds spending);
- spending (use of income and possible consumption of capital);
- inheritance transfer.

Then, depending on the investor's age and need for liquidity, an investment time horizon can also be determined.

38.2.3   Choosing a reference currency

This step simply involves defining a reference currency according to the investor's country of **residence**, **expenditure** and **income**. The portfolio's performance will be assessed in this currency.

38.2.4   Evaluating the risk profile

First, this means identifying the investor's **ability** to **take risks**, i.e., defining his or her **financial limits** according to his or her various commitments, available assets and liquidity needs. In other words, it is necessary to conduct a personal assessment like a balance sheet (assets *versus* liabilities).

Then an evaluation is required to see if the investor is **risk averse (to losses)** or if, on the contrary, he or she likes taking risks when investing, within his or her financial limits. This means finding out if the investor is a "player" or instead looking for more certain returns. The advisor plays a key role here; it is he or she who has to determine this sensitivity to risk.

Finally, it will be necessary to ensure that the investor is **conscious** of the **risk** taken when making investment decisions. Indeed, we have seen that depending on their level of experience and the strength of their psychological biases, investors can react irrationally, and therefore under- or overestimate the risks taken.

According to these three aspects, it will be possible to qualify the investor as more conservative, moderate (balanced) or dynamic. In **practice**, banks often use **questionnaires** that aim to define a risk profile based on these three aspects, which will help determine the **asset allocation**.

As such, it is interesting to note the approach developed by Bhfs[6] (Behavioural Finance Solution) to evaluate investors' risk profiles and suggest the asset allocation. We suggest comparing this allocation with the strategic allocation resulting from our process, as in our opinion, adjustments and additional discussions are always necessary.

38.2.5   Estimating a return target

An expected return estimate can also be established. This return target should then be compared regularly with the actual return resulting from the chosen portfolio construction and the decisions made. The idea, in a way, is to set the investor's **individual benchmark**. Investors may also mention a benchmark at which they would gain personal satisfaction from their investments.

It must be highlighted that this return target should not be used as the basis for constructing the portfolio. Our approach does not concentrate on returns, which are difficult to anticipate, but rather on **managing the risks** that make up the portfolio.

Investors may first express this target as an **amount** of money, which often corresponds to their spending or cash requirements. Sometimes, investors aim for a certain level of income at retirement age. The practical example at the end of this chapter will serve to illustrate this.

An **expected rate** of **return** may also be mentioned, and this usually is based on average historical returns for the different asset classes.

However, the target indicated must be **realistic**, considering interest rate levels and market conditions. Furthermore, historical returns should be treated with caution, as at best they can only help formulate estimates for uncertain future returns. As we noted earlier, we favour an approach based on risk management over one based on return estimates.

Furthermore, the desired return must **correspond** to both the available **capital** and the investor's **risk profile**. Any inconsistencies must, without fail, be identified at this stage of the analysis.

Finally, as we noted to begin with, the desired return must obviously be **positive** and, if possible, **higher** than the **average inflation rate** in order to preserve the investor's real wealth over time. In our opinion, the rate indicated should be adjusted for inflation, unless the investor has already incorporated this into his or her target. Furthermore, net return – that is return after tax – should ideally be taken into account.

---

[6]See www.bhfs.ch.

38.2.6   The investor's tax rate

Next, the rate of **income** and **capital gains taxes** should be taken into account to define the investment universe more precisely. For example, in a context of high income tax and no capital gains tax, low dividend stocks with high growth potential should be favoured for the stock component.

38.2.7   Determining the proportion of risky assets

The next step involves deciding on the share of risky assets that the investor can hold in the portfolio, given his or her financial limits and ability to take risks. In other words, investors have to decide how much of their capital they are willing to risk and, in the worst-case scenario, lose completely.

However, the degree of capital loss can be distributed and qualified. For example, an investor may accept to lose 10% of his or her initial capital entirely, and to lose a large proportion (50%) of 20% of his or her capital, instead of simply asserting a willingness to "risk" 30% of the total capital.

Once this proportion has been established, it should be distributed between the different categories of risk that we defined earlier. This step makes it possible to set the upper limits of exposure to each asset class.

38.2.8   Evaluating the expected degree of liquidity
(share of illiquid assets)

The investor should also define the required speed at which assets can be realised, which will help determine whether less liquid assets can be included in the portfolio. This proportion will designate the investor's potential exposure to hedge funds.

If he or she accepts this exposure, the investor will need to choose one or more investment strategies, which will be included in the corresponding asset class as an alternative strategy in that class.

38.2.9   Portfolio construction and management

We stated early on that future returns are hard to predict, and estimates of the different probabilities associated with these returns are hard to make. Consequently, any portfolio construction method that relies on these criteria is likely to give random or uncertain results; it is difficult to obtain a reliable, precise result using estimates.

Portfolio management involves managing the various risks that make up the portfolio, by deciding whether or not to be exposed to a particular asset class. Portfolios should be constructed using the same reasoning: guided by risk constraints and not expected returns. We believe that managers should not manage expected returns but risks, and this is how they create added value. They can do this using the framework we are about to define.

a) Strategic allocation and type of management

Based on the investor's risk profile, the final step of the process is to determine the portfolio's strategic allocation, i.e., to define a targeted distribution of capital between the different asset classes. As Swensen points out, "policy asset allocation dominates portfolio returns".[7]

Depending on the investor's profile, some asset classes will be excluded and others favoured.

In terms of weighting, it is possible to define fixed weights. However, we recommend more flexibility within each class and avoiding an excessively narrow range of fluctuation, to ensure the greatest possible **flexibility** of investment choices.

We suggest defining first of all a **maximum proportion** per asset class, according to the type of risk profile. A maximum weight per position can also be defined at this stage (for example, a maximum of 5% per bond or 2% in an individual stock). As Swensen notes, "committing more than 25 percent or 30 percent to an asset class poses the danger of overconcentration".[8] So we suggest also defining a limit by category.

A **minimum weight** for each of the asset classes should also be set. The degree of fluctuation, which will allow the lower limit to be set, will ultimately depend on the degree of freedom that the investor wants to have or to allow his or her manager, as well as the desired magnitude within each asset class. In other words, it is important to decide if an entry into or exit from an asset class should be total or partial, and therefore if the investor wants to maintain a minimum exposure per asset class. To refer again to Swensen, he says that "committing less than 5 percent or 10 percent of a fund to a particular investment makes little sense; the small allocation holds no potential to influence overall portfolio results".[9] So, once the decision to invest has been made, we suggest an investment of at least 3–5% in an asset class so that it can have an impact on the portfolio's final return.

The investor's **degree of conviction** about the ability to apply this approach will, in our opinion, define this lower limit. For example, investors with a weak conviction will prefer a bigger "fixed" component and a smaller "flexible" component. Conversely, investors whose conviction is strong will allow a much wider margin for fluctuation so that they can achieve optimal positioning in relation to market conditions.

Our Advice

We suggest first defining a **maximum weight** per asset class, and possibly per individual position. An exposure of 75% should be the general maximum limit for an asset class. Individual positions ideally should not exceed 10%. It is obviously possible to set lower limits (5% maximum per individual position, for example).

The **minimum weight** will depend on the minimum degree of exposure sought and on the desired degree of flexibility within the asset class. The limit may be 0%, but once a decision to invest has been made, we believe that an investment should represent at least 3–5%.

---

[7]Swensen, p. 132.
[8]Swensen, p. 135.
[9]Swensen, p. 135.

Next, the investor needs to determine the **type of management** he or she prefers for each asset class, namely passive or active management.

Passive management seeks to replicate the performance of a benchmark index; index management (using tracker funds or ETFs) is the most common form. This offers enough diversification, good liquidity and helps achieves a performance consistent with the underlying, "neither more nor less", with low management fees. However, there is a risk of concentration, as market capitalisation weighting of indexes can sometimes lead to a significant concentration of large cap stocks.

Conversely, **active management** aims for a better performance than the benchmark index by making specific bets on the stocks that make up the index, and offers greater performance potential (stock picking in equity funds, for example). Besides the risk of under-performance and the risk related to the manager's decisions, the fees entailed by this type of strategy are higher.

Our Advice

We suggest evaluating, for each asset class, the **opportunities for outperformance**, i.e., the degree of efficiency of the class in question.

If these **opportunities** are **weak**, as is usually the case for bonds, **passive management** using tracker funds or ETFs should be favoured.

If, on the other hand, these opportunities are more common or significant, such as for stocks (depending on the region in question) or less liquid markets, then **active management** is better. A combination of passive and active management is entirely possible.

In the classic, so-called **"core-satellite" approach**, passive management of the core component is combined with active management of the satellite component.

Some, like the Wegelin bank,[10] takes things further for the core component by making a selection within the passive section aimed at eliminating certain securities from the benchmark index while maintaining sufficient diversification. Various criteria, such as historical earnings and free cash flow or the return on equity, are used to make these choices, but the end result should stay close to the reference index.

The minimum variance portfolio, as it is constructed and managed by Unigestion, discussed earlier, adopts a sort of improved passive management approach. The performance of such a portfolio is practically identical to its benchmark index, but with less volatility, which means it can outperform the benchmark in the long term. Thanks to their selection of stocks within the original investment universe and different weightings, they are able to determine a better allocation in terms of risk.

---

[10]See pp. 152–156, Tolle, Hutter, Rüthemann, Wohlwend.

Our Advice

We readily recommend **improved passive management** in order to achieve a more homogeneous exposure to a market, and to reject stocks that are "only" in an index because of their large capitalisation – which are excessively weighted in the index – or securities that we don't want to hold in the portfolio temporarily or at all.

In terms of portfolio construction, it is also possible in a given asset class to define a minimum investment for the "core" component – held, for example, in a tracker fund (market index, improved or not) – and to allow a certain margin of fluctuation for the "satellite" component, which will constitute the active part of this class. The investor can then either increase exposure to the tracker fund, or pick individual stocks or favour certain sectors, but can under no circumstances go below the minimum threshold. For example, if this threshold is set at 10% (situation no 1), he or she will have a lesser margin than in the situation of total freedom (situation no 2) – see Table 38.1.

Table 38.1 Example of possible Min. and Max. ranges for an asset class

Situation no 1	Asset class	Min.	Max.
	Stocks	10%	20%
Situation no 2	Asset class	Min.	Max.
	Stocks	0%	20%

We could even imagine situations where tactical decisions are no longer made directly in relation to the basic strategic allocation, but delegated to the different managers in the active component. A strategic allocation is therefore defined for each asset class, with a part managed passively and another part managed actively. The tactical decisions will be made for the active component by the manager or managers of the chosen investment funds (situation no 3) – see Table 38.2.

Table 38.2 Example of possible distribution between active and passive management for an asset class

Situation no 3	Asset class	Passive	Active
	Stocks (20% total)	10%	10%

Our Advice

Once the decisions are made regarding active and passive management, the investor must also decide on the **level of delegation** he or she wishes to allow.

Indeed, besides the resources and time necessary for all these analyses, investors have to reflect on whether they have the **skills** necessary to manage their portfolio.

> If their answer is yes, they can manage the portfolio themselves according to the investment model presented here. Otherwise, we sincerely advise delegating this management to a professional (manager).

Note also that investors or managers themselves tend occasionally to manage a portfolio more conservatively and take fewer risks than necessary. Past experiences of financial crises and sharp market corrections, which encourage increased caution, can lead to a **conservative bias**. The use of objective criteria and keeping "emotions" at arm's length help limit this bias.

In the end, the upper and lower limits for each asset class will be defined depending on the risk profile, and can be summarised in a table – see Table 38.3.

Table 38.3   Asset allocation chart

Degree of risk	Asset class	Min. %	Max. %
Categories presenting the **lowest risk**	**Money Market Funds** **Fiduciary Deposits** **Government Bonds**		
Categories presenting a **low to moderate risk**	**Real Estate (Direct)** **Investment Grade** **Corporate Bonds**		
Categories presenting a **moderate to high risk**	**Real Estate (Indirect)** **High Yield** **Bonds** **Metals** **Commodities**		
Categories presenting a **high risk**	**Stocks from developed countries** **Stocks from emerging countries** **Private Equity**		

Management of the portfolio will therefore be governed by these limits. The different weights assigned within each asset class will depend specifically on management choices and the attractiveness of each asset class at the time of analysis. For each class, passive (improved or not) or active management will be informed by diversification requirements and opportunities for outperformance.

For stocks, we recommend adopting a more detailed approach that includes the various industries and sectors we described earlier, and the main geographical regions. Within this asset class, defined by the upper and lower limits, managers will make specific investments according to their view of the cycles, and choose the industries and sectors they believe to be positioned the best.

The table below (Table 38.4) will help them to categorise and improve the monitoring of their investments.

Table 38.4   Stock allocation chart by sector, industry and region

Sector	Industry	Europe	Switzerland UK	USA Lat. Am.	Asia
Energy	Energy				
Materials	Chemicals Construction equipment Metals and minerals Pulp and paper				
Industry	Capital goods Business services Transport and logistics				
Consumer Discretionary	Automobiles and automobile components Consumer durables, apparel, textile and luxury goods Hotels, restaurants and leisure Media Distribution				
Consumer staples	Food and staples retailing Beverages Food products Tobacco Household products and personal care				
Health	Health equipment and services Biotechnology Pharmaceuticals				
Finance	Banks Diversified financial services Insurance Real estate				
Information Technology	Software and services IT equipment Semi-conductors and equipment for their manufacture				
Telecommuni-cations	Diversified services Mobile communications				
Utilities	Utilities				

For bonds, once the level of credit quality has been defined, the choice of different issues will depend mainly on the desired duration and therefore on the expected movement of interest rates.

For real estate, we recommend first favouring investments in the country of the investor's reference currency, then looking at foreign currency investments. It will therefore be necessary to decide on the regions or countries to favour.

These considerations on the incorporation and management of different asset classes have brought us to the point where we can address tactical allocation.

b) Tactical allocation

Once the strategic allocation has been determined, the various **tactical weights** must be chosen according to the **attractiveness** of each asset class, macroeconomic and psychological factors and also the results of fundamental and technical analyses.

An overall market analysis should therefore be carried out to determine the asset classes to favour in constructing the portfolio, according to the set margins of fluctuation. While selecting asset classes, we suggest constantly asking the following question: "If I had cash right now, what would I invest in?"

Our approach stops short of market timing, which aims to anticipate market movements in order to position investments optimally. Use of the multi-force approach does not seek to forecast market movements, but rather to determine, on the basis of current conditions, whether or not it is appropriate to invest or remain in the market. This analysis should be carried out on a regular basis, ideally weekly, and at the very least monthly.

Going back to our earlier barbecue example, market timing seeks to advise our sausage-lover whether or not he should go to the butchers on Monday in anticipation of the weather we're going to have at the weekend. Our approach, on the other hand, aims to help our friend do his shopping on Saturday according to the weather outside at the time he has to make his decision.

Swensen recommends avoiding market timing, which tends to weaken portfolio performance. For **institutional portfolio** management, where the time horizon is very long, much longer than that of private investors, management should indeed respect the **basic strategic allocation**, rebalanced regularly to maintain the chosen proportions.

However, for **private investors** whose time horizon is usually shorter and whose objectives change more quickly, a **more flexible approach** should be applied. We asserted earlier that this process is not focused on expected returns but on managing the various risks that make up the portfolio. Any element of forecasting should therefore also be rejected, to focus on current conditions.

i) Choice of investments

Once a particular asset class has been retained, investment choices must be made within the asset class using the **top-down approach**, which means deciding first on a region and sector and then on an individual security.

As we indicated earlier, we recommend following a core-satellite management strategy by building a core of, for example, index funds, and then making a few bets on individual stocks.

The index fund used in the core component should be sufficiently diversified and should faithfully represent the movement of the market the investors wish to be exposed to. To avoid excessive concentration in a particular sector, or to avoid exposure to certain stocks, it is possible to adapt the composition of the benchmark index by eliminating stocks that don't meet certain criteria or that represent too great a weight in the index. So it can be wise to carry out some stock selection.

In terms of the **form of investment** in individual stocks, structured products can also be used depending on the outlook. Instead of buying a stock on the market, buying an option, a reverse convertible, a capital protected product or a maximum-return product in a set fluctuation range can also be considered. In this way, real exposure to a market or sector can be modified.

In terms of individual stock picking, it is worth mentioning an observation of Jesse Livermore's, a trader who wrote his memoirs of the early 1900s.[11] In a bear market most stocks fall, and in a bull market most rise. However, the average investor doesn't want to be told whether it's a bull or bear market, but prefers to hear which particular stock to buy or sell. He wants to have something for nothing, doesn't want to work and doesn't even want to bother thinking about it. It's certainly easier to think in terms of individual stocks but, above all, it's the **general market movements** that are worth studying, as they are what make the difference.

Finally, in terms of stock selection, it can be worth determining an observation period (six–twelve months, for example) and a holding period (three–six months, for example).

> **Our Advice**
>
> We believe it is better to define trends and use index funds accordingly, with a few bets on individual stocks. It is not these few positions that will make the difference, but rather the general market movement or movement of a particular sector.

ii) Foreign currency management

Foreign currency exposure must also be managed according to currency forecasts, although their development is very hard to predict in practice. As Swensen notes, "At more than 20 to 25 percent of portfolio assets, the currency exposure constitutes a source of incremental risk, suggesting consideration of some corrective action."[12]

In our opinion, analysing the **outlook** of the investment currency is crucial. Indeed, as we mentioned before, short-term fluctuations can be very violent and affect the portfolio's total performance. The investor's or manager's **degree of conviction** will essentially determine the level of currency risk hedging.

Technical analysis is perhaps the most useful tool for determining the outlook for exchange rates. Some use the notions of absolute and relative purchasing power parity (PPP) to determine the expected currency movements.

Absolute PPP: The exchange rate between two currencies equals the ratio of the two countries' price level of a fixed basket of goods and services.

Relative PPP: The expected rate of depreciation of the local currency is determined by the difference between domestic inflation and foreign inflation. Empirically, it has been

---

[11] Taken from Lefèvre, p. 71.
[12] Swensen, p. 219.

observed that the currencies of countries with high inflation depreciate. The inflation rate differential between two countries may indeed play a role in exchange rate movements. For example, if inflation is stronger inside the country than outside, domestic products become more expensive and economic agents will tend to look towards foreign markets (increasing imports), while foreign agents will buy fewer domestic products (reducing exports).

The country with the higher inflation rate will see its currency pushed down in order to conserve purchasing power parity. This variation in exchange rate lets domestic prices adjust so that the values exchanged in goods, services and assets are perpetually equalised.

Furthermore, note that capital tends to be invested in the currencies of countries offering the most advantageous compensation. These inflows can lead to an increase in demand for the currency and therefore an increase in its price.

iii) Rebalancing rules

When holdings invested in an asset class remain within the acceptable range of fluctuation, no particular decisions are required. However, when the maximum limit is exceeded, the portfolio needs to be reconfigured according to the established rebalancing rules.

First, we might consider simply reducing the inflated component enough to bring exposure to the asset class back down to the maximum limit. Another option is to pull right back to the minimum level of exposure, or to an intermediate level. Ultimately, the choice will be linked to the attractiveness of the asset class at the time the threshold is crossed and to its future prospects. Depending on market conditions, it could be better either to maintain a maximum exposure or, on the contrary, to book the profits and favour a more cautious approach for the future by reducing exposure to a lower threshold.

Proceeds from the sale can be allocated between the other asset classes, or to one class in particular.

Independently of the final thresholds chosen, it is essential to set **precise** rebalancing rules and to apply them **rigorously** in managing the portfolio.

c) Comparison of actual returns with target returns

The process that we have described is dynamic. Consequently, the expected return target should be compared regularly with the actual return resulting from the chosen portfolio construction and the decisions put into effect.

We often tend to assess portfolios on an annual basis. It is entirely possible to modify the observation period by setting, for example, a monthly or quarterly comparison, with rates adjusted accordingly.[13]

---

[13]For example, an annual rate of 5% corresponds to a monthly rate of 0.4074% on a 360-day basis. Actual monthly performance should be compared to this figure.

If the actual return deviates from the expected return, **explanations** must be sought using recent data, to determine whether the difference is due to:

• an unrealistic target;
• poor tactical allocation choices (under- or over-weighting of one or more asset classes);
• poor basic strategic allocation that can never or rarely generate the expected return;
• poor application of the model;
• luck/bad luck.

We also recommend performing this analysis when the actual return is close to or higher than the expected return target.

38.3 A PRACTICAL EXAMPLE OF PORTFOLIO CONSTRUCTION

To conclude this chapter, we will illustrate our reasoning with a practical example. Mr Dupont, aged 45, has savings amounting to 750 000 euros, to which can be added the proceeds from the sale of his magnificent yacht that he recently sold for 50 000 euros, and an account with 250 000 euros invested in short-term deposit. In terms of investment, he is willing to grant considerable flexibility to his manager.

Under his savings plan (interest rate set at 2%), he can expect to have a sum of 1 470 000 euros at retirement age, which would provide him with an annual income of nearly 90 000 euros for 20 years.

He doesn't want to touch the 750 000 euros, and hopes to constitute enough capital to live comfortably after 65. He says he is willing to "risk" the 250 000 euros but only 100 000 euros can be risked "in full". The 50 000 euros will soon be spent, as he is intending to buy a new car.

Mr Dupont is still working and has no major expenses. He is in perfect health and expects to live to 85. According to his estimates, and taking into account his various commitments (particularly his mortgage), he hopes for an annual income after retirement of about 120 000 euros.

Mr Dupont pays wealth tax. He is taxed on both capital gains and income. Liquidity is very important to him, especially if he is faced with unexpected expenses.

Mr Dupont lives in France, but spends a lot of time in Verbier (Switzerland) where he owns a chalet bought some time ago by his parents. In winter, he goes there almost every weekend, and he stays there for at least a month each summer (about two months a year in total).

In view of these details, Mr Dupont's profile seems fairly conservative and his ability to take risks is limited. With his fortune of 1 000 000 euros (750 000 in savings and 250 000 from his account) and the sum he is willing to risk, we can consider that 25% can be invested in risky assets, but only 10% in really risky assets.

In terms of reference currency, we can consider the euro as the reference currency, but with a possible exposure in Swiss francs of 15% to 20% (2/12) to cover his need for cash in Switzerland.

As for expected returns, Mr Dupont has indicated that he would like an annual income of 120 000 euros, but it is important to make a distinction between the capital made up of savings and the capital he intends to invest to generate additional income.

In view of the desired annual income of 120 000 euros and the income generated by savings (90 000 euros), the additional amount required is 30 000 euros. At this stage, two fairly complicated calculations need to be made.

Firstly, we need to determine the amount of capital required at retirement age in order to provide the additional annual income for a certain number of years. Note that after each payment, the remaining capital generates a return. For our example, this amounts to calculating the present value of capital that our investor will need at retirement age in order to earn an additional income of 30 000 euros a year for a period that we will set at 20 years (with a life expectancy of 85 and retirement at 65).

Using the formula for discounting annuities over a period of 20 years and a rate of 2%, we arrive at the sum of 490 543 euros that will be required at 65 to allow for 20 annuities of 30 000 to be paid for 20 years.

$$\text{Present value of an annuity} = \frac{\text{Annuity}}{k} * \left(1 - \frac{1}{(1+k)^n}\right)$$

where k = discount rate and n = number of years.

Secondly, now that we know the capital required at age 65, we need to calculate the amount of the annual instalments to be paid from now until retirement age to build up this capital, also taking into account an annual return on this capital being accumulated and potentially accumulated. For our example, given Mr Dupont's current age, these instalments will be paid over a 20-year period. To simplify things, we can deduct the 250 000 from the 490 543 at this point. We will leave the 50 000 euros for Mr Dupont's cash needs.

This time, using the future value formula over 20 years and a rate of 2%, we arrive at an annuity of 9900 euros. This is the sum that Mr Dupont will have to set aside each year in order to constitute a sum of 240 543 euros in 20 years' time, or by the age of 65. Thus, at 65 he will have the total amount of 490 543 required.

$$\text{Final value of an annuity} = \text{Annuity} * \left(\frac{(1+k)^n - 1}{k}\right)$$

where k = discount rate and n = number of years.

Besides the length of the payment period and life expectancy, the really decisive parameter is the discount rate. We suggest using a fairly conservative rate of 2%, or 3% at the most.

Finally, by dividing the annual sum to be generated by the capital available for investment, we obtain the target rate of return. Given the available sum of 250 000 euros and an expected revenue of 9900 per year, the return target is 3.96%. This is a nominal rate and the annual income indicated does not include taxes.

In terms of the rate of return, the real rate can be obtained by adding the inflation rate, but we are considering here that our rate covers an average inflation rate of 2–3%, so will not need adjusting.

However, in terms of taxes, we recommend considering the amount obtained after taxes. Therefore, the gross income needs to be recalculated so we can then infer a new target rate of return. Ideally, for the annual amount generated by investments, the capital gains component should be distinguished from the income component, so the corresponding tax rates can be applied.

The target return arrived at, whether gross or net of taxes, should be regularly compared to the portfolio's actual return.

In terms of strategic allocation, we will only consider asset classes with low to moderate risk. As Mr Dupont is happy to grant considerable flexibility in terms of investments, we can allow for almost total fluctuation within asset classes.

Looking first at money market funds (or fiduciary deposits) and government bonds, the entire portfolio can be invested in these classes, however with a minimum exposure of 15% to 20%. For corporate bonds, the minimum is set at 15% with a maximum of 35%. These three holdings represent the "fixed" 50% of the portfolio, with the manager able either to increase these weights or invest in other asset classes.

It is possible to incorporate up to 5% real estate, or commodities/precious metals up to 3%.

In terms of equity, the proportion can vary from 0% to 25%, which is the limit "indicated" by Mr Dupont. However, for an exposure of 25% to risky assets, we need to include indirect real estate, stocks and commodities/precious metals. In our opinion, if these three holdings are present at any one time, exposure to stocks should not represent more than 17% or 20%.

Finally, considering Mr Dupont's requirement for liquidity, hedge fund investments are unsuitable. On this basis, we could propose the following strategic allocation (Table 38.5).

Table 38.5   Strategic allocation proposed to Mr Dupont

Asset class	Min.	Max.
Money Market Funds/Fiduciary Deposits	20%	65%
Government Bonds	20%	65%
Corporate Bonds (high grade)	10%	35%
Indirect Real Estate	0%	5%
Developed Equity (80% index and 20% individual stocks)	0%	25%
Commodities/Precious Metals	0%	3%

According to the attractiveness of each of these classes and to market conditions, the manager will determine specific (tactical) allocations, culminating in a portfolio with different weightings at any given moment. Then, according to market movements and choices that will have been made, these weightings will change, delivering a certain performance which will need to be compared with the target.

Part X
Attractiveness of the Different Asset Classes

Now we can examine the attractiveness of each asset class. The method of portfolio construction we propose combines the following four approaches based on:

- macroeconomic movements;
- fundamental analysis;
- trends (technical analysis);
- behavioural finance.

The idea is to identify the **forces** that are likely to push prices up or down. The **resulting force** should give us the direction of the market and therefore help us decide on the **attractiveness** of that class.

The table below (Table X.1) summarises the possibilities available to investors:

Table X.1 Consequences for investment according to the decision and the market

Decision	Bull market	Bear market
Enter / Hold position	Positive decision	Negative decision
Exit / Stay in cash	Bad decision (Opportunity cost)	Good decision

In the event of a bull market, the decision to invest or hold a position is the most profitable. If investors decide to exit the market or to stay in cash, they will obviously not participate in the rise, but the most they will have lost is an investment opportunity.

In a bear market, the decision to hold a position or enter the market clearly leads to the worst possible situations, as investors will make a capital loss. However, if they decide to exit the market or to stay in cash, they are making a good choice that will preserve their capital.

An analysis using the four forces will allow the market movement to be identified. Then, according to the margins of exposure allowed for each asset class (minimum/maximum exposure), investors will have to decide whether or not they want to invest and in which proportions. The answer to this last question will depend on their **personal experience**, their **knowledge** and **analytical abilities**, as well as their **conviction** about the market.

Before reviewing the four forces, we would like to go back over the attractiveness of each asset class for investors. We should reiterate that their incorporation into the portfolio must depend on their attractiveness at the time of analysis, and should fit within the framework defined by the strategic allocation.

Asset Classes

39.1 MONEY MARKET INVESTMENTS

This asset class – the least risky – usually represents a significant part of **conservative portfolios**. It also includes government bonds with a maturity of less than 12 months. Depending on the configuration of the portfolio, a fixed proportion of money market instruments may be necessary. However, because of their low real return, this asset class should be limited in every portfolio.

The return from a money market investment will essentially depend on the market **interest rates** and the **rate of inflation**. If inflation is high and the nominal rate is low, the real rate (nominal rate minus inflation rate) will be low, which may lead investors to consider other asset classes to prevent inflation "eating up" their capital over time.

As such, it is important first of all to compare the money market rates with the rate of inflation to determine whether the investment will at least cover inflation. Then it is useful to compare these rates with the returns of high-grade government and corporate bonds.

If the money market investment is considered worthwhile, the **counterparty** and **maturities** should then be carefully selected according to the investor's need for liquidity and the outlook for interest rates according to current and expected inflation.

When using our model, the most important factors to examine are the various forces acting on interest rates.

39.2 BONDS

Bonds should be incorporated into a portfolio according to the attractiveness of this asset class at the time of analysis, but their integration also depends on the investor's need for **regular income** to be generated over time. They usually represent a significant proportion of conservative portfolios.

Generally, the interest rates at longer maturities should be considered for bonds. These depend on the markets' ability to control inflation and are also influenced by the future financing needs and capacities of public and private agents.

Bonds are selected according to the issue's **rating**, **yield to maturity** and the **maturity** in question or, more precisely, the **duration**, which depends on expectations for interest rate movements. So, it is best to be positioned at the point on the yield curve that will be the least sensitive to interest rate variations. Interest rate developments and the control of inflation should be analysed.

If interest rates are expected to rise, it is better to buy short-term bonds which are less sensitive to interest rate variations due to their low duration. Conversely, when interest rates are expected to fall, long-term bonds should be favoured. The "exact" positioning in terms of maturity will depend on the expected evolution of the yield curve (flat, normal or inverted yield curve).

If fairly high inflation is expected, which portends rising interest rates, investors may decide to stay in cash or to choose short-term bonds. However, if they are very keen for regular income, by necessity perhaps, they can use inflation-indexed bonds to guard against the negative effect of a rates hike on prices.

It is also useful to examine the **difference** between **government** and **corporate** bonds to determine both the attractiveness of the latter and, especially, the overall economic situation. Indeed, this gap increases during a recession and decreases in periods of economic growth. Sovereign bonds, because of their usually modest returns and their negative sensitivity to inflation, should only make up a limited proportion of a portfolio.

The multi-forces model can be used to determine the various forces that will influence the price of bonds. However, the use of this approach is limited when the investment is held to maturity. In this case, investors seek simply to block a return over a given period, to earn coupons and recover the invested capital at the moment of final redemption. However, it is useful to be aware of the factors that influence bond prices.

39.3 STOCKS

As two independent analysts justly note, "investors should therefore base their expectations of gain on earnings growth".[1]

When buying stocks, investors are above all buying **economic growth**, in the expectation of future earnings that the company will generate. They want to participate in the resulting **creation of wealth**. In addition, because of their higher historical returns than those of other asset classes, stocks usually provide good protection against inflation. However, investors must accept the fact that they are investing in risky assets in absolute terms and may potentially suffer losses.

This asset class is essentially considered in order to generate higher capital growth, as limiting a portfolio to money market and bond investments may prove insufficient to cover average inflation. However, as we pointed out earlier, there are times at which it is desirable to invest in stocks and other times where it is wise to avoid this asset class.

---

[1]Rodet and Giacoletto in *Le Temps*.

We favour the use of a so-called **top-down approach**, which involves studying the major macro-indicators, firstly, to determine the general trend and the attractiveness of the asset class. Secondly, the best-positioned market sectors or industry groups should be selected, then finally the individual stocks from within those groups that are the most attractive in their industry.

Then, it is best to follow the so-called core-satellite approach, with more or less flexibility for each of these two components (definition of upper and lower thresholds within each part). This involves, for example, using an index fund (the core part under passive management – improved or not) and making specific bets on certain companies (the satellite part under active management). The use of stop loss orders is recommended for protection from downside risk, as is placing sell limit orders which can be useful for booking profits in the event of a rise, according to a return target set at the time of purchase.

It can be advantageous to use capital protected products, which are more consistent with investors' loss aversion; investors find losses more painful than they find gains satisfying. It can therefore be preferable to participate in market upswings while benefiting from capital protection at maturity. The use of options is also possible depending on the scenario expected for a position.

For the approach we propose, a detailed analysis of the four forces is essential in order to determine the resulting force that will push the stock market either up or down.

39.4   REAL ESTATE

Direct real estate usually offers a low correlation with the other asset classes, especially stocks, with a return that is often more stable over time. Conversely, indirect or securitised real estate has a high correlation with stocks, and can undergo large fluctuations in the markets.

In practice, it is advisable to invest between 15 and 20% in direct real estate and about 5 or 10% in securitised real estate, through a property fund or index, for example. For this analysis, we have decided only to consider indirect real estate.

The attractiveness of this asset class depends essentially on the level of **supply** and **demand** for real estate in a particular geographical region and for a particular type of real estate (residential or commercial). **Demographic factors** should also be taken into account as they stimulate both supply and demand. **Interest rate** levels also influence the value of real estate.

Because each property market has specific characteristics, a given market must be analysed with the utmost care. Therefore, we recommend making use of **market studies** carried out by industry experts, which allow the market and its outlook to be evaluated. There are various market studies, which are usually carried out annually.

The multi-forces approach can also be used for this asset class.

39.5   COMMODITIES AND PRECIOUS AND INDUSTRIAL METALS

The level and development of certain commodities will influence investor decisions about other asset classes and some sectors. High crude oil prices will benefit oil companies, but will set companies that are strongly dependent on energy, such as airlines, at a disadvantage.

Regarding energy in general, the levels of supply and demand influence prices, but these also depend on other factors as we mentioned earlier.

For agricultural products, supply and demand are the predominant influences on prices. Structural conditions in terms of production, the climate and natural disasters will have an impact on the price of these commodities. Speculation can also be very strong, and the psychological impact of excessive media coverage can have consequences on the attractiveness of this category.

However, from a **social** and **ethical** point of view, we recommend that investors avoid this category and concentrate instead on the **energy** and **precious** or **industrial metals** industries.

Finally, in our analysis, we will concentrate essentially on industrial metals, apart from a few remarks about gold. Demand for industrial metals is strongly linked to the growth of industry, which uses them in the production process. The growth of developed and emerging countries helps maintain the price level.

As for the other asset classes, the multi-forces approach can be used to better distinguish the various factors acting on prices.

The Four Forces of the Investment Model

40.1 THE MACROECONOMIC FORCE

40.1.1 The Macroeconomic Force and money market investments

The return from money market investments depends primarily on the movement of **short-term interest rates**. These are given by the money market and influenced by the Central Bank's policy in terms of **inflation** and **growth**.

Upward pressure on interest rates results from a context of uncontrolled inflation and excessive growth. Conversely, controlled inflation or the beginning of a recession pushes rates down or keeps them stable.

Therefore, investors must follow the **indicators** for the country's inflation and growth in order to identify potential for interest rate hikes or cuts. Furthermore, the meeting schedule of central banks (which are the dates for decisions about interest rate levels) should guide investors, particularly in their choice of maturity.

Interest rate levels essentially depend on the country's economic situation and on central bank policies.

The level of **exports** and **imports**, and therefore the balance of trade, are also factors that may affect interest rates. A central bank can take steps to avoid excessive appreciation of its currency against foreign currencies, either by intervening directly on the foreign exchange market, or by changing its short-term interest rate policy.

Finally, a country's **current account** balance can also influence interest rates. A deficit can push interest rates up.

In terms of the form of investment, a short-term fiduciary investment is most appropriate when interest rates are rising, as it allows investors to take advantage of any new rise. On the other hand, when rates are falling, money market funds are more suitable as they are less sensitive to further short-term interest rate cuts, precisely because they are invested in instruments with longer maturities. In the end, the choice between these two forms of investment will also depend on the investors' tax regime.

40.1.2 The Macroeconomic Force and bonds

As we pointed out earlier, key factors to be determined are the potential increase or decrease of medium- and long-term interest rates, and expectations for **inflation** and **growth**. The **10-year rate** is often used as a benchmark in practice.

High or uncontrolled inflation is likely to result in a future interest rate hike and, consequently, a drop in bond prices. Conversely, low or controlled inflation prompted by economic slowdown usually leads to a future drop in interest rates and therefore an increase in bond prices.

In addition, it is important to determine the way in which short-term and medium- to long-term interest rates will develop. A **parallel movement** of yield curves[1] is more dangerous for bonds, as they are all affected, whereas movement of a **part** of the **curve** only affects those that are located at the point experiencing the movement.

So, depending on the outlook, investors need to position themselves correctly on the curve and choose a specific **duration** accordingly.

To do this, investors must first examine:

- the structure of the yield curve, to evaluate the potential for rising or falling interest rates;
- inflation (controlled or not);
- current short-term and long-term interest rates (high, low);
- the outlook for short-term and long-term interest rates.

It can also be useful to track the development of the **budget deficit** and the measures used to cover it. As we saw earlier, to finance its expenditure, the State can either increase its taxes, raise capital on the markets by issuing bonds or obtain funds from the central bank.

The deficit shrinks in periods of economic growth and grows during recessions or economic slowdowns. A budget deficit can stimulate growth and employment in an economy in recession, but an increase in public debt can have negative long-term consequences, both on stocks (low growth) and bonds (risk of inflation and interest rate hikes).

We suggest the reader refer to our above comments on money market investments, which also apply to bonds.

40.1.3   The Macroeconomic Force and stocks

This analysis should be performed by studying a certain number of **macroeconomic indicators**, and must take into account their **calendar** and the calendar of earnings announcements.

Moreover, we recommend examining the level of market activity by comparing current **volatility** with its **historical average** (index VIX), as well as the trading volume. Strong volatility involves violent upswings or downturns. Such an environment is particularly risky, and wise investors should avoid this type of market.

---

[1]Graphical representation of interest rates by maturity.

Although this pertains more to the field of market psychology, a study of the **put/call ratio** can also help determine market sentiment.

Growth is the major driving force that pushes stock prices up. Conversely, an economy in **recession** drives stock prices down.

Inflation and short-term interest rates have an influence on stocks. Falling or controlled **inflation** is a positive factor for stocks. Uncontrolled or rising inflation, on the other hand, is likely to lead to interest rate hikes, which is negative for stocks. As we saw earlier, it is essential to identify the type of inflation in order to correctly evaluate the implications.

A stock investment mainly signifies the purchase of future growth, and consequently it is important to follow the indicators for growth and recession (particularly unemployment) to identify potential increases or decreases in growth rate. Investors must bear in mind that the stock market cycle anticipates the economic cycle and that the GDP report, which is published quarterly, only covers the past quarter.

Along with growth, **interest rates** are one of the most significant factors affecting stocks.

To begin with, interest rates influence company **valuations** using discounted cash flow (a higher discount rate implies a lower present value).

Furthermore, higher interest rates have a negative impact on corporate **investments** and the **cost of borrowing**, curbing companies' development. So an increase in interest rates has a negative effect, and vice versa for a decrease.

Finally, the **strength** or **weakness** of the domestic **currency** can have an effect on stocks. A strong currency favours importing countries and companies, whereas a weak currency favours exporting countries and companies.

A study of the **balance of trade** and of the **current account balance** may also prove useful.

40.1.4   The Macroeconomic Force and real estate

Interest rate levels can influence price developments. An environment of low interest rates favours real estate transactions and can therefore keep prices high. Conversely, high interest rates can reduce returns because of the high cost of mortgages and tend therefore to push or keep prices down.

Moreover, when valuing real estate with discounted cash flow, low interest rates increase the value of the property and high interest rates tend to decrease it. Similarly to stocks, a rise in medium- to long-term interest rates is therefore negative for this asset class.

Economic growth or **recession** have a considerable impact on the price of real estate. Indeed, the levels of housing sales or construction are important indicators for assessing a country's growth.

40.1.5 The Macroeconomic Force and commodities, precious and industrial metals

The overall **economic situation** (growth or recession) will have a direct impact on the demand for crude oil and industrial metals. A recessionary context will lower demand and, consequently, prices. The reverse is true for strong economic expansion.

For crude oil, **stock** levels, especially American, will also play a role in setting prices. High stock levels will not encourage demand, while falling stocks will tend to increase demand and, hence, prices.

Geopolitical factors also add a risk premium which pushes prices up. This is especially true for oil.

Next, **central bank interventions** can have an impact on prices. When central banks are building up their gold reserves, prices are often pushed up, but when they are selling their reserves, prices fall.

The **strength** or **weakness** of the **currency** and, more precisely, of the US dollar, can also affect the price of commodities, which are nearly always listed in US dollars. A weak dollar can help hold prices up and a strong dollar tends to have the opposite effect.

We saw earlier that the **price** movements of commodity **futures**[2] depend on changes in **interest rates**, on **storage costs** and finally on the so-called "**convenience yield**".

Interest rate levels also influence prices. High interest rates help increase the price of futures while low rates, on the other hand, will decrease their price.

Storage costs can indeed vary over time, but the magnitude of this variation is not usually very large. In general, an increase in storage costs is reflected by an increase in the futures price.

As for the convenience yield, this depends on inventory levels and seasonal fluctuations. Thus, depending on the context, holding the commodity can confer advantages that the futures holder doesn't have. We gave the example of heating oil in winter. The spot holder had an immediate advantage over the holder of the futures contract, implying in this case a high convenience yield and therefore a lower futures price (situation of backwardation). In other situations, this convenience yield will be lower, with the futures price higher than the spot price (situation of contango).

40.2 THE FUNDAMENTAL FORCE

40.2.1 The Fundamental Force and money market investments

As we stated to begin with, the money market rate also depends on the **counterparty** (quality of the borrower) and, consequently, any change in **rating** will have an impact on rates.

---

[2]Future price = Spot price * (1 + risk-free rate) + storage costs − convenience yield.

A drop in the issuer's rating, whether for a fiduciary deposit or a money market fund, will increase returns but with a corresponding increase in counterparty risk. Conversely, an increased rating will result in a decrease in the rate offered while at the same time reducing the risk of the investment.

40.2.2   The Fundamental Force and bonds

From a fundamental point of view, the **credit quality (rating)** of the issue and its development will influence the bond's price. A drop in rating will result in a lower price (with an increase in the bond's return, as it becomes riskier) and an improved rating will increase the price (while pushing down the bond's return as it becomes less risky).

The type of issuer and its ability to satisfy its commitments will also determine the attractiveness of an issue. An increased **level of debt** has a negative effect on prices, while an improvement in the level of debt helps keep prices up. Therefore, it is important to examine the issuer's level of debt by analysing, for example, the debt ratio or the interest coverage ratio. A study of the current ratio and the quick ratio can also be useful in determining the company's short-term liquidity.

The **fundamentals** of a particular industry or country can also influence price levels. When issues from a particular industry are more sought after, prices can be pushed up, particularly when the healthcare industry or the outlook of this sector is better than others. Conversely, neglected industries can see their issues lose value, due to the lack of investor interest.

40.2.3   The Fundamental Force and stocks

a) Sector analysis

We suggest that investors undertake a **detailed strategic analysis** of the various sectors of the economy, like the one we presented in Part III. This will help determine the sector's prospects according to the impact of macroeconomic events, the legal, political and tax environment and especially the barriers to entry which denote the existence of one or several market niches. The outlook for the sector to which a company belongs has a major impact on the company. Once this first level of analysis is complete, investors can move on to identifying the strongest and weakest companies within the sectors.

The **SWOT table** (see Table 40.1) can be used to summarise this analysis and provide an overview of the sector under consideration.

i) Consumption and spending

First, the levels of **private consumption** and **public spending**, as well as investments, should be analysed, according to the type of customer for each sector, namely **(household) consumers**, **companies** or the **government**.

The consumer confidence index, retail sales and personal income are all indicators to follow, as they help determine the attractiveness of businesses that depend on private consumption.

Table 40.1   "Threats – Opportunities – Strengths – Weaknesses" table

THREATS	OPPORTUNITIES
STRENGTHS	WEAKNESSES

As we noted previously, the computer and leisure sectors depend on sales to consumers. A drop in these indicators can lead to a drop in sales for the companies operating in these sectors.

The development of the State budget and planned expenditure is key to determining the attractiveness of sectors that depend on the government, such as defence, aerospace or infrastructure. An increase in planned spending will boost them, whereas budget cuts will hold these companies back.

Finally, indicators such as new orders and the industrial production and capacity utilisation rate will indicate the level of investment in sectors dependent on the consumption of companies, such as manufacturing or chemicals. Rising indicators will have a positive effect on these companies, while deteriorating indicators will do the opposite.

ii) Production process

Depending on the production process used (workers, machinery, oil, mixed), macroeconomic factors will have different impacts.

The rise and fall of interest rates has a greater impact on capital-intensive companies such as utilities, as it can affect the cost of borrowing capital.

Labour-intensive companies, such as those in the retail sales sector, are more exposed to rising and falling unemployment rates and wage inflation.

Fuel-intensive companies, including those operating in the transport sector, are greatly affected by oil price fluctuations.

iii) Growth and cycles

Whether or not the economy is growing or in recession will also influence which industries to buy and which to avoid.

In a growth phase, **cyclical** sectors, such as the automotive industry, construction or transport, should be favoured as they react more strongly. However, they should be avoided in periods of economic slowdown or recession, where the so-called **non-cyclical** sectors are preferable, such as healthcare, pharmaceuticals or food.

iv) Currency

The **strength** or **weakness** of the domestic currency can have an impact on a given industry. A strong currency benefits import-oriented sectors, while a weak currency favours export-oriented sectors, like agriculture, industrial equipment, computers or pharmaceuticals. Export dependent sectors react more strongly to the balance of trade and currency fluctuations.

v) Energy, metals and commodity prices

The price of energy (crude oil, gas) also has an influence. An increase in oil prices benefits oil companies, but has a negative effect on airlines and road transport companies.

A rise in the price of metals will benefit mining and producing companies, but will penalise companies that use the metals, such as construction companies.

Similarly, an increase in commodity and staple food prices which can be reflected in their retail prices will favour producing companies, but the impact can be limited by a strong currency. On the other hand, the impact will be negative for companies that buy these commodities, and for those that produce them but cannot easily reflect the price rise in retail prices.

vi) Climate

The climate can also influence sales and therefore corporate margins. A favourable climate allowing abundant harvests helps push prices – and therefore producer margins – down, but will increase margins for buyers whose purchase costs are lowered. Conversely, small harvests due to poor weather conditions will push prices up, which will benefit producers but not buyers.

b) Analysis of individual stocks

The second step is to complete a **detailed analysis** of the company, in the light of several different criteria.

It can also be worthwhile to classify stocks in one of the **six categories** outlined by Lynch to determine not only the attractiveness, but also the holding period of the investment. In Chapter 5, we mentioned the following categories:

1. Slow growers;
2. The stalwarts;
3. The fast growers;
4. Cyclicals;
5. Turnarounds;
6. The asset plays.

i) Business model and competitive advantage

As we noted earlier, it is essential to understand how the company makes money, i.e., to be familiar with its business model, which should be easily understandable. As an investor, it is advisable to have at least some knowledge of a particular sector before investing in it.

Company websites are a good place to start, as they provide a good description of the business's activities, and financial statements give a more precise idea of how these activities are distributed.

It is also important to determine the company's **competitive advantage(s)**, as this is what defines its positioning in the relevant market and allows it to develop. As such, the following points should be examined:

- the company's market share;
- its revenue, including distribution of sales;
- its growth rate;
- its customers;
- growth of the sector;
- the competition;
- sector regulations.

We favour solid, enduring businesses (large companies), whose product or service is durable, i.e., is unlikely to become obsolete. Regular sales are necessary, so the product's sales percentage (impact of the product on the company's sales) should be examined.

Finally, it is easier for a company to develop and win market share in a low growth sector.

ii) Management

The management team is what drives the company, and this role must be occupied by top class individuals. A company run by its founder is obviously ideal (Bill Gates, Michael Dell or Warren Buffett, for example), but if **stocks are held** by the company's **managers** and **executives**, this is also a positive sign.

So, the quality aspect should be taken into account. For example, the arrival of a new manager with a lot of experience in the sector should be regarded as positive for the company.

The company's website will provide information about the management team and their experience (CV, careers). CEOs sometimes appear on television and regularly grant interviews to major newspapers or specialised magazines.

Corporate governance rules, which define the relationships and responsibilities between management and shareholders, help gauge the degree of independence in decision-making and the degree of protection of shareholder interests.

The fact that the Nobel Prize in Economics in 2009 was awarded to Elinor Ostrom and Oliver Williamson for their work on economic governance and the organisation of cooperation demonstrates the importance for the economy of these rules.

iii) Financial health

First, the company's short-term **liquidity ratio** must be examined, essentially by studying the current ratio and the quick ratio. Then the company's long-term debt should be studied, by examining the **debt ratio** and the **interest coverage ratio**.

The company must have adequate liquidity. It can also be useful to calculate the net cash value per share,[3] then subtract this from the market price, and finally divide it by earnings per share.

These ratios are available on financial information websites or calculated using the balance sheet, which indicates what the company owns (assets) and owes (debts).

As we noted earlier, it is especially important to examine the development of these ratios over a three–five-year period. This first step will help determine the company's default or bankruptcy risk.

In this regard, the **ratings** attributed to companies by credit rating agencies can influence their stock prices, as these ratings represent their financial soundness. A drop in rating often leads to a fall in stock price, not to mention the impact of the higher interest rate the company will have to pay on the market to raise capital.

iv) Earnings per share, P/E and P/B ratios

A stock's return consists primarily of a share in the company's earnings. The company should ideally have a continuous record of **dividend** payments, i.e., **stable** and, if possible, **increasing** dividends.

It is therefore important to examine the earnings per share by studying the income statement. This document indicates what the company generates and spends, with the difference representing a profit.

An increase in earnings over time, thanks, for example, to improved sales, has a positive effect on the stock price. Spending should ideally remain constant, or at least increase at a fairly low rate – lower than the rate of earnings growth.

Companies with high margins are obviously preferable, particularly because they have a larger safety margin for coping with a difficult environment.

It is useful to track the development of earnings per share (EPS) over time, and to study the estimates made for the company. Using the EPS, we can calculate the **Price to Earnings Ratio (P/E)**, examine its historical development and analyse the estimates for the future. Obviously, this should be compared to the P/E ratio of the industry in question, as the P/E is a relative measure. Very high P/E ratios are usually to be avoided.

As we mentioned previously, it is also useful to examine other ratios, such as the **Price to Book (P/B ratio)**, ideally situated between 1 and 2, or the Price to Cash Flow ratio.

---

[3]Current assets minus long-term debt, divided by the number of shares outstanding.

Finally, it is worth comparing the stock price movement to earnings growth and the P/E ratio graphically.

v) Earnings and future prospects

When buying a stock, investors are buying future growth, so it is essential to determine the company's **ability** to **increase** their **earnings** in the future.

The announcement of **good results** generally has a positive impact on the stock price, especially when the company has exceeded expectations, or publishes good figures in a difficult economic environment. Obviously, the same is true for forecasts for future results, even if they are only estimates. This estimate will help determine an intrinsic value, which can be compared to the stock price.

A programme of **cost reduction** or the **sale** of certain company **divisions** – for reasons of profitability, price or a willingness to focus on its core business – will also have a positive impact on the stock.

Stock repurchases, undertaken by the company itself or by its management, will have a positive effect on the stock. The same is true of a tender offer on the company.

It can also be useful to examine the **results** published by **competing companies**, to get a better idea of the sector's growth prospects and those of the company in question, as in principle they operate in the same environment.

vi) Free Cash Flow

The company's ability to generate cash is probably the most important criterion for investors. A high free cash flow enables the company to repay its debts, pay dividends, undertake stock repurchases and especially to ensure its future growth.

A company has three sources available for generating cash, namely operating activities, investing activities and financing activities. All these factors appear on the cash flow statement.

vii) Inventories

It is also useful to study the development of inventories. A growing inventory can be a negative sign for the company, which eventually will have to lower prices to liquidate stocks or wait longer to sell them. Conversely, diminishing inventories are a positive sign for the company.

viii) Specific risks

Finally, it is a good idea to study the political risk of any **new regulations** applying to the business, of **nationalisation** or even **boycotts** driven by consumers. The media (newspapers, official reports, political debates, etc.) usually provide this type of information.

40.2.4   The Fundamental Force and real estate

The fundamentals of the real estate market in question will mainly depend on **supply** and **demand**, and on **demographic development**.

The demography of the region will strongly influence prices. An increasing number of inhabitants or individuals requiring housing will push up the price of existing real estate. Furthermore, the **size** of the **territory** and the **area authorised for construction** will also influence prices.

Excessive construction and mortgage levels should be studied closely, as these factors can lead to a **real estate bubble** which, when it bursts, will see prices collapse. The collapse of the Dubai real estate bubble, which had indeed been fed by excessive construction and borrowing, is a perfect example.

A **specialised real estate study** will allow these fundamental factors to be evaluated.

40.2.5   The Fundamental Force and commodities, precious and industrial metals

Population growth and the **appearance** of a **middle class** in emerging countries, whose needs will increase over time, have an influence on prices.

A country's or industry's **limited reserves**, or the **scarcity** of an energy **resource** or particular metal will also contribute to price rises. The development of renewable energy or alternative materials may limit this impact, but the cost of research and development must be taken into account.

To a more limited extent, the **climate** and **natural disasters** can have an impact on prices, but these affect supply and production capacity, which must be placed in the context of overall demand. Interruptions in production due to natural disasters will probably have a limited impact on prices in a context of weak demand.

Finally, **State interventions**, particularly in terms of new or increased taxes, can have an impact on prices.

40.3   THE TECHNICAL FORCE

40.3.1   The Technical Force and money market investments

Interest rates usually follow a **cycle** that alternates a series of increases towards a peak, then a series of declines, leading to a trough.

Using a **chart** to study interest rate movements helps determine the current point in the cycle. The main objective is to identify the turning point. An initial rate hike increases the prospect of future hikes and an initial cut suggests more cuts to come. Investors should use these pivotal moments to position themselves correctly and to choose the appropriate maturities.

In the event of an initial increase in interest rates, it's important not to choose too long a maturity, so as to avoid getting stuck while rates continue to rise. Conversely, after an initial drop in interest rates, long maturities can be considered, this time to lock in attractive terms for a long period in the expectation of lower interest rates in the future. A comparison with the returns offered by bonds is essential in order to choose the more appropriate instrument.

The search for specific technical patterns is of little use in the case of money market investments. Expectations for inflation and growth are thoroughly decisive (macroeconomic force), as it is these expectations that will influence central bank policy and therefore short-term interest rates.

40.3.2   The Technical Force and bonds

Regarding bonds, it is important to distinguish between an investment held to maturity from a short-term investment. In the first case, technical analysis is somewhat superfluous as investors seek simply to block a return over a given period, to earn coupons and recover the invested capital at the moment of final redemption. Interest rates and their expected development are the decisive factors here.

In the case of more speculative investments, forecasts of upcoming price increases or decreases can be used to make a profit, so a chart analysis of the interest rate cycle and bond price movements may prove useful.

However, for bonds, the macroeconomic and fundamental forces, and even the behavioural force, will have a more significant impact than chart patterns.

40.3.3   The Technical Force and stocks

A detailed chart analysis is necessary, because some investors base their investment decisions mainly on the technical aspect. It's worth being on the same side as the technical analysts.

It is important to look for **specific patterns** and **support** and **resistance** levels. Indeed, some investors buy or sell on the basis of a technical pattern in the observed price, or an ostensibly relevant level being broken through. In our opinion, Fibonacci retracements can also provide very useful indications.

Most important is to determine the **trend**, whether it is bullish (higher highs and higher lows), bearish (lower highs and lower lows) or sideways.

40.3.4   The Technical Force and real estate

Interest rates usually follow a cycle that alternates a series of increases with a series of declines.

A chart analysis of historical movements helps investors situate the current point in the cycle and thereby determine the prospects for interest rate hikes or cuts, which will have an impact on real estate. Medium- to long-term interest rates, or the three, five and 10-year rates are those to consider in this case.

40.3.5   The Technical Force and commodities, precious and industrial metals

A chart analysis of prices and patterns can help determine the direction in which prices are moving in this category, which is generally subject to speculation. Note, however, that the development of prices for industrial metals is strongly linked to the economic cycle.

40.4   THE BEHAVIOURAL FORCE

40.4.1   The Behavioural Force and money market investments

This force is of limited importance for money market investments.

However, for fiduciary investments, a **particular counterparty's attractiveness** to investors can justify a lower interest rate being offered. If investors want to lend their money to a particular borrower because of its credit quality in a context of strong uncertainty, the borrower can afford to offer lower rates due to the strong demand.

Conversely, a borrower which is subjectively regarded as more risky, even if its rating remains unchanged, may be forced to offer higher interest rates by this psychological force sustained by investors.

40.4.2   The Behavioural Force and bonds

At the psychological level, **major insecurity** or a **risk aversion** to stocks or other asset classes can strengthen the attractiveness of bonds and push up prices, sometimes higher than they should be. Thus, such an "exaggeration" can originate in an irrational behavioural force, not based on return criteria, for example, but simply on the desire for the additional security offered by bonds.

The recent financial crisis drove many investors to buy bonds in 2008; this asset class alone was favoured and the stock market was neglected. Some investors, affected by this force, threw themselves on lower-quality bond issues that they would not have considered under normal market conditions.

40.4.3   The Behavioural Force and stocks

First to be considered is the **optimism** or **pessimism** of investors or market players. **Confidence indices** provide an initial impression by indicating the economic climate in which economic agents are operating (consumers, business managers).

A study of the **media**, particularly newspaper headlines, articles and especially the **vocabulary** used, helps to pinpoint this sentiment and any risk of a speculative bubble forming. We are referring here to the **strength of association** that we talked about earlier. Noise and excitement generated around an industry or stock can also provide precious indications. It is better to avoid investing in companies whose popularity is solely due to a fad.

Moreover, in a context of asymmetrical information, investors tend to believe that others are better informed, which causes mimicry (the "herd" effect).

Investors also tend to underreact to news due to a **conservative bias** that leads them to underweight recent information compared to prior information. Furthermore, the **self-attribution bias** leads them to overweight information that confirms their first evaluation and underweight information that is inconsistent with it.

As such, it is worth reiterating that in pre-crash periods, individuals tend to underreact to extremely negative news and overreact to extremely positive news. These under- and overreactions subside after the crash, but remain present nonetheless.

It is obviously very difficult to determine this force and its direction, if only because of the large number of individuals interacting in the market. However, exploiting these lags in price adjustment to information can help investors to position themselves properly in the market.

We have also seen that individuals underestimate the frequency of repetitions and see cycles as **mean reverting**. Therefore, these "psychological" turning points should be taken into account.

Fads (trends) or **rumours** should also be taken into consideration as they can occasionally push investors to buy stocks or favour a particular sector, as was the case with Internet companies in the lead-up to the speculative bubble of the 2000s.

Finally, the attractiveness of other asset classes can determine the attractiveness of stocks and push prices up or down.

40.4.4   The Behavioural Force and real estate

Real estate speculation obviously contributes to price rises. So the establishment of a real estate bubble must be monitored very closely because of its possible collapse and consequent impact on prices. Unfortunately, the subprime crisis is not yet a distant memory, any more than the Dubai crisis.

The **desire** to **become** a **homeowner** or **landlord**, linked to a country's culture or to tax incentives, can also help push property prices up. Finally, a preference for **more regular income** and capital that fluctuates less over time can also lead investors to favour this asset class and therefore contributes to price rises.

40.4.5   The Behavioural Force and commodities, precious and industrial metals

Media coverage, the **proliferation** of **articles** and **features** on commodities and metals can have a psychological impact that strengthens the attractiveness of this asset class.

41

Table Summarising the Different Forces

Finally, we propose to summarise what we believe are the most relevant factors for each force, in regard to each of the asset classes we have selected.

All throughout our analysis, we have tried to identify the elements that can influence prices in the financial markets. Table 41.1 on pages 274–5, although comprehensive, is not necessarily exhaustive.

What we are providing here, above all, is an investment framework based on these four forces, and we leave it to each investor to determine the factors that he or she considers the most appropriate for judging the attractiveness of an asset class, and to make decisions accordingly.

Table 41.1 Major factors for each force for each asset class

	Macroeconomic Force	Fundamental Force	Technical Force	Behavioural Force
Money market investments	– short-term interest rates – inflation – growth/recession – current account balance – balance of trade	– counterparty (borrower quality)	– chart analysis, focused on short-term rate cycles – nearness to historical highs/lows	– attractiveness of a particular counterparty – aversion for the other asset classes
Bonds	– long-term interest rates – inflation – growth/recession – current account balance – balance of trade – budget deficit	– borrower quality (default) – rating – sector fundamentals	– chart analysis focused on mid- to long-term rate cycles – nearness to historical highs/lows	– risk aversion stronger for the other asset classes – preference for more regular income

Stocks	– level of market activity (volatility)
	– short-term and long-term interest rates
	– inflation
	– growth/recession
	– leading indicators
	– Baltic Dry Index
	– unemployment
	– price of commodities
	– current account balance
	– balance of trade
	– budget deficit
		a) at the sector level
		– sector fundamentals (strategic analysis)
		– sector P/E ratio (historical)
		– P/B ratio (historical)
		– private consumption and public spending
		– strength/weakness of the currency
		– crude oil prices
		– metal and commodity prices
		– climate
			– detailed chart analysis focused on
			  i) trends
			  ii) supports & resistances
			  iii) particular patterns
			  iv) other technical indicators
				– risk aversion
				– consumer confidence (optimism/pessimism)
				– psychological biases
				– the media
				– rumours (tender offers, results, etc.)
				– trends, fads

b) at the company level

- business model
- strategic analysis (products, etc.)
- management
- corporate governance
- financial health (liquidity, level of debt, rating)
- Earnings
- Dividends
- P/E, P/B ratios
- Free Cash Flow
- inventories
- specific risks (political, regulations, boycott, etc.)

Real Estate	– mid- to long-term interest rates – inflation – growth/recession	– liquidity – supply/demand – demography – territory size – area authorised for construction	– chart analysis focused on mid- to long-term interest rate cycles – nearness to historical highs/lows	– real estate speculation – desire to become homeowner/landlord – preference for a more regular income

Commodities Precious metals	– overall economic situation
	– inventory levels
	– geopolitical factors
	– central bank interventions
	– strength/weakness of the currency (esp. $US)
	– convenience yield
		– demography
		– limited reserves
		– climate
		– natural disasters
		– State interventions
			– detailed chart analysis focused on
			  i) trends
			  ii) supports and resistances
			  iii) particular patterns
			  iv) other technical indicators
				– speculation
				– the media

42

A Final Example: Analysis of the Subprime Crisis

We would like to conclude our analysis with one last example: the recent subprime crisis and the financial crisis that followed. Using this example, we can briefly illustrate the attractiveness of an asset class in the light of the proposed investment model.

We have decided to focus on stocks and to analyse the most relevant factors. With the United States as a point of reference, let us now reconstitute an analysis of early 2008.

a) The Macroeconomic Force

By examining the **volatility** index (VIX index), we could see that over the previous months, the level of market activity had exceeded the historical average, which is generally situated around 15–16% (average volatility of the S&P500). In January 2008, it was positioned at about 24%.

Furthermore, **short-term interest rates** had been falling since August 2007, and the Fed had decided on 22 January 2008 to lower the official market rate to 3.50% – a drop of nearly 2% in less than six months.

It was also interesting to analyse the development of and the **difference** between the **short-term** and **long-term rates**, taking the three-month LIBOR and the 10-year US Treasury yield as benchmarks. Besides the short-term interest rate cuts, we could see in particular a fall in the 10-year yield, indicating a rise in bond prices, the beginning of expectations for a crisis and of weaker inflation to come.

Looking at the report published on 21 February 2008 by the Conference Board, the US leading index had fallen for the fourth consecutive month in January. According to the OECD report of 11 January 2008, the composite leading indicators were signalling a slowdown in growth prospects for the biggest OECD member economies, with a downturn in the US.

In terms of **growth**, we also noted the drop in the Gross Domestic Product (GDP) in early 2008.

Finally, examining the development of the ISM Manufacturing Index, we noticed a contraction of **industrial activity**, with the index falling below the threshold of 50. The Baltic Dry Index indicated a major slowdown in worldwide commercial activity.

Therefore, in January 2008, all these factors pointed towards a Macroeconomic Force that would push stock prices down. Some indicators were beginning to deteriorate, showing that the bullish trend of 2003–2007 was reversing towards a new bearish cycle, whose magnitude was, at that stage, impossible to determine.

b) The Fundamental Force

We will not undertake a detailed strategic analysis of industries and individual stocks. However, with the subprime crisis having erupted in summer 2007, we believed that banks were the most exposed (specific risk of this sector that was therefore best avoided).

Nonetheless, it was worth studying several factors in order to determine the attractiveness of certain industries.

Looking at the price of **crude oil**, we found that this had jumped dramatically, reaching nearly 100 dollars a barrel. This favoured oil companies, but was beginning to disadvantage industries dependent on oil (airlines, transport). We know now that it continued to climb, reaching almost 150 dollars.

In terms of the **EUR/USD exchange rate**, we could see that the dollar had depreciated sharply, reaching the historic level of 1.50 to the euro. This favoured American exporting companies, and European companies that could obtain supplies from the US at better prices.

The **commodities** index showed a strong appreciation, due particularly to the weakness of the dollar.

Examining the level and development of the **P/E ratio** (S&P500), we noticed that it had fallen sharply, reaching historically low levels, with more attractive stock prices. However, as we have mentioned, it is important to treat this ratio with caution, as it mainly depends on the company's earnings per share, which can fall.

We also noted that the **P/B ratio** (S&P500) had dropped, returning to more reasonable valuation levels (as a reminder, during the excess of the Internet years, P/B ratios had reached levels of 5).

Fundamentals were more difficult to estimate and opposite forces could prevail depending on the sector in question. However, we considered the banking sector to be avoided, or at least highly risky.

Incorporating the macroeconomic indicators, we believed that a weak to moderate downwards pressure was acting on stocks.

c) The Technical Force

From a technical point of view, the S&P500 chart for the previous 10 years showed a magnificent example of the "double top", where we could also see that the bullish trend begun in 2003 was starting to reverse, with the appearance of "lower highs" and "lower lows". The resistance of around 1520 had been tested several times without breaking and could not be used as a new support level.

The Technical Force was therefore pushing down on stock prices, but only generally speaking, as we have taken the S&P500 index alone into account.

d) The Behavioural Force

During this period, other than the **abundance of articles** on subprime mortgages, we could sense the beginning of a climate of mistrust, fed strongly by the press which, in general, was using a **negative vocabulary**. The strength of association would gradually take effect.

Moreover, a certain **pessimism** had begun to take hold, as shown by the American consumer confidence index, which had worsened considerably in 2008. The University of Michigan index had dropped below 80 in late 2007, and in March 2008, it reached 69.5, the lowest since 1992.

The Behavioural Force had also begun to pull stocks down.

e) Conclusion

In the light of all these factors, it appeared in early 2008 that the resulting force was pulling **stocks** down rather than pushing them up.

The extent to which equity was to be reduced in a given portfolio depended on the investors' degree of conviction about a (strong) correction in this asset class – the element the most difficult, if not impossible, to predict at that time. Market movements follow cycles and a bearish cycle alternates with a bullish cycle over time.

For **money market investments**, the drop in short-term interest rates suggested blocking fiduciary deposits into a long maturity to profit one last time from the high prevailing rates. Money market funds would then take over.

Considering the drop in long as well as short-term interest rates, **bonds** were to be favoured and their maturity to be chosen according to expectations for inflation and future possibilities for rate hikes. At this time, durations of three to five years were usually advised.

Given the weakness of the dollar, **commodities**, especially energy, remained attractive.

Real estate, in the context of the subprime mortgage crisis, was obviously an asset class to be avoided, or at least seen as extremely risky.

Finally, in this context, the **investment strategy** to be favoured was one that aimed for a positive performance regardless of market movements. Thus, especially as an alternative to stocks, we believed that a particularly well-diversified **hedge fund** strategy could be incorporated into a portfolio. This strategy provides the necessary degree of investment flexibility.

In late 2008, the MSCI World stock index was showing a negative performance of −42.08%, while the HFRI Fund Weighted Composite Index[1] and the Credit Suisse/Tremont Hedge Fund Index[2] had achieved respective performances of −19.03% and −19.07%. Admittedly, these were negative, but almost 2.5 times less so, and the negative performances were mainly generated at the end of 2008. As their liquidity periods are usually quarterly, many investors were unfortunately forced to suffer the massive correction over this short period, that no one could have foreseen. Indeed, these indexes resisted very well in the first half of 2008, but given the size of the correction and the panic reigning over the markets, almost all asset classes were affected.

In 2009, these two indexes generated a positive performance of +19.98% and +18.57%, which leads us to consider the second half of 2008 as exceptional, with a completely unpredictable crash in October 2008. To sum up, caution was imperative regarding stocks, unlike bonds that we believe were to be favoured. Commodities could be kept and hedge funds adapted to the context that we have described.

Finally, we reiterate that such an analysis must be carried out regularly, as the attractiveness of each asset class changes over time. Portfolio construction and especially management must be regarded as a truly dynamic process.

---

[1] Source: www.hedgefundresearch.com.
[2] Source: www.hedgeindex.com.

Conclusion

We have now come to the end of our analysis, having defined more precisely the framework within which investors operate and select their investments.

Firstly, we concluded that volatility (standard deviation), beta, VaR and CVaR are not appropriate measures of risk and that approaches based on normal distribution are unsuited to the financial markets. In our opinion, the markets are risky in absolute terms, with the risk being taken at the moment the decision to enter or exit a market or an asset class is made.

We then defined the various asset classes and the diverse risks associated with them – risks that can often be managed or reduced. We also proposed a classification according to their degree of risk, but which is not based on the sole criterion of volatility.

We noted that the market is not perfectly efficient: it is in fact directed by many emotions and psychological biases. Basing investment decisions solely on fundamental and technical analysis is inappropriate, as these behavioural biases must also be taken into account.

In terms of asset valuation, various approaches were presented based on principles, ratios, or particular methods of analysis that have been tested empirically in the context of fund management, for example.

In relation to the forecasting of market movements, we suggested combining all these approaches. As such, we have developed an investment approach that relies more on human reasoning than on the use of mathematical models based on fragile assumptions.

In our opinion, it is necessary to take into account both the general market conditions – or macroeconomic trends – and the sentiment of the various market players, as well as carrying out fundamental and technical analyses. By determining each of these four forces, investors can identify the resulting force that will give the direction of the market or asset.

In terms of portfolio construction, we recommend performing a strategic allocation that offers considerable flexibility and, above all, that is not based on the criterion of volatility. The choice of different weightings for tactical allocation depends on the attractiveness of each asset class at the time of analysis, and should be made using the "multi-forces" investment approach.

Indeed, portfolio management in the future will amount to managing the various risks that make up the portfolio and deciding whether or not to be exposed to a particular asset class.

In the introduction, we stated that it was time to try to understand how markets work, the process of price formation and the way risk should be measured. We hope to have provided answers to these questions, and to have defined a more precise investment framework. It is now time to invest intelligently.

Bibliography

Arabadjiev, B., Understanding Risks Embedded in Portfolios of Hedge Funds, Credit Suisse Asset Management.

Baker, N. and Haugen, R. (1991) The Efficient Market Inefficiency of Capitalization-Weighted Stock Portfolios, *Journal of Portfolio Management*, 17(1), 35–40.

Behr, P., Güttler, A. and Miebs, F. (2008) Is Minimum-variance Investing Really Worth the While? An Analysis with Robust Performance Inference, Research Paper, EDHEC-Risk, November.

Beiner, Dr N. (2009) Risk Management in Financial Institutions: An Overview, AZEK Campus, 1 April.

Bessiere, V. and Kaestner, M. (2005) Sur- et sous-réactions des analystes financiers: une étude des évolutions post-krach, Université de Montpellier.

Boujelbene Abbes, M., Boujelbene, Y. and Bouri, A., Les profits des stratégies momentum: sous et/ou surréaction ou phénomène rationnel? Cas du marché français, Faculté des Sciences Economiques et de Gestion de Sfax (www.iae.univ-poitiers.fr/affi2006/Coms/096.pdf).

Bulletin "Métaux" (2008) Le magazine du Crédit Suisse, 4(Octobre/Novembre).

Cappocci, D. (2004) Introduction aux Hedge Funds, *Economica*.

EDHEC (2009) A Long Road Ahead for Portfolio Construction Practitioners, Views of an EDHEC Survey.

Fama, E. and French, K. (1992) The Cross-section of Expected Stock Returns, *Journal of Finance*, June.

FINMA (Ex-Commission Fédérale des Banques (EBK CFB)) (2007) Hedge-Fonds Marktentwicklung, *Risiken und Regulierung*, September.

Financial Times (2008) "Magic formula" defies all the rules, Monday, 15 September.

Garessus, E. (2008) L'objectif absolu: limitation et contrôle du risque, *Le Temps*, 1 December.

Graham, B. (2003) *The Intelligent Investor*, Revised 1973 edition by Graham, B. and Zweig, J., Harper Business Essentials.

Grandin, P., Hübner, G. and Lambert, M. (2006) *Performance de Portefeuille*, Pearson Éducation France, 2006.

Greenwald, B.C.N., Kahn, J., Sonkin, P.D. and Van Biema, M. (2002) Investir dans la valeur: de Benjamin Graham à Warren Buffett et au-delà, *Valor Éditions*.

Hens, T. and Bachmann, K. (2008) *Behavioural Finance for Private Banking*, Chichester: John Wiley & Sons, Ltd.

Hoesli, M. (2008) Investissement immobilier, *Economica*.

Jegadeesh, N. and Titman, S., (2001) Momentum, University of Illinois Working Paper, 23 October.

Kahneman, D. and Tversky, A. (1979) Prospect Theory: An Analysis of Decision under Risk, *Econometrica*, XLVII, 263–291.

Kahneman, D., Slovic, P. and Tversky, A. (1982) *Judgment Under Uncertainty: Heuristics and Biases*, New York: Cambridge University Press.

Kim, M.J., Nelson, C.R. and Startz, R. (1991) Mean Reversion in Stock Prices A Reappraisal of the Empirical Evidence, NBER Working Paper No. W2795, August.

Künzi, A. (2008) Le market timing parfait, *PME Magazine*, October.

Lazzaroni, A., Snopek, L., Tripiana, J. and Vazquez, C. (2002) Le projet genevois e-voting sur le risk management, *Les cahiers de l'ASO*.

Lefèvre, E. (2006) *Reminiscences of a Stock Operator*, New York: John Wiley & Sons, Inc.

Lynch, P. (1999) *Et si vous en saviez assez pour gagner en Bourse*, Éditions Valor.

Malkiel, B.G. (2007) *A Random Walk Down Wall Street*, W.W. Norton & Company, Inc.

Mandelbrot, B. (2009) Une approche fractale des marchés – Risquer, perdre et gagner, *Éditions Odile Jacob*.

Markowitz, H.M. (1959) *Portfolio Selection: Efficient Diversification of Investments*, New Haven, CT: Yale University Press.

Martin, I. (2008) La volatilité constitue-t-elle une chance ou une malchance pour l'investisseur?, *L'Agefi*, 26 November.

Michaud, R. (1989) The Markowitz Optimization Enigma: Is "Optimized" Optimal?, *Financial Analysts Journal*, 45(1), 31–42.

Morningstar Advisor (2009) Morningstar Conversation, A read on risk, February/March.

Murphy, J. (1999) Technical Analysis of the Financial Markets, New York, *New York Institute of Finance*.

Navarro, P. (2002) *If it's Raining in Brazil, Buy Starbucks*, The MacGraw-Hill Companies.

Novello, P. (2000) *Guide de l'investisseur*, Éditions Pierre Novello.

Pardoe, J. (2007) *Warren Buffett – 24 leçons pour gagner en Bourse*, Paris, Maxima.

Piaget, M. (2002) *Demain j'arrête d'être salarié*, Genève: Georg Éditeur.

Risques Particuliers dans le Négoce de Titres (2009) Swissquote.

Robert, M. and Devaux, M. (1994) *Penser stratégie*, Dunod.

Rodet, A. and Giacoletto, E. (2009) Faut-il surpondérer les actions?, *Le Temps*, 4 May.

Rouwenhorst, K.G. (1997) International Momentum Strategies, Yale ICF Working Paper, February.

Rüthemann, P., Hutter, B., Ganz, R., Tschudi, T. and Lindauer, T. (2010) Swiss Derivative Guide.

Sharpe, W.F. (1964) Capital Asset Prices – A Theory of Market Equilibrium Under Conditions of Risk, *Journal of Finance*, 19(3), 425–442.

Snopek, L. and Tripiana-Snopek, J. (2008) *Devenez entrepreneur en 10 leçons*, Fédération des entreprises romandes, 3e édition, August.

Swensen, D. (2009) *Gestion de portefeuilles institutionnels – Une approche non conventionnelle de la gestion de portefeuilles institutionnels*, Paris: Maxima.

Taleb, N.N. (2007) *The Black Swan*, New York: Random House.

Thetaz, M. (2009) Trois raisons pour éviter les hedge funds, *PME Magazine*, June.

Tolle, S., Hutter, B., Rüthemann, P. and Wohlwend, H. (2005) *Les produits structurés dans la gestion de fortune*, Éditions Neue Zürcher Zeitung.

Vlcek, M. and Hens, T. (2005) Does Prospect Theory Explain the Disposition Effect, NCCR FINRISK Working Paper no 247.

Weinberg, N. and Condon, B. (2004) Les hedge funds, un marché de dupes, *Magazine Bilan*, November.

Zaker, Dr S. (2008) CFA, The Hedge Fund Allocation Problem: An Institutional Perspective, AZEK Campus. See also: Solving the hedge fund asset allocation puzzle, www.hfmweek.com, 24–30 May 2007.

Index